The Secret Diary of an ADHD Martyr

A GIRL GONE WILD
BY
HANNAH HUXFORD

Copyright 2023 by Hannah Huxford all rights reserved.

No part of this publication may be reproduced in any form without the permission of the author.

The Secret Diary of an ADHD Martyr
A GIRL GONE WILD
By
HANNAH HUXFORD

PERSONAL ACKNOWLEDGEMENTS

I acknowledge the use of a selection of inspirational lyrics, used as chapter headings and used in various chapters, by the following artists; Madonna, Duran Duran, Britney Spears, TLC, Soft Cell, Colin M & Janez.

I acknowledge various inspirational quotes & quotes throughout the chapters by the following inspirational people & artists;
Madonna, Shakespeare, 'This Might Help ADHD Social Media', Andy Warhol, Director Serio Leone, Kate Moss, Bob Dylan, Arnold Schwarzenegger and Wikipedia.

Disclaimer Warning; this diary contains adult content, and possible ***Trigger Warnings*** that may cause upset.

The publication of this diary has been a personal heartfelt and proud moment of my life. Successfully achieving my dream of writing my very own book has been empowering. The grammar may not be perfect, but it's written in the most authentic way of my own voice. So you can truly understand my journey of discovery, through my neurodiversity mind.

This diary, is my own personal account, based on a true story.
Its views and opinions of various events are mine and mine alone. Names and locations may be fictional. Names may have been changed to protect the rights and anonymity of individuals mentioned in my book.

This diary is for everybody with an undiagnosed disability, always keep fighting for your truth. Never give up! And for those who are diagnosed, always keep spreading the word to help others. It's OK to be different. Never be afraid to seek help and support if required.

Thank you, Navigo Health & Adult ADHD Social Care Services, for their professional support in officially diagnosing my ADHD in June 2022. Thank you for all the support in helping me finally understand how my neurodiversity affected my life. A Huge Thank you to Stella.

I want to acknowledge my present employers. Who, knowing of my neurodiversity, along with accepting my renowned past. Have truly stood by me, supported me and trusted me to fulfil and execute my role in their business. I also want to personally thank all my work colleagues. Especially all my teammates at GY, for their support and understanding.
My special thanks goes to Tom, Nathan and Emma.

I want to acknowledge some of my wonderful friends; Sy, Jambon, J9, Bra, JoBo, Bell, Roch, Pe, Fi, & Niki. I know we don't always see each other. 'Out of sight out of Mind.' However I know you are always there. Picking up from where we left off. Thank you for understanding me. Xx

I want to acknowledge and thank everyone who has played a significant part in my journey of life. You all know who you are! Each and every one of you have given me a lesson to learn. Whether it's been good or bad, I regret nothing. Without making mistakes, how can we ever learn? Life is to be experimented, without these experiences how do we grow. Unfortunately this book is just not big enough to include every single person or story I've experienced, but I thank you all.

I want to acknowledge the powerful influence Madonna has had over my life. She has unapologetically taught me it's OK to be different. It's Ok to be controversial and fearless. She taught me the facts of life. Through her art, I've learned the importance of reinvention. To live life without no regrets and to stand up to judgement. To always be strong and never be the victim. Through Madonna, I had a lifeline. A reason to keep existing, I could have easily given up. She helped me spiritually through all my traumas. She is the reason why I 'Never gave up.' Through her wise words of wisdom, she taught me to stand up to all the haters and say 'Fuck You' this is who I truly am. I thank you Madonna.

This diary was not written to embarrass, shame or hurt anyone. Especially my family. Throughout these pages, you hopefully will gain a better understanding as to how my neurodiversity has affected my life. I hope it will be read with empathy, in a non-judgemental way and with full understanding. Thank you to my Mum, Dad and Sister for all the love and support you have given me. Xx

A huge thank you and appreciation to Kate from Taptree Therapy. We reconnected after 30 years and thank you for helping me with the final arrangement and publication of the book. You have helped make this book real.

Finally I want to thank Allen for all his help, and his knowledgeable guidance. I cannot thank you enough for all your help and support in the writing of my very first book. I appreciate how precious time is. Thank you for believing in me. Xx

I WOULD LIKE TO DEDICATE THIS BOOK TO

My wonderful rock, my soulmate, my heartmate, my world, my lifelong best friend & husband, Ed.
Without you I couldn't have done any of this. Thank you for putting up with me and believing in me, when I didn't.
We were always meant to be together, life, coming full circle, to reconnect us together again.
You, Ed are the only person in the whole world that gets me and I love you and I dedicate this book to you. Xx

I would also like to dedicate this book to my beautiful daughter. I know it hasn't been easy for her. My story, impacting on her life in so many ways. However, she's been a warrior, stayed strong, steadfast and true and I'm so proud of you. I shall love you, forever and a day.
I love you for all eternity. Mum xx

The Secret Diary of an ADHD Martyr
'A GIRL GONE WILD'

A Madonna classic close to my heart, the lyrics echoing my rollercoaster ride through the ups and downs of my extraordinary life. So why not join me on my exploratory adventure through life. Sharing my journey to enlighten. Explore the experiences that took me away from my beloved Grimsby in search of knowledge and self-awareness. A voyage of discovery of unbelievable hardship and trauma. A journey that would come full circle and bring me safely back to Grimsby. It's taken all my life to achieve my goal and come to understand my disability. I invite you to share in that voyage. And finally get to know the real me so where to begin?

PROLOGUE

ADHD AND ME

So all through my childhood, my teens and into adulthood my ADHD disability was undiagnosed. All my life I've always known that I was different to other people. My brain functioned differently to others. A fact no one would believe, so I spent years masking my disability. Resulting in me ending up with post-traumatic stress.

This book, I hope will inspire people to get a better understanding of ADHD, and its effects, and if possible seek an early diagnosis and receive help.
However it's never too late, as my diagnosis came when I was 47 years old.
ADHD is recognised under the Disability and the Equality Act 2010.

The ADHD symptoms highlighted in this book are based on my own personal experiences and may not reflect the effects it may have on another neurodivergent.
We are all unique and exhibit different symptoms.
I don't offer solutions or advice on dealing or coping with ADHD.
I'm not a professional therapist, psychiatrist, or an expert on the disorder, but offer an understanding of neurodiversity through my own complex personal journey.
ADHD is a complex neurological brain disorder that I'm still trying to understand how the effects of the disability manifest itself.

My ADHD diagnosis has given me more confidence and understanding.
I've finally found my truth. I am educating myself to truly understand who I am.

Why do I behave the way I do? Why do I think the way I do? Having my ADHD confirmed, has given me the strength to fulfil this goal in writing my heartfelt book. By highlighting all these struggles, with my then undiagnosed ADHD. I hope my reader will be able to empathise with my struggles with it. To understand why I made some of those very bad decisions I made in my life. However what works for me may not work for another, as neurodiversity is so diverse...

I've been diagnosed as a 'Neurodivergent' In other words my brain works differently than a normal brain. Such differences include my mental and learning disabilities along with other related conditions, these will be explained throughout these pages. My ADHD has been diagnosed as combined moderate to severe.
This is characterised by impulsive hyperactive behaviours and intense distractibility.
Now, within the pages of my book, I can finally feel liberated. I can finally take that mask off, stand up and say, here I am, and this is the real me...

Before I realised ADHD was part of my problem I couldn't understand how people around me were able to successfully organise themselves into functional role models. Those who can't, that's me, are labelled executive dysfunction.
I thought, forgetting details, tasks, appointments, struggling preparing meals and not being able to finish the household chores, was the result of me having a bad day, but no as it turned out, my ADHD was manifesting my executive dysfunction. I believed I was a failure at nearly everything in my life, especially being a new mum, because I just couldn't handle high energy moments, I would crash and burn out. Self-esteem was always rock bottom, always the feeling of never being good enough and not being able to cope.
Over stimulation is often referred to as a sensory overload. Your senses overwhelming your brain. An intense urge to escape the environment you're in. Triggered by the simplest of things. For example fixating on minor things, such as high-pitched noises, especially kids screaming, the cat meowing, crumbs on the kitchen floor, my daughter's bedroom being messy, tangled electricity cables, to name certain irritating situations that wouldn't annoy normal people but trigger a sensory overload to me.
ADHD invokes sensory overwhelm, and creates unmanageable character mood swings, manifesting as out of control temper tantrums and erratic behaviours.
I'd upset and offend people, often without reason or understanding. This is the effect of sensory overload that I couldn't handle or comprehend at the time.

If under-stimulated, my ADHD makes me feel exhausted. I have what the experts call, a low frustration tolerance, and emotional dysregulation. I experience emotional highs and lows, and I've to regulate my emotions thus creating emotional periods of disorder. Many people with ADHD have a hard time finding dopamine, the neurotransmitter that leads to increased motivation. My brain requires more stimulation so I seek unusual, and exciting environments.

Got to get that dopamine buzz.

My hormonal imbalances were made worse by a dopamine deficiency.

Through puberty and having my daughter, I went through bloody hell with it. I'm now in the perimenopause stages of my life, and the change in hormones is making my ADHD symptoms worse. It can flare, it's a bad trait, so be warned..?

At school, taking my GCSEs with then an undiagnosed ADHD crippled with dyslexia created major problems in understanding questions and what was expected from me. I spent most of my time doodling on the exam sheets, my brain meandering in no man's land. My schooling suffered. My brain was unable to function normally with school routines and learning situations.

I was mentally paralysed.

I got bored and suffered from attention deficiency. I become disruptive. My brain unable to cope with any sensory overload. My undiagnosed ADHD plays a major role in my ability to learn. So I would cause disruption in class and was regularly known as the class clown...

Out of sight, out of mind, is a great way to describe the majority of my friendships throughout my life. However, it's important to understand. It's never intentional and I always pick up from where we left off on those forgotten friendships. I struggled to keep relationships, but endured them in a vain hope that I'd fit in, and feel that sense of belonging. Friends and acquaintances have said how friendly and bubbly I appear to be and always so popular, but the truth is I'm socially masking myself to appear this way. The reality is I'm actually a loner, and prefer my own company. Being around too many people can cause me to melt down and then I feel emotionally exhausted and drained...

I have a crippling inability to relax. My brain at night is a minefield of sleepless thoughts, overthinking over analysing and I have had many sleepless nights.

My inability to concentrate and focus my attention on people or subjects.

I'm easily under stimulated and if my environment doesn't provide enough interest I crave hyperactivity and chaos.

At times you feel you're an imposter, colleagues not believing you're struggling, with the simplest of tasks. You get the feeling, they think you're making it all up, seeking sympathy or getting out of doing it.
Not true.
They don't understand, it's a genuine discomfort, the distress is real. Not believing in yourself is hard. Knowing you're an intelligent being, and finding it difficult to accomplish goals you set out to achieve. The knowledge is there, but my brain just cannot organise itself to perform efficiently. That's a difficult thing to handle, especially when you're ignorant of the fact, it's actually your ADHD that's creating the problem.

Understandably, I am masking my disorder.
I sometimes use fake eye contact, adapt to the imposter syndrome, and appear to be interested when in reality my mind is elsewhere. Fake smiles and forced facial gestures and expressions enable me to appear normal, when deep inside I'm struggling to be interested. I've been guilty of modelling people's traits and interests, in order to be accepted, and appear normal. I've even scripted conversations, to mask my real personality.

Masking my true feelings is exhausting, and leads to insecurity, anxiety, depression, and a total loss of identity. Before being diagnosed, I unwittingly masked my true feelings in order to be accepted and appear normal. It came as second nature, a tactic that allowed me to survive, in a world that wasn't the same for me as it was for others. I wouldn't disclose this for fear of being judged abnormal, and have to face the stigma of being different. I've probably spent most of my life being judged for being loud and demonstrative. I still fear failure and go overboard to please and be accepted.

Annoyingly, I've been told, I'm too loud, difficult to handle, too difficult to cope with. A real pain in the arse. So, the solution to my dilemma was simple: mask my true feelings, pretend to be someone else, and be accepted. I'm so impatient, my mind wanders off.
I fidget, doodle, unable to listen. Classic conditions of ADHD that frustrates so many people, especially those not understanding my disability. So often, when confronted with adversity, I feel like a child, not an adult, in trying to solve the dilemma.
ADHD makes us very sensitive to criticism and we go on the defensive. We have low self-esteem and have impulsive hyperactivity behaviours. Alongside these debilitating conditions, we easily get distracted.

My brain never switches off, it's permanently hyperactive.

Inattention sensitivity creates emotional pain and we become people pleasers, simply to gain approval from friends and family...

Having ADHD, is a Topsy-Turvy world of decision and indecisions. Fear of being judged and upsetting people...

When I was first diagnosed with ADHD. My Mum had her own reservations about it. Fair enough. I respect my Mum whole heartedly. I tried to understand why my Mum found it hard to come to terms with. I felt Mum was blaming herself, thinking she'd let me down. This is so far from the truth, my Mum has been incredible throughout my life, and never once has she let me down. However Mum didn't really understand the implications of the diagnosis.

For Mum, she felt it was just another label to hang around my neck. For me, it's been a life-time of having an undiagnosed disability finally confirmed. It gave me that affirmation that my brain was different to everyone else. It gave me a chance to finally understand exactly who I actually am...

ADHD creates a wandering mind that can abruptly change from one topic to another without warning. Your mind becomes a meander mess of conversational confusion. You feel guilty for being abrupt or for changing the topic of conversation without warning. My attention deficiency has created problems when socially interacting with people. With the need to increase my levels of dopamine, I can get very hyperactive around people in social situations and sometimes I have been known to behave inappropriately.

It's a lot to take in, I know. Not everyone will understand, but my brain really does work differently. Hiding that fact, and masking the real me, has helped me feel safe, and avoid the stigma of being some kind of freak, in the eyes of the uninformed. Masking has helped me avoid ridicule and bullying. However, my condition has at times allowed unpleasant individuals to bully and mistreat me.

I didn't stand up for myself at the time and was taken for granted. I take things literal and I struggle to sometimes comprehend if someone is being serious or joking. Literally believing what people tell me, this makes me very vulnerable and trusting, so much so people have taken full advantage of me, causing me upset and trauma. I've now developed my own coping strategies, to overcome such pain and deep rooted trauma...

My ADHD disorder would encourage anorexia and bulimia, creating confusing challenges and irregular eating habits. Dopamine seeking behaviours, especially from dieting, weight loss and restrictive eating compulsions, would boost my dopamine, but create unhealthy relationships with certain foods. Such compulsion over food, affected my self-esteem...

Simply put, ADHD can be hereditary. So it's worth exploring one's family history for tell-tale signs and behaviours. Possibly, as in my case. ADHD might have gone undiagnosed in your families' past or you suspect a family member, either past or present, who are displaying underlying symptoms. Early diagnosis is essential. So, it's time to make people more aware of ADHD.
We're not all born the same. We're unique, each with our own personalities. Hopefully, the next generation will be made more aware of ADHD and understand what people with neurodiversity have to endure...
To summarise; hopefully educating more people about ADHD, will help remove the stigma. Having a diagnosis of ADHD is important...
When I got my official diagnosis, I grieved, I went through all the emotions. I felt grief, I cried, I felt pain, and then I felt relief. It was a lot to take in. It was hard to process. A whole lifetime of not being diagnosed. Decades of knowing you are very different from the norm. Having my diagnosis gave me some clarity to all those years of confusion. It gave me affirmation that it wasn't in my head...
However, ADHD as always, has been a part of my life. It doesn't go away. So you learn to live with it. My impulsive behaviour has led me down many a never ending road. Roads that have led nowhere even to complete disasters...We do things on impulse. Start projects or tasks that never get finished.
A classic example; I had tried so hard to write a book many times over the years, but every time I would just give up on my dream. Receiving my diagnosis for ADHD gave me the drive and determination that I could actually do it...

In conclusion; I want to share my neurodiversity journey with you....
This diary has been written in my own true authentic voice. Spoken in my own vocabulary, the grammar will not be perfectly written ... I don't want it to be...
My thought process is very different from the norm.

So I ask you, my reader, to read this diary organically, with all its imperfections. I want you to truly experience how my neurodiversity mind works!

Be warned; It will get frustrating at times, I know, I live with it... I will go off on tangents, I tend to repeat myself unknowingly, which some readers may find highly annoying... I want you, my reader, to be open minded.

To authentically experience and gain a realistic understanding, on how it felt living with an undiagnosed ADHD. And how it hugely impacted on my life. Unapologetically, I have opened up Pandora's Box. To give you a true insight into my colourful past. Deep hidden secrets, locked away in the abyss of my mind, resulting in years of post-traumatic stress.

I hope my reader will find empathy, and try to understand how I have spent a lifetime masking my authentic self. This resulting in developing my own coping strategies, protecting me from trauma. These strategies enable me to appear normal to the outside world. I can't change what has happened in my life. It is part of my past. Everything in life happens for a reason. I've taken many wrong roads. However, each road gave me a lesson to learn. I live with no regrets. I've narrated my journey to the best of my ability, it's an honest account of various life events that may be uncomfortable to read at times...I make no apology.

So come with me and explore my adventures at the time. For me it's been a form of therapy to enable me to heal. Finally I reveal the truth, it's not been easy. This is who I really am...

Hannah Huxford

INTRODUCTION

MADONNA

From the moment I saw Madonna I fell in love with her. I was nine years old, entranced by a beautiful black and white Athena postcard of her. I knew nothing about her, other than she looked so glamorous and so beautiful. I was captivated by this image and would follow her career for most of my life...

I believed I was her number one fan...Something in the way you love me won't let me be...

Madonna is a living legend there is no doubt about that. She has spanned a very successful career for over forty years from the 80s all the way up until the modern day. She's always been on the cutting edge with her music, a controversial icon, with outspoken views and artistic expressions.

It was all so innocent, that first time. I knew from that moment in time she would become something to me. I know I was young, but just looking at that postcard, I knew I was hooked, fixed for an eternity.

My Sister had a few of her albums on vinyl, and she used to let me use her record player to listen to them. A favourite one of mine was Madonna's first album. 'Borderline.' I'd listen, captivated, as she sang one classical hit after another. Hits such as 'Holiday,' 'Borderline,' and 'Lucky Star.' She had other albums too, and I'd become mesmerised staring at those album covers. Her 'Like a Virgin,' album cover would transfix me for hours.

Inspired by my Sister's scrapbook cuttings, I decided to make my own scrapbooks on her. I'd trawl through every newspaper and magazine I could find, to cut out pictures and articles on Madonna.

I had one particular friend at junior school called Emma, and she was also a fanatical Madonna fan. We instantly became friends because of our mutual love of Madonna. Her parents had bought her a VHS video of Madonna's, 'Virgin Tour.'

I remember having sleepovers at Emma's house and obsessively watching the VHS video. Over and over again we'd rewind, play it, and again rewind and play. Probably wore the tape out. We used to physically copy the dance routines and learn all the words to the songs. The opening scene of Madonna's 'Virgin Tour' sees her speaking into the camera, in black-and-white, looking and speaking like Marilyn Monroe...

"I want to be famous, I want to be a star, and I want everybody to love me"...

Words to encourage my outlook on life...

I remember standing in Emma's living room putting on an American accent playing over and over again the start of the video. Mesmerised by Madonna, and stimulated by her aspirations, I too wanted to be famous, wanted everyone to love me. I truly believed in those words and my undiagnosed ADHD fixated on that. It'll probably be difficult for someone with a normal neurological brain to understand my fixations.

My obsessions become a compulsive routine and I'd go for it...

However, in addition to my neurodiversity. I had learning difficulties, my junior school placing me in remedial classes.

Mum suspected I had dyslexia as well, and voiced her concerns to the school. In their wisdom, the school refused to accept I had dyslexia, and I continued to struggle, without help, in those remedial classes. As it turned out, I did have dyslexia, and ADHD, as well, but neither were diagnosed. So for the rest of my life I would struggle with these debilitating conditions.

My Mum really did try, but it fell on deaf ears...

So, along came Madonna, with her inspirational songs, her fame and stardom. I just wanted to be the next Madonna. I clung to this belief, my life lived with this in mind. It wasn't until I gave birth to my daughter, that I finally realised fame was not what I wanted after all. I'd spent most of my early life chasing a superficial fix.

We only have to look at society now, the world we're living in, with its easy access to the internet and social media. Everybody wants to be famous.

You can be an Instagram star, get a following on Facebook. Make a video, get a million hits on YouTube or TikTok. Become a 'Reality TV' star on programmes like 'Love Island,' 'Big Brother.' Fifteen minutes of fame,' famously quoted Andy Warhol. 'In the future everyone will be world-famous for 15 minutes.'

Fame for the Hell of it.

The death of her mother shaped her into the Madonna we see today. The loss of her mother was a devastating blow. Feeling abandoned taught her a valuable lesson. She would have to remain strong, overcome the grief, and never be seen as being weak. So, Madonna decided to take on 'World Domination'.

She wanted everybody to love her, she'd lost her Mother's love, such a tragic loss, at such a young age, so she looked to the people of the world to replace that love. I, on the other hand, had my Mother's love. So I didn't crave it...

I craved fame back then for multiple reasons; I wanted to be somebody.

I wanted to be someone's inspiration. Madonna was my inspiration. Having been told by my teacher, I was destined only to stack shelves for the rest of my life, as I wasn't academically clever enough to excel in any other career. It was confidence destroying especially to a young neurodivergent vulnerable girl. I never thought I would be ever good enough to excel in achieving anything. Literally taking those teachers' words to heart...

Okay I'm not as successful as Madonna. I'm no pop star, but I tried. You can read all about my attempt to win 'Pop Idol,' later in the next book. I certainly don't have the money or stardom, Madonna commands but I took it upon myself, when I was younger, to make Madonna my role model. She's been with me nearly all my life, and it's uncanny how similar our lives had overlapped. We've certainly been through similar upheavals and traumas.

I've never met Madonna, seen her in concert, many times, but never personally had the pleasure of a face-to-face meeting. Should that miracle ever happen, I often wondered, would we be friends, or would our personalities clash? We're so alike, having so much tragedy in common, I'd like to think we'd be friends.

I can still dream can't I?

Okay, back to Emma's living room, when we were young girls, watching Madonna's 'Virgin Tour' video. We'd dress ourselves up, grab pieces of lace and tie them in our hair. I used to borrow mum's Avon lipstick and eyeliner and create the Madonna look...

In 1987, Madonna went on a world tour with 'Who's That Girl'.' The tour venue had her performing in two UK cities, at Roundhay Park in Leeds and Wembley Stadium in London.

For my twelfth birthday dad bought me a ticket and Emma's stepdad, Allen bought her one too. Allen took us both to see Madonna in concert. Tickets must have been expensive, in those days, so we felt privileged and very excited to have had the opportunity to see our mentor. At the time, Madonna launched a video to coincide with the name of her tour. To this day, 'Who's That Girl,' the movie is one of my favourite movies starring Madonna.

My own daughter loves watching it, and we've had many nights over the years putting on the DVD and having a girly night, on the sofa watching it over and over again. I will never get bored of watching it, such a typical neurodivergent thing to do watching the same movie over and over again.

Madonna is unique, authentic and different to those who'd come before. Her voice is raw and distinctive. She was controversial, and still is, the voice for women and their rights...

So there we were at Wembley. I remember waiting, for what seemed like forever. Madonna never arrived on stage, as scheduled. She would always be fashionably late. This was to build anticipation, create fervour, preparing her fans for a rip roaring crowd cheering, Madonna entrance on stage. She eventually came on stage and the crowd were electric, the screaming, the cheering was nothing like I'd ever seen or heard before in my life.

Her entrance was fanatically inspirational.

Wembley shook with noise and admiration for this singing sensation. I can remember the atmosphere was electric, exhilarating, thrilling. I'd never experienced anything like it, I could feel my nerves tingling with excitement.

Arron Smith
Henrikson, a
makeup artist
with Madonna.

Madonna's
Manager,
Guy Oseary.

Watching Madonna rehearse

Ricardo
Gomes,
Madonna's
Artistic
Director.

This was the old Wembley, and I remember watching, 'Live Aid,' on TV, and those famous white towers it had. I remember looking up at them, not quite believing I was actually there at Wembley watching my Madonna.

It was my dream come true.

We stood with the sound engineers, literally in front of the stage.

We felt a little overwhelmed with the crowds, all around us, after all we were quite young. People were drinking and having a great time. Everyone was singing, everyone was excited. It was Madonna's first tour, in the UK.

She was at the height of her fame, at the beginning of her long lasting career. On either side of the stage were two very large video screens, so if you couldn't see the stage, which I was struggling to do, you could view her on a big screen.

Everyone, of course, being taller than me, could see. Not me.

I stood on tiptoe trying to see, but my view was restricted, so I looked towards the giant video screens. I just couldn't believe my icon, Madonna, was on stage, not that far away from me. She was energetic around the stage, dancing to, 'Open Your Heart,' I just wanted to get on that stage and join her...

She danced with a young lad who she regularly danced with. He looked my age,
I wanted to be him, and it made me feel really jealous. Everybody wanted to be that young lad, I'm sure. What a time we had. Unforgettable. I will never forget a moment of Madonna's Wembley, 'Who's That Girl.' World tour.
So from there onwards I became the biggest avid collector of Madonna pictures, and memorabilia. Sunday markets would see me searching the stalls, buying any old pop tat, anything that had her face or name on it. With my saved up pocket money, which wasn't a lot, I'd buy specialist magazines and picture books about Madonna. At Christmas I'd get Madonna bits and bobs. Vinyl, cassettes, posters, postcards, and every year a calendar. All of course featuring Madonna.

I was completely obsessed...

Madonna was always in the tabloids. She caused controversy wherever she went, hounded by the paparazzi over things she did and said. She used to run for miles, in order to be fit, to do her strenuous tours. She wore controversial outfits by fashion designer Jean-Paul Gaultier, the iconic Gold Bask attracting so much media attention. She graced just about every newspaper with her outspoken views, her 'Blonde Ambition Tour' attracting controversy. She'd bought homosexual dancers, sex and religion together in this artistic display of theatrical performance. It was mesmerising. It was a revolutionary show. It set the tone for how pop concerts of the future would look like. She set a bar and she set it high.

There has never been quite an artist like her before. She did everything outside the recognised box. Everything she did or said had a message.

She represented so much for so many people. She became an icon for homosexuals, for freedom of speech and a voice against racism. She wasn't afraid to incorporate political and sexual religious themes in her music videos and concerts.

She was different, no one quite like her. She generated both controversy and critical acclaim. She expressed her art through her music, through her tours and through her videos. Madonna originally launched herself on MTV, a visual platform to introduce herself to the world.

I'd be Madonna anywhere and everywhere, always singing and dancing to 'Vogue,' and 'Hanky-Panky. In secondary school, I was forever entertaining people in the school common room, but the headmaster put a stop to it. I'll never forget the look he gave me. It was my free time, and I wasn't causing trouble. I was being musical and artistic.
Looking back, maybe he should have come over and taken an interest in what I was doing, instead of shouting me down in front of everybody and chastising me.

I was doing something good for a change, something that I loved. Had I back then been diagnosed with ADHD my tutors and peers might have dealt with it more understandable?

But I hadn't and they didn't.

I had an ability to be creative. Had the school offered me more help and guidance with my creative side, I possibly wouldn't have been the pain in their arse, they saw me as. That's the thing with life. If you don't fit inside somebody's box, then they don't want to know. I fit inside my own unique box, no one else's. I was meant to be that different person. So Madonna taught me never to be afraid to express myself, and that's what I did.

So to fixate on Madonna helped me face the pain of society's betrayal. When listening to Madonna or collecting her memorabilia, I could switch off from all the shit and trauma I was going through at the time. Madonna's philosophies of life have taught me a lot, and as sure as hell influenced my attitudes to life.

Madonna had the dream of becoming a star. She was a talented dancer and in the 1970s moved to New York. She was literally dropped off in Time Square, with very little money. She wanted to pursue a career in modern dance, and New York was the place to achieve such ambitions. She was fearless, unafraid. She had the dream. That burning sensation in your gut, I'm going to be somebody.

She made friends with artists. Ironically, all incredibly famous for their art. Andy Warhol, Jean-Michal Basquiat, whom she dated, befriended the legendary Keith Haring. Whether deliberate, or accidentally, she got the attention of very talented people. She was destined for big things, influential people could see she was special, very special indeed.

So liken this to everything that happened to me in my teenage years. My dad's illness when I was thirteen, the secret traumas I encountered. So like Madonna, escaping to New York, for a better life. I thought that escaping from my home town of Grimsby would give me a better life.

I was trying to recover and getting out of Grimsby was my escape. I wasn't going to New York like Madonna but I had that desire to work hard to escape my hometown and make something of myself elsewhere. So, you can now understand how Madonna has influenced my decision-making throughout my life. I thought if she can do it, I certainly can. She taught me to be true to myself, and be fearless in its execution. I left Grimsby, hoping for a better future...

Madonna launched a book called 'Sex'. The book featured adult content including soft-core pornography and simulations of sexual acts including sadomasochism. Madonna developed 'Sex,' a book based on erotic photographs. She wrote it as a character named 'Mistress Dita.' Nobody had done anything quite like this ever. It had beautiful photographs and sexual positions showing homosexuals, lesbians, and people of culture. It showed dominatrix and all forms of artistic sexual images. She was living out people's sexual fantasies in art. The book was a work of art. She used a top photographer, Steven Meisel, and artists, Vanilla Ice and supermodel Naomi Campbell to name a few...

The book was wrapped in foil so you had to buy the book to see inside. A collector's item to be sure. Everybody wanted the book, the first batches sold out quickly and were only available to over eighteens. My Sister bought one and I too obtained a copy. I opened mine, as I was too impatient and impulsive. I recall looking at the images, totally mesmerised. Yes, the sexual nature was explicit, but very artistic. People voiced a barrage of complaints.

Madonna didn't care.

She was fearless, true to her principles. She knew exactly what she was doing. True it caused controversy but this was my Madonna, she'd always evoked disagreement and people played right into her hands.

You see Madonna pushed the boundaries of artistic expression. She controlled every aspect of her career...

Madonna released a VHS video afterwards to coincide with her tour and it was a very controversial documentary. It was called, 'In Bed with Madonna'. Directed by Alek Keshishian.

She decided to give Director Alek Keshishian, *Carte Blanche,* during her, 'Blonde Ambition,' tour. The result is a controversial rockumentary with live performances, filmed in colour, and backstage scenes, in black & white. The film, a first of its kind, gives fans a look behind the scenes of a Madonna tour, with a focus on Madonna's relationship with her dancers and tour crew.

So, Madonna's documentary, 'In Bed with Madonna,' reminded me of when I had the opportunity to film student life in college. I filmed hours around the college making a real documentary. When I left the West Midlands to go to Manchester, Madonna had changed her genre. Her music was reinvented...

She was the Queen of reinvention. It was the mid-90s and she launched her 'Bedtime Stories,' album. I was living in Manchester.

Madonna has always stood up for multicultural relationships and I guess, when I started dating Wayne I never saw dating a black guy as any different from dating a white guy. Madonna had educated me about multi-racial and multicultural relationships. To me it wasn't controversial. It was normal. I learnt more from Madonna about relationships than I ever learnt from my education at school. She taught me to love everybody. We're all equal under the skin.

When I got into the Adult Entertainment Industry, I didn't seek it. It was a coincidence. That day in that photographic studio in Manchester, when I met Ross, life then spiralled me into a life of debauchery, not planned. Madonna taught me not to be ashamed. You see I grew up being ashamed about sex because, if I'm honest, I can't recall ever being told about sex. Not at school or by my parents, not that I can remember. So my first encounters were horrific. I blame no one for this omission.

Madonna also taught me to live out your fantasies and not be ashamed of them. She made a soft porn movie before she got famous, called 'Certain Sacrifice' Madonna posed nude, for photographs, as a student to make money. Years later those photographs were being sold for substantial amounts of money.

She's been on the front cover of Penthouse.

She has never been ashamed of any of it, and this is why I don't feel ashamed of my past or the things I did. However, people have in the past made me feel ashamed. Shame on them...I've felt silenced to talk freely without any judgement..

'Ray of Light,' Madonna's seventh album, launched in 1998 the year I started working in the adult entertainment industry. Her music played loudly in my car as I travelled up and down from Manchester to London, to keep me company. Metaphorically speaking her music would transport me away from my troubles, and take me to much better places.

'Ray of Light' is an incredible album, possibly one of my favourites. She recorded it with William Orbit and again, she changed her style, and reinvented her genre. Everyone eagerly awaited her next tour. I kept on collecting Madonna memorabilia as normal and sending it all back to my parents in Grimsby who put it in my Madonna chest along with all my other Madonna memorabilia...

Photographs:
Hannah Huxford

Many thanks to Google for
making my seagull a star!

CHAPTER ONE

DON'T FOLLOW THE RULES

'Don't Follow the Rules'... Quotes my mentor Madonna...
She influenced my thinking, my behaviour, and taught me to be independent. Probably taught me more than I realised. In fact Madonna has been with me a lifetime, influencing the events and experiences that have forged my life...

I wanted to be famous, and dreamed of one day being the next Madonna...I wanted to be adored and admired. I just wanted to be accepted, that was my reality if truth be told...The crazy thing is, I hate attention but that's a contradiction, because I crave it. A most bizarre emotional situation, don't you think? Confusing to be sure, but that's part of my condition of ADHD. Always wanting the need for the next fix of dopamine.
So, trouble is always an honest outspoken word. The truth hurts, but I say it as it is.
I really don't have any filters. I say it how I see it and see it how I say it.
If you want the truth then I will always give you the truth.

My mind is constantly racing at a hundred miles an hour, foot on the gas not coming up for air. You will never get a word in edgeways. Interruptions make people with ADHD lose their train of thought. That's me...
       I see things in pictures.
My brain works as a camera. Like a video so to speak, constantly playing. As images flash up I just can't get the words out fast enough or get the right words to explain what I see. This is why I'm very good at being creative. I can visualise things that others struggle with. I have the perfect eye for the perspective. So this enables me to create the most beautiful photography.

One Christmas my parents bought me my very first instant camera, it was red and had a flash. I would document and take photographs of everything.

I'm good at photography despite ADHD hindering my self-confidence and lack of self-esteem and belief. It's a trait that has hindered me throughout my life. Looking back I really could have been a great photographer. Probably could have made a career out of it...

Like my hero, Madonna, fame has crossed my path. In 2010, I took a photograph of a seagull eating a chip, on an iPhone 3. It went viral on the internet. In 2021 I was contacted by a London based Design Consultancy. Their client Google loved my iconic photograph so much that they paid a licensing fee to use it in a huge summer billboard advertising campaign. I was then interviewed by the BBC and the story went global. Fame at last...

Let's start my life... right back to the very beginning. I was born in Grimsby at a Maternity Home in the hot summer of 1975. My Mum informs me, she knew from the moment I was born, I would be trouble. I came out screaming. Somehow Mum knew I'd be different from other children. My screaming continued, prompting the midwife who delivered me, to tell Mum, what a little madam I was, and what a good set of lungs I had. Mum would certainly have her hands full with me. How right she was. I was a handful...

A true Grimbarian, as were my parents. I've spent most of my life in Grimsby attending school and in later years being employed in one of the town's car dealerships.

I'm married to my beloved Ed and we journey together through life's little challenges, one of those challenges being me.

I've known Ed since 1976, when our Mums went to the same baby weighing classes together. Ed is a twin, he and his brothers also went to the same Playschool, Infants and Junior school as me.

Ed was the first boy at five years old to hand deliver my first Valentine card. We shared birthday parties together along with his brother's. We were always close, and our families knew each other very well.

Destiny would have Ed and me meet later in life fall in love and get married...

My Mother's Mum, Granny Rose, sadly died a few years prior to my birth. I never had the opportunity to physically meet her. My Sister however did, and had a wonderful photograph taken with her, where my Sister is sitting on Granny Rose's knee. I'm a spiritual person, I truly believe I'm psychic...
Although I never got the opportunity to meet my Granny Rose, I always felt her spirit was around me, protecting me.
In my dark days of sadness, which have been many, she would appear in the form of a Pied Wagtail Bird. I tell it as it is, so believe me or not...
It's up to you...
I know when I'm in a bad place, as that Pied Wagtail Bird will always come to visit me, a sign from Granny Rose that everything is going to be okay...

Growing up I saw things differently. I have a sixth-sense that enables me to witness supernatural events. As a child, I was convinced my bedroom was haunted.
I have experienced my head being touched by something paranormal in my bedroom. I would see people appear and disappear and hear strange sounds and voices. I once saw a man in a World War II soldier's outfit. He was smoking a cigarette while standing at the side of my bed. He smiled.
Such strange paranormal happenings. But as a child I didn't want people to think I was lying or it was my overactive imagination...
I never did sleep properly. So was it my neurodiversity at work, or was it real? I'll leave you to make up your own mind... I slept with my head under the sheets. And still do. I still believe I'm psychic with a sixth-sense. Which enables me to experience a knowing sensation that I'm in the presence of spirits.

My parents bought a bungalow in 1970. It needed a lot of renovation. To them, it was a labour of love project. Dad did most of the interior renovations himself. A lot of land came with the property. It was full of trees, had a beautiful brick walled garden, with vegetable patches and an old greenhouse. It was a fantastic place to play. Hide and seek anyone...

A quick word about my Sister, the intelligent sibling...

Mum insisted my Sister included me in her plans, so I got to share my Sister's passion for horses. So, we went horse-riding together at a local riding school, a leisure activity I found very exhilarating. We had the usual list of animals, rabbits, a guinea pig and a dog called Shannon. I had a tortoise called Hickory, found wandering in the garden and lots and lots of cats.

Across the road lived a little girl called Lucy. Sue and David, her parents, had a small holding, and a pony called Muffin as well as a foal called Firecracker.

I became obsessed with Muffin, my undiagnosed neurodiversity creating another uncontrolled dopamine fixation. Muffin, I felt, was my own little pony, me and my Sister took it in turns riding it.

David, my friend's dad, used to work away on the oil rigs for months. He used to play football at the local school hall, but sadly he had a heart attack and instantly died. I was devastated. Life is so cruel, and always will be. I was unbelievably sad. David was a kind and caring man. How sad, and how tragic life can be...

Let's talk about my parents; Mum has always been obsessed with computers, and achieved a degree in Web design. Well done my clever Mum, I'm proud of her!

Her first computer was the ZX Spectrum by Sinclair. It had cassette games like The Hobbit, Morris Minor, and Jet Set Willy that we used to play.

Dad on the other hand wasn't really into computers he was more into his history especially 'Napoleonic wars' along with Robin Hood they are his favourite.

He is beyond a very talented model builder. His intricate work in designing model buildings is genius!

Mum back in the 1980s, was a member of a dance troupe called Rainbow. As a child I used to go along and watch Mum and my Godmother dance at Lillian's Dance studio. Mum and my Godmother would perform incredible dance routines to disco hits like Michael Jacksons 'Thriller' and Anita Ward's 'Ring my Bell' to name a few. There she was, my Mum in a sequined green leotard, on the studio floor dancing to The Jacksons, 'Can you feel it'. While I ran crazy around the studio making loud noises, getting very impatient and fixating on Mum taking me to Tate's supermarket afterwards for a treat.

I look back and remember how fantastic it was. Memories that I will treasure a lifetime. Mum and her dance troupe became well known in the area, even appearing on local television on ITVs Calendar News.

I recorded a song called 'No Regrets' after appearing on ITVs Pop Idol. And with the help of my Sister she edited the original video footage of my Mum and her dance group. She then synced my song over it. It looked fantastic.

I never did achieve pop star status but what the hell, I nearly did...

Mum enrolled me into ballroom dancing classes when I was younger.
I found them really boring, I was far too impatient to learn the strict routines.
My elder Sister, by five years, was far better at it than me.
After only two classes I left, I was bored. Undiagnosed neurodiversity controlling my reasoning.

However, I do love dancing. I'm a very creative dancer, I'm not into structured choreography, and my body is in tune to the beat of the music. I freestyle my own movements. I express myself through music and probably inherited such traits from my Mum.

The 1980s were a great time to be growing up. Technology had yet to alter the framework of life so I was fortunate to have lived before mobile phones and social media took control of your life...
Summers would always be spent out in the garden in the fresh air, my parents encouraged my Sister and I to experience nights outside camping. This I also did with Louise, she lived up the road...

Louise, she copied me in almost anything I did. I guess I should be flattered to have been that icon...

I had a love for 'My Little Pony' and 'The Care Bears', and she'd follow suit and would have to have the exact same ones.

Her parents were a lot older than mine, Louise was usually left to her own devices. Mum regularly cooked meals for Louise as her parents were always late home from work. Everything I collected she would have to collect too.

Louise and I loved camping out in my parents back garden. Like hedgehogs we'd hide in our tents, the noises in the night keeping us excitedly awake. My Dad, in the middle of the night, would sneak into the garden, with a torch and scare us. Fond and forever memories of the 1980's that's for sure.

My ADHD dopamine fixations were always high as a child. So many exciting activities that were stimulating for my neurodivergent brain. My mind wanders back to these happy times, everything seemed so rose tinted perfect, but it really was like this, my childhood to me was perfect. Long warm sunny summers and staying out all day seeking adventures. I was told to be back inside when it got dark, when the street lights came on.

Each week I would find a different new friend to play outside with, creating dopamine high outdoor adventures.

Raleigh bikes with baskets and bells, walks to Weelsby woods and up the farm track to feed the horses. Even getting stuck on a barbed wire fence just to stroke a pony. Graffiting my dad's garden brick wall with emulsion paint, 'Blacksmith Keep Out' Dad was none too pleased and chased me across the cornfield.

Collecting Storyteller cassette tapes with the weekly magazine. Smash Hits, Just Seventeen and Jackie along with all the agony aunt problem pages.

My nature table that I made, literally collecting everything. It even had live snails on it! Collecting pen pals from all over the world, and sending handwritten letters. Swapping photos that you'd ask to be sent back, then waiting weeks in hope of a letter of reply. It was the original old school Facebook of the time.

I like to surround myself with things that bring me happiness. Memories of renting and watching VHS classic video films with my family like Gremlins, ET, The Goonies and Ferris Bueller's day off.

Played on a VHS video player, stimulating those happy thoughts.

I loved it. The perfect stimulation raises my dopamine levels.

Christmas was always magical with my family. Traditional Christmas decorations and a real Christmas tree. Nativity plays and carol concerts.

Music by Band Aid 'Do they know it's Christmas' released in 1984, to raise money and awareness for the famine in Ethiopia. Nearly 40 years on it's still a relevant Christmas song creating memories. Advent calendars with little picture squares with images of festive glitter scenes. Pretty Christmas cards that were sent to absolutely everyone, in the hope you would get one in return. The Queen's Speech, followed by the traditional Christmas film that was usually on ITV. Radio and TV times were the guide to Christmas TV, back then there were no more than 4 TV channels the main film would usually be 'Indiana Jones'. Selection boxes and the token tangerine.

Boxing Day traditions would be at Nanna and Grandads, my Dad's parents.

We would spend it with all my Aunties, Uncles and Cousins. My Grandparents would decorate their front room in lots of magical tinsel, paper chains and everything festive. It was the most Christmassy room you could ever imagine.

They would always buy wonderful gifts that would be magical to open on Christmas morning. Nostalgic memories never to be forgotten.

My childhood was perfect in my eyes, it was magical and exciting for a neurodivergent like myself. Forever I will be eternally grateful to my parents.

We had family holidays in the North Yorkshire Moors. My parents would rent a cottage, and invite my Godmother with her partner and their kids. We loved the countryside and explored all the walks in the area. It was a fantastic way to have a holiday. No phones, no computers. Our transport would be a purple MK2 Ford Escort car, that ironically would now be a vintage classic, but at the time I hated it.

I will always treasure and remember with fondness, Mum's home cooked meals. They were a family affair. We all sat around the kitchen table, ate and talked as families rarely do. Our living room was out of bounds during meals. No one dared upset Dad at the dinner table. He was quite strict with us and insisted on draconian table manners. Which we followed on pain of retribution.

Once, I back chatted with Mum at the dinner table. Dad was quick to react. He grabbed the back of my head and pushed my nose into my meal. Gravy and food went everywhere. Mum came to my rescue, as she screamed at him to stop. I never did it again!

Lesson learnt Respect!

I always had a high level of respect for my Dad and still do.

He was the classic alpha male. If we misbehaved, Mum would put the fear of God in us. 'You wait till your Dad gets home,' she'd threaten. When he did, we knew we were in trouble. A strict upbringing but that's the way it was. I have a lot of respect for my parents, especially my Dad, but would never want to cross him.

Our local village Playschool expelled me after only one day, the teacher telling my Mum she didn't want me back as I was far too disruptive to the other children. I was too loud and very boisterous. Well, I wasn't a naughty child, or a bad kid. No one knew of my neurodiversity. Mum eventually found me another Playschool, one that accepted me for me. There I took a shine to one of the teaching assistants.

My neurodiversity likes fixating on people. I know a lot of people but I don't seem to be able to keep consistent, long lasting friendships...They tend to fizzle out after a short period of time. I become fascinated, obsessed and engrossed with one person.

After Playschool, I attended Infant school. I enjoyed my time here as well, it was imaginative and creative. I again had another lovely teacher. She was very imaginative and inspired my imagination. The perfect recipe, for someone like me with neurodiversity, as I get restless and bored.

I certainly didn't get bored in her class, my mind was stimulated. I had lots of friends, I seemed very popular. I flitted around everyone, but in my own neurodivergence head I felt I really didn't fit in. My neurodiversity disorder creates self-doubt and insecurities at such a young age.

I recall a figure of an eight shaped playground, and walking around its edges on my own. That bizarre feeling of being weird and alone. The craziest thing was I wasn't alone. I had lots of friends but in my neurodiversity mind I created such loneliness.

In Infant school, I had a pair of beautiful Clark's shoes. They were bright red. I loved and fixated on them. I wore them all the time. Eventually they wore out and I couldn't wear them anymore. In fact they fell apart around my feet. Such was their influence. I love red shoes and still wear them today.

I don't like certain textures against my skin. It makes me feel weird, uncomfortable, and itchy. I like things that are not constricting. I dressed for most of my childhood as a 'Tom Boy,' always in dungarees and running wild, splashing through mud and running wildly across fields. I was never trendy and had my own very different style. Definitely a loner, bent on being completely unique.

My thoughts wander back...

At the age of two, I managed to climb on to a kitchen workbench, found a bottle of Calpol and drank it all. I was rushed into hospital and had my stomach pumped. I cried for my Mum while being left in the hospital. Mum believes this traumatic incident with the Calpol caused me to have emotional attachment issues. My Mum was not allowed to stay with me at the hospital. Causing me panic and distress.

I was born differently, no two ways about that. Unfortunately back in the early 80's no one had professionally diagnosed me with my then undiagnosed ADHD and dyslexia. As a child, I did slip through the net in mainstream education. Had I been at school in modern day times, I'm sure it would have been picked up on. How this has affected my life and those around me will now be addressed through the pages of my book.

When I started junior school, I was put in remedial classes. This confused me,

I just couldn't understand why. I always felt my brain was intelligent. It is intelligent. It's just wired a little differently. However, I did find some junior school work difficult academically, I used to write my words backwards and had difficulty pronouncing words, clearly presenting dyslexia from a young age.

Even my Mum went into the junior school to express her concerns with my then undiagnosed dyslexia.

Surprise,

It fell on deaf ears saying, I was just immature for my age and that I would eventually grow out of it! If only I'd been diagnosed then?

Oh well! I wasn't.

And that's exactly how it's been nearly all my life, constant struggles with an undiagnosed neurological disorder.

Recent research into ADHD, especially in females, suggests we are harder to diagnose than males, as females spend more time masking the disability.

So yes, my childhood was lovely, but my undiagnosed ADHD has unwittingly dominated my behaviour. I was always too talkative, boisterous, and loud and labelled a drama queen. Not being academically clever, I tended to experience life through visual stimuli. I enjoyed creating art through patterns and colours.

I have a huge passion for music, I love lots of genres, not just Madonna.

I love songs with meaningful lyrics. I'm particularly drawn to music that creates emotional stimuli. I absolutely love orchestra strings.

My all-time favourite song is probably Massive Attacks 'Unfinished Symphony'.

It heightens my emotions, creating sensations, raising dopamine.

Throughout my life music has created memories, I can be transported back to a place and time, by listening to music.

Throughout the pages of my book, it features references to music artists as it's my way of remembering those memories to share with you.

I also loved to sing, I was a good singer. I enjoyed singing hymns and belonged to my junior school choir, which was most fun. Expressing myself through singing and music. I performed in many of my junior school choir concerts, and even performed in a few junior school nativity plays, once I even played the Virgin Mary. As long as it was creative, and had an opportunity to sing then I loved it.

After my third year in junior school, my Mum wanted me to go to a certain secondary school, because that's where she and my sister went.

However my junior school teachers, at the time, said I was far too immature, so I was kept on at junior school for another year.

You can imagine how that made me feel. My neurodiversity created mental misery. When I finally got into secondary school, people had already formed established friendships and there was me, the new girl...

It was very awkward to begin with. I felt upset. My junior school friends who I had formed relationships with, had all gone on to a different secondary school.

My Mum was adamant I went to her choice of school. Her intentions were good as her choice of secondary school back then had a good reputation.

At secondary school I really did struggle which I cleverly masked. True, I had learning difficulties and wasn't the brightest pupil in the school, but troubled with trauma that happened in my early teens did not help matters...

My School Report, branding me 'out of control' I needed more 'self-control.'....

I was thirteen, going on fourteen, when my life changed dramatically.

My stable family home was torn apart by my Dad being very poorly on a life-support machine. Don't follow rules came thundering through the chaos as my life began to fall apart...

So let me explain that in more detail.

My Dad was critically ill in hospital. My Mum, trying her best to keep the family home together under terrible circumstances. Keeping everything afloat financially was a big strain for my Mum. My Mum was incredible in this period of time, if only I realised that back then. Instead of making things worse with my erratic behaviours. I did not take my dad's illness well and I went off the rails.

I felt unable to cope... I became a pain in the 'arse'... I just didn't understand what was happening to our once perfect home...

I stayed a lot with Helen. Now Helen wasn't someone you would not want as a best friend. More of a school acquaintance to be honest. But my circumstances warranted a friend, so I hung around with her a lot during my Dad's illness.

Now all the boys fancied Helen, and she knew it. Boy did she play on the fact too. She had the body of an athlete, strong sporty legs and a figure any girl would kill for. I felt so unattractive next to her. I felt plain and frumpy...

Now, Helen had a boyfriend called Neil and her Mum would allow him to stay over on occasion. Helen's Mum was engaged to her new fiancé and was spending more time with him than Helen. Her Mum's absence at home allowed her to do what she wanted.

Neil had a friend called Mark. An ugly youth. I would have fancied him but his face was a turn off. Shallow of me, I know, but he looked like a frog.

So while Helen was getting off with Neil I was lumbered with Mark. I was to encounter Mark in an old school doorway, where he demanded an inappropriate act. I was thirteen, an innocent bystander in Mark's adult world. I was not yet an adult. Pure in thought and mind. I still played with toys, listened to Madonna sing 'Like a Virgin,' and here I was, confronted with grownup things.

It was unpleasant and I felt ashamed. I felt sick and disgusted with myself, that feeling I'd done something very wrong. After which, Mark told me I was frigid.

Mark, unashamedly, was eager to tell Helen and Neil what I'd done. He did this to humiliate me. I felt very uncomfortable. I withdrew mentally.

At the time, I wanted my life to be innocent but it was tarnished by Mark.

It did have an effect on my mental stability at the time, wishing it never had happened. It was a lot to cope with, I just wasn't mature enough to comprehend such things.

Helen lost her virginity to Neil, it happened in front of me and Mark while we were listening to Neneh Cherry's Buffalo Stance. Mark, encouraged by Helen and Neil's behaviour, tried it on with me. I was thirteen, and certainly wasn't ready.

Mark and I argued while Helen lost her virginity.

Remembering what Mark had forced me to do in that old school doorway, a feeling of disgust overwhelmed me. I told him to stop and get off me.

I was strong. Stood up for what I believed in. No! I insisted again. No!

Mark was angry, and again told me I was ugly and frigid. He vowed to embarrass me even further by informing all of our friends, I was still a virgin.

Peer group pressure is a strong persuader, and I wanted to be accepted. But I stood my ground and said NO!

I love Neneh Cherry's music. She is a Swedish singer-songwriter, rapper, who was huge amongst my generation in the late 80s. Still to this day. When I hear her Buffalo Stance, I'm taken back to that vile memory at Helen's Mum's house.

My parents were very sensible with money, so I was dressed in what was affordable. Her parents were affluent, and could afford to spoil her with the latest trends. She always wore the latest fashions. Her Reeboks were bright and colourful, and the height of fashion in the 80s. These she flaunted, to my detriment.

My Mum could only afford to buy me Velcro Asda Zoom trainers, dull and inferior when seen against Helen's Reeboks.

Was I embarrassed? The hell I was! Especially when standing next to Helen in her high fashion footwear and I in my untrendy Zooms!

So in later life, when finally earning my own money, I somehow became addicted to trainers, always buying the best, top of the range styles. In the light of my recent diagnosis, I realise why I exhibited such incredulous impulses.

All the boys fancied Helen with her 'cherry' curly permed hair and her big hooped earrings. Such styles were very fashionable at the end of the 80s.

Mum refused to let me have my hair permed, informing me it was 'common'. I had to wait for my Mum's permission before I was even allowed to have my ears pierced and only then to have little studs and not trendy earrings.

Helen was so 'trendy' and here was me wearing my Asda Zooms. An unfashionable outcast, trying to cope with the complexities of growing up and surviving in a very confusing world.

In my life I've known lots of people, in fact many people. People will say comments like I know everybody I'm so popular.

I've engaged with and interacted with most of them. But if the truth be known I actually don't really like being with lots of people which is another contradiction as I'm also known as a people person confusing yes I know. But the real me can be a real loner, as a young girl I was popular but lonely. I lived inside my own bubble of thoughts and my brain would create really bad low self-esteem issues due to the lack of dopamine.

This bad trait of low dopamine has hindered me throughout my life. I never really thought I would have a successful career due to thinking I wasn't good enough...

At the time that is what I truly thought, crippled with self-esteem issues.

You see how I've diverted off the subject, that's ADHD for you.

I need to get back on track with my story...

So where was I? Yes Helen, Neil and Mark.

Helen continued to go out with Neil. I eventually got bored of them, I didn't really fit in with their lifestyle so I deserted Helen and found another dopamine buddy called Kelly. My school work, around this time, was rapidly going downhill. Mum came to my rescue, explaining to my teachers, my Dad was in hospital seriously ill, and this was affecting my learning. So, what was the school's response to this? Did they help me? Well you know the answer to that.

That was the problem back then, we just had to get on with it. No sympathy, no counselling, you were on your own, you just had to continue the best you could. So I just went further down that rabbit hole, the school giving up on me. I was put in detention given lines. Lines!

The worst thing to do with someone with neurological issues. Had I been in school now in the same position, I would have hopefully had the correct support. It makes me so sad, even now, recalling how I was treated. So I just kept on masking my problems as I always...

Kelly, my new dopamine buddy...

Kelly was very popular at school. She was always great fun and all I remember was we laughed a lot, boy did we laugh a lot!

She understood my love and devotion for Madonna. Kelly nicknamed me Madonna, encouraging me to dance and sing to anyone who would listen. I recall doing my Madonna routines in the common room, much to everyone's delight.

Reflecting on my school days, I remember being shit at sports. Crazy that, considering in my late thirties I would complete two marathons and win awards for my running. Here I go again, drifting off the subject...

Kelly made PE classes funny. Encouraged by her lust for fun, we'd both run around the girl's changing room flashing our bits and tits, much to the annoyance of everyone and of course our PE teachers. I'd end up in detention, but what the hell we had fun. So being labelled 'Lack of self-control', I took it upon myself to prove them wrong!

It wasn't a pleasant time for anyone in the family.

Soon after Dad's admission, Grandad was taken ill and he too was taken to hospital. Uncle John had a heart attack and at one point we had three male family members in hospital at the same time. Sadly, Grandad died alone in the hospital, which only added to my Dad's distress. So the late 80s was not a nice time for me or my family.

I'll stop there, hopefully tempted to read more... To delve deeper into my life and explore more in greater detail my extraordinary journeys to come...

Defined by my inspiration Madonna. 'I don't follow rules!'

CHAPTER TWO

VIRGIN

So let me tell you more...
My Dad was seriously ill in hospital and I was too young to visit him in intensive care. I was thirteen going on fourteen, with a lot of anger and frustration to channel somewhere, confused why my perfect family home was torn apart by my Dad being critically ill. It wasn't my Dad's fault he got ill, and I never want my parents to ever feel any blame because there isn't any.

My Mum did everything she could to keep the house together and provide for my Sister and me. My Mum desperately needed emotional support herself, I just didn't understand this at the time, and I really didn't know or mentally understand her struggles...

Earlier I introduced you to Kelly, a new friend of mine, at the time. Kelly lived in a local village. She was the oldest sister to Vicky and the youngest sister to an older brother.

I loved staying at Kelly's house on the weekends. It was a fun house.

Her parents used to let me stay over. We had great fun, with sleepovers, in a static caravan they parked in their driveway. Kelly, me, Vicky and Jane plus a few others loved exploring the village.

Gangs of boys and girls, aged between thirteen and fifteen, used to meet at the village pub car park on Friday nights.
We also met up with older eighteen-year-old boys who had cars. It was quite normal, then for fourteen-year-old girls to date eighteen-year-old boys.

Back then it was the era of Rita Sue and Bob Too. Rita, Sue and Bob Too was a 1987 British comedy-drama film set in Bradford. It was about two teenage schoolgirls who have a sexual fling with a married man.

Back then it seemed normal, and nobody batted an eyelid. But, today Bob would possibly be looked upon as a sex offender. It was the late 80s, the early 90s and it was the start of the House Music culture. To be more precise, for me it was a fabulous era to be living in.

I loved House Music and still do.

Acid House Music was a subgenre of House Music. It was developed around the mid-1980s by DJs in Chicago, its style characterised by the deep baselines and squelching sounds of an electronic bass synthesiser-sequencer. It gave rise to many derivative forms that included two of my favourites, Detroit Techno and Chicago House. I listened and danced to Detroit Techno legend, Derrick May 'Strings of Life,' the opening strings, creating emotional stimuli for eternity.

Reminiscing Old School Classics by Todd Terry the pioneer of House Music. Todd was influential in moving House music beyond the early Chicago House sound of 1984–86. He crossed the sounds of House with Hip Hop breaks to create a more energised and popular sound that was able to reach commercial success outside the underground House scene.

I recall being lost in a world of Acid House & Hip Hop music, while I danced the night away. I felt free and uninhibited, the music masking, if only for a moment, the mental torment I was going through at the time.

A quick mention; this book just isn't big enough to talk more about my favourite House Anthems!

Obsessed with the old skool mainstream classics, by DMob 'Acieed', Yazz 'The only way is up' and Technotronic 'Pump up the Jam'. Dancing erratically, moving my arms up & down, then lifting my legs in time to the beat at the Friday night youth club. It was a memorable decade for this genre of music that will forever live on in my memory.

The village pub car park, with its ghetto blasters, blaring out Acid House music, and us dancing unashamedly around the cars to Lil Louis 'French kiss, and A Guy called Gerald 'Voodoo Ray.' Fashion styles were wild, Wallaby shoes, Kicker's, hoody tops, MC hammer pants and pink baggy trousers.

Everything was bright, everything was colourful, and everything was different. Life was returning to normal, but was it?

The crazy thing is, even today, I can get lost in Acid and old Skool House.

I love it. There's nothing better than getting in my car, putting that music on full blast, and just losing your mind to it.

To me it's relaxation for my crazy neurotic head. To the uninitiated, it is probably a racket of absolute shit.

But to me, a life saver.

I used to incorporate Madonna's Vogue dance moves and just lose myself in the dance passions I loved...

Yes, I'm repetitive in retelling my story, but boy I am still proud to have been in that generation revolution that was Acid House!

So let me get back on track. I'm going off on a tangent, but you should be used to that by now. I recall things in no particular order, so you'll appreciate the problems I have in retelling my story.

That's my ADHD mind for you!

So every Friday night, Kelly and us girls would leave school and go straight over to Kelly's house.

We were having a weekend sleepover. Where? Who cares? We lived for our Friday night get together, so whether it was in Kelly's or Vicky's bedroom or in the caravan stuck outside Kelly's it didn't matter.

Remember Helen? Well I'd knocked her on the head for now.

Bored with her. My fixation and dopamine level was now focused on Kelly.

Right, back to Friday nights.

We would meet up with eighteen year old boy racers.

Their GTis and XR3i cars would impress us fun seeking girls in the hope of 'getting off' with one of them!

One of the lads, Mike, who I was at school with, he was in the year above me, he was a little different to the others, and we became good friends.

In time, he would become Kelly's full-time boyfriend. Mike had dark skin and wore dreadlocks. He smoked and was a good dancer. Everything about him looked cool and trendy.

I loved Mike...but as a friend...

Mike was a DJ back in the late 80s and 90s. The trend was to mix vinyl records on the Technic 1210's decks. Nostalgic memories of him mixing Strictly Rhythm vinyl, MK Burning, being a classic and one of my favourites.

His Technics 1210's decks looked cool, and had an attractive satin black look. You could adjust the sound through an adjustment controller on a slider.

Mike was fantastic at mixing music and as our Friday nights progressed, we used to end up having raves on an old disused airfield in an abandoned old brick building.

Mike & his best mate Pete, would bring their decks and some of the lads would bring a generator with speakers. These nights on the airfield became popular, so much so that the police eventually got involved, it even made the front page of the Grimsby Telegraph branded us all Acid House ravers!

I never took drugs.

My friends? Yes, maybe, but not all! Ecstasy and Acid was popular, but I was too scared at the time to try so I never did.

The main thing in my life is, my head doesn't like to be out of control. I smoked cigarettes back then, because you did. It was cool. The normal grown up thing to do. Not frowned upon.

Friday night rave parties on the airfield field were incredible times. Acid House Music, blaring out, everybody happy. No violence, no fighting, no arguments, just happy people having a good time.

Back then I would try drinking cans of lager, but only in small moderation. I was always in fear of being out of control. In truth, I actually hated the taste of alcohol and never got drunk.

The fear of being out of control that was to resonate throughout my life.

I have a fear of losing it, mentally, so I must be in control of my behaviour at all times. Maybe I'm a control freak who knows. But to me it's important I'm in command of all my faculties. So substances like alcohol have always been taboo.

I can picture those Friday nights as if it were yesterday. Walking down to the village pub. Waiting and wondering which boys would turn up. We girls, dressed up as attractively as we could afford in our unique fashion, smelling of cheap Dewberry oil by Body Shop. The laughing, the giggling, the joking, and of course those great tunes, a mix of House, Techno and Acid House music blaring out.

Such great memories. Such great times.

A regular guest to our raves was a lad called Ben. Ben was eighteen but hell was he cute. He drove a car and he had a reputation, the girls loved Ben.

Yes you've probably guessed it, Ben took a shine to me.......

On reflection Ben was charming, though. A cheeky Chap, with the ability to get into girls' knickers.

So was I his next pair of knickers?

Ben asked me out and I guess he was my first, proper attempt at having a boyfriend. I was fourteen and he was eighteen. And boy did I think I was kingpin and cock sure of myself.

I never told my mum and certainly didn't want my dad to find out that I had a boyfriend, but I sure as hell did tell all my friends at school...

At first Ben and I just kissed. It was nothing more than just a kiss.

It was a New Year's Eve party at Jane's house. I can remember one of the lads having a VHS video of a porn film and he put it on. I'd never seen one before.

I didn't even know they existed, that's how naive I was. I can remember watching it and feeling somewhat uncomfortable.

God it didn't feel right. Was this kind of thing legal?

Ben started to kiss me and said shall we go upstairs? Innocently, I said yes. Everyone was everywhere around the house, so I thought nothing of it.

How wrong I was... I really had no idea what was going to happen, that's how inexperienced I was. I really wasn't ready for what happened next.

Jane's house was weird and I found myself, with Ben, in Jane's parents' bedroom.

I remember it having a huge mirror. Ben didn't even put me on the bed.

With both of us still fully dressed, I found myself on the floor.

I was confused, I kind of didn't know what to do with myself. I just laid there stiffly, feeling awkward, and very uncomfortable. I even still had my shoes on!

This was far from what I'd expected it to be, my first time with a boyfriend...

I could hear the party going on down below. I could hear the laughter and the music. Just wishing I was down there enjoying myself with them... My childhood innocence flashing through my eyes.

That feeling of guilt and not being able to say No!

It was wrong, it felt wrong, but fear had me speechless and succumbed.

I was only fourteen and he was eighteen...

I went back downstairs to join everyone at the party. I sat down on a stool and put my blue bandana over my face, feeling very awkward and embarrassed.

I remember everyone was having fun, and enjoying the party. Life to everyone carrying on as normal. I was silently crying underneath that bandana. I felt confused, a sense that I'd done something wrong. I was only fourteen years old, not ready to be exposed to what had just happened to me...

My home life was in complete tatters. My Dad was seriously ill, my childhood dreams were crushed. I didn't want anyone to look at me underneath that bandana and I don't recall Ben even asking if I was ok?

At the time truth be told, I just wasn't ready for such adult encounters, I was still a child. Not emotionally mature enough to understand such things...

A very confusing time, it was all too much for my neurological brain to understand.

However, I don't hold any hate or malice towards Ben. Time is a great healer.

So I wish him well. That's what I always do, I always try to find the good in people, and I try to understand why. I don't hold onto grudges. I like things to be set free, so I can move on...

At the time, my school work went further and further spiralling downhill. I became disruptive, my mind racing all over the place.

I just couldn't concentrate or focus on anything, my thoughts racing constantly and I had a feeling I was seriously out of control...The truth is I was totally out of control.

The head of year at my secondary school tried in vain to humiliate me. By making me stand on the stage in front of everyone in the morning assembly. Telling everyone my attitude was like I was flicking two fingers up at the school.

They were right, I was rebellious! Oh how I rebelled...

I just didn't care anymore, against my better judgement I acted as if I was proud...

When my Dad finally came out of hospital, my home life was completely upside down. My perfect childhood was destroyed. My relationship with both my parents was strained. Dad was still not very well and I hadn't seen him for months...

I recall the day when Mum brought my Dad back home from the hospital. I was dreading seeing him again. My big alpha male Dad now looked like a frail and poorly old man. My Dad, our family protector, had been very ill on a life-support machine.

I was not allowed to visit him while he was in intensive care, because I was too young. My neurological brain just couldn't comprehend not being able to visit my Dad, my childhood hero! In his absence my childhood innocence was taken away from me. It was far too much for my neurological brain to comprehend.

The first thing I impulsively shouted when I first saw my Dad walk through the front door was, "Send him back, that's not my Dad!"

Hurtful cruel words that deeply upset my parents.

The truth was, seeing my Dad for the first time in a long time traumatised me. His illness traumatised me. I missed him, I missed being the perfect family.

It wasn't my Dad's fault he got ill, I never want my Dad to ever feel he was to blame because he wasn't. I just wasn't mature enough to cope with it all that was the real problem. So I had to lash out somewhere...

Dad became frustrated as he wanted to get better and get back to the life he knew.

And there was me, the problem child, to hinder his recovery...

The deep truth be told I was hurting inside, deep rooted pain that I couldn't tell anyone about.

My head was full of confusion, a swirl of crippling brain fog. Mentally paralysed. My rose tinted childhood was ruined, tarnished never to be the same again.

I was lashing out at home masking my true inner feelings of pain. That is what I have done all my life, masked out my traumas, kept them all a secret, an eternity of masking my true authentic self just to fit in and be accepted.

To the outside world I physically appeared normal, always appearing loud and confident, a rebel without a cause, little did people know the real truth.

My ability to pay attention, riddled with learning difficulties and emotional trauma, are sure to be a very good reason why I failed my GCSEs the first time round. I had no idea I suffered from neurodiversity back then, so this was a huge contributing factor. In retrospect, I also find it difficult, believing an extra year in junior school would have improved my maturity. However, my failure to get my GCSE grades the first time around, forced me to spend an extra year retaking those exams again, only added to my mental instability.

When I found out my GCSE grades were not good enough, I was gutted. All my friends got better grades than me. I was so embarrassed. Embarrassed because I knew I was intelligent but my then undiagnosed disability was hindering me.

But I didn't stay on the floor for long. I picked myself up and got back on track.

I contacted the school and arranged to re-sit my exams again, this time I was determined to pass. I would make it my mission to pass them, through pure hard work and determination...

CHAPTER THREE

FROZEN

My Sister went to a college in Sheffield before eventually going on to Oxford University. She had student digs in Sheffield, so I used to travel by train on a weekend to visit her. To be honest, we've a love-hate relationship. I love my Sister to pieces but we do clash in personalities. We can, at times, dislike each other immensely, but we'll always be there for each other should we need to. It's a very bizarre sisterly relationship.

We're not close but we are, if that makes sense.

Mum didn't mind, me staying the weekend with my Sister.

In order for me to go with her to nightclubs and bars I would need ID.

Fake ID was easily obtained in those days.

Mine displayed I was part of the student's union, so I would go out with my Sister to the bars and nightclubs around Sheffield.

I'd go with my Sister to the Leadmill on the bus. The Leadmill is a live music venue and nightclub in Sheffield. It opened in 1980 and featured bands, such as the Human League, Cabaret Voltaire, Heaven 17, and ABC.

I never drank whilst attending these venues. I actually never liked the taste of it.

Alcohol takes control, and I don't like to be out of control, but you already know this, see I told you I like to repeat myself!

I loved it in Sheffield, I just wanted to have a great time. All I wanted to do was dance and party. I loved it, expressing myself on the dance floor, dancing of course to Madonna, who at this time, was at the height of her fame. Her music was blaring out everywhere. I would show off on the dance floor, dancing to Madonna's Vogue or any artist's music that motivated me to dance. I also loved dancing with my Sister to her favourite dance track, 'What would we do' by DSK.

I knew I was a good dancer. A true exhibitionist and attention seeker. People in the nightclubs would stand around me in a circle to watch me dance. Creating the shapes that I had learnt from Madonna's dance routines.

'Only when I'm dancing can I feel this free'....

I danced to perfection. Lost myself in the music.

I loved the attention and wanted to be famous, loved and adored. Not cast aside, as a failure as my neurodiversity mind thought at the time.

My Sister was in Sheffield for one year. She then returned to Grimsby, before embarking on to Oxford University...

Whilst in Grimsby, my Sister, myself and her friends spent time at Gulliver's nightclub. My Sister and her friends were all very stylish, wearing the latest designs by Manchester Born Fashion Designer John Richmond. The Designer launched a diffusion line of fashion called 'Destroy,' this being popular amongst my Sister and her friends. As well as the legendary Dame Vivienne Westwood.

My Sister's friends had cars so they used to pick us up. We'd start off at Cleethorpes in Willy's Wine Bar, which was a really cool place to be. We'd meet up with trendy new people. DJ's who would regularly be in Sublevel, an underground vinyl record shop in Grimsby, played the latest dance tracks. The place was full of lads looking cute, with their 90's trend of long hair called 'curtains'. Girls in tight hot pants, cropped tops, with scrunchies in their hair, dancing the night away...

Being underage and getting away with it, made me somewhat big headed...

It was the 90s music scene, and it felt great to be alive. I was having the time of my life. We also used to go to Cleethorpes's Pier then on to JDs nightclub, with all the 'Sharon and Tracy's' a term used for girls dancing around there handbags...

I remember great memories of going to the Flam's 'Sunday under 18's Night' dancing erratically, to House Music, and drinking soft drinks. I recall entering a dance competition at the Flam, it was on the stage, and winning a 12" vinyl record, by Sueno Latino, an Italian Ambient House Classic. Fantastic memories to saviour for eternity.

So here was me, hanging out with my Sister and her friends. Meeting up with new people, and having a great time. I was living the life. Mum knew I was safe with my older Sister, so there was no need for her to be concerned.

I would go night clubbing in a mix and match set of my Mum and Sister's clothing. I had also got myself a part-time job at Hobo, which was a trendy boutique in Grimsby town centre. It was owned by a local beauty queen, she had won Miss England and competed in Miss World. I used to buy clothes from her and pay weekly for the privilege.

Boy did I have some really trendy outfits...

Thrift stores provided me with trendy fashions and I always dressed uniquely. I like to be different from other people, so I dyed my hair black, Mum used to style it for me in curls, so it was just like Madonna's in the blonde ambition tour, a roller and set. I wore my make-up just like Madonna, danced like her and tried to do everything like Madonna.

I was strongly influenced by everything that Madonna said and did.

I used to have false eyelashes and painted my lips with bright red lipstick.

My eyebrows always arched like Madonna, and I had tight velvet hot pants like the ones she wore on her blonde ambition tour. So I fixated on wearing the same. I bought and wore underwear as outer wear and had the same pointy bra as she did.

Yes! I was certainly the wacky one. I was way out there with my unique sense of clothes.

There were no boyfriends after Ben. However I did have a huge crush on a lad called Stuart who would always be in Willy's wine bar. He was a lot older than me but beautiful with it. He had long curly hair and a pretty face. He looked very much like my husband Ed when he was younger.

I can remember being brave enough to ask him out and he refused, explaining I was far too young. That I now respect having been exposed to the type of lads that took advantage of young girls. I was absolutely devastated. I could not believe he didn't want to go out with me.

So that was the gorgeous Stuart.

Reflecting on my ADHD I can possibly now understand why I fixated on him. A symptom of ADHD. I can remember feeling hyper fixated on him creating dopamine. I craved to see him, literally wanting to go out into bars and nightclubs, to find him, so I could look at him. It was an addiction, Stuart being the greatest aphrodisiac one could ever have. That's ADHD for you. So yeah I had a huge crush on Stuart and Stuart totally rejected me...

Let me set the scene.

One weekend, whilst walking through Grimsby Town, I bumped into Kim, an old acquaintance. We'd first met at a local riding school, where my Sister and I went horse riding. I was eleven then, and four years later, fate had brought us back together. We talked, I told her I had just secured part time work at weekends at Leon's Fish Restaurant and also about my part time work in trendy fashion boutique Hobo. Kim was a lot older than me, a bit rough around the edges, if truth be told. Reflecting back, to that chance meeting with Kim, I recall her being somewhat shocked at my appearance. She'd commented on how much I'd changed.

The last time we'd met I was, in her eyes, a young innocent girl. Now look at me, all grown up. Kim had just had a baby, and was a new mum. She was living with her partner Dean, in a house literally doors from where... I dare say it...I lost my virginity to Ben...and now she knew...

My ADHD started taking over me, I started boasting in my own maniacal fashion, wanting to impress, so I started romancing the truth. I can remember boasting to Kim about how I'd lost my virginity and how I loved to drink and smoke.

My mind lost total control of reason and I confessed to going out at night and visiting nightclubs and all manner of things. In truth, I really didn't know what I was saying. True to form, my ADHD caused me to show off trying to impress, building an image that wasn't really me. I wanted Kim to think I was a big girl now, and how grown up I'd become. Cool and outgoing.

Sadly, I'd sown the seeds of my own destruction and at the age of fifteen I was about to walk. Naively into the lion's lair.

Kim was older and far more experienced in the ways of the world than me. I really didn't know what I was getting myself into, so when she suggested I should come and visit her at her house.

I naively unwittingly agreed.

We parted, the best of friends and arranged to meet again at her house...

I never really thought much of it other than I thought, fine, Kim wants to see me. She's got a baby and I never thought of her as a predator, and had no inkling of her intentions or the danger I was putting myself in.

So that following Saturday, at the vulnerable age of fifteen, I went and stayed with Kim and her baby. All appeared very innocent. We ate, watched television, and put the baby to bed. The baby slept in a cot in her and Dean's bedroom. Soon the baby was fast asleep and Dean joined us. At this point Kim fetched out the drink and we all started drinking. Innocent me, thought nothing untoward was happening.

However, there I was showing off trying to impress. The more I drank, the more out of control I became.

For the first time in my life I was drunk...

This is my own personal account, in my own words, of what I can still remember from this traumatic night. It is uncomfortable to write and I know it will be uncomfortable to read.

Kim put on a porn film on a VHS video player just like the night I lost my virginity to Ben.

Alarm bells rang.

I instantly felt uncomfortable. Yes I was drunk, but why a porn film? It was all getting a bit weird and uneasy.

The next thing I remember was Kim and Dean kissing passionately. Encouraged by the porn film, it was obvious they would eventually go all the way.

I watched, feeling very uneasy not sure what to do. I was drunk but I still remember that feeling of being uncomfortable.

I froze, my mind racing back to my encounter with Ben. What do I do now? I remembered asking myself. How awkward is this? The night was turning into a nightmare. This is not what I envisaged or had planned. I thought I was there to have a nice night with Kim, Dean and the baby.

It was obvious to me now, they had other intentions. Despite being drunk, I should have left then. Got the hell out of this pornographic nightmare, but I didn't. Why I didn't, has haunted me for most of my life.

I sat there, like a spare prick at a wedding. Then, Kim started making advances towards me. To my horror she kept touching me up. I of course resisted. No, I shouted, refusing to join in. I can remember moving away from them as they were getting quite carried away with themselves.

I took myself into a bedroom, where their baby slept. The child was fast asleep in its cot and I laid on the bed. I just wanted to get the hell out there before, God knows what will happen.

It all seemed somewhat bizarre, on reflection, I just laid on that bed trying to gather my thoughts and fathom out what to do next. I must've passed out, the drink finally taking its toll on a girl not used to drinking.

I awoke to find my knickers on the floor.

What the hell was going on? I'd no idea what was happening.

I lay there, the room black and red and everything spinning around. Had I been drugged, or were these the effects of the booze? All I knew, I felt ill, my mind unable to focus on the reality of my predicament.

What in hell was going on?

Reality returned when I felt pressure on my body. Kim and Dean focused into view and I heard Kim telling Dean to hold me down.

I must have passed out again.

When I finally awoke, much later, I remember feeling confused and struggling to remember what had just happened to me. Slowly my memory returned to my ordeal gradually unfolding.

It was then I realised what had happened.

I was horrified...

I can't remember Kim and Dean coming into the bedroom. I really can't remember that part. I was drunk and I've even questioned if I drugged. I had definitely passed out...

More drifted into mind. The smell of Dean as he held me down. I recall vaguely calling Dean the 'Devil,' then it all fades into a black and red blur...

I felt ashamed and violated.

What had I done? What had they done more like? I was fifteen, Dean a twenty six year old and Kim nineteen.

What indeed had they done? Raped an underage minor, that's what they had done.

I can only describe my rape as a nightmarish blur of black and red.

A pornographic film unwittingly not of my making. For me it was a fuzzy, confusion of muffled voices and inaudible noises. An overwhelming sense of helplessness.

I can remember turning my head and seeing their baby sleeping innocently in its cot. How disturbing is that?

If I'm honest, it happened so long ago, time makes reality fade into memory.

Had I been drugged? I know I was drunk. I kept on going in and out of consciousness, my body completely comatose. It was early in the morning and getting light.

I really have no idea how I actually got out of the house, I only remember fleeing the scene, and half dressed. I ran in chaotic confusion in a hectic dash to escape.

Panic overwhelmed me and I told myself to get to Kelly's as quickly as I could. Kelly lived on the other side of the village. Her parents kept a static caravan parked in the driveway for sleepovers and my hope was to seek shelter there.

Scared and confused, I opened the caravan door, and walked in. Kelly and Jane were in there, fast asleep in their bunks. My intrusion woke them but they were not at the least surprised to see me, and said good morning. We often hung out together having sleepovers. This was normal to them, unaware of the trauma I'd been through. I was shattered and just curled up in a ball next to Kelly and fell asleep.

I know I was raped.

Was I drugged? Possibly. Only my rapists know that.

I never saw Kim and Dean again. I really have no idea where they are, whether they still live locally or whether they moved away. I couldn't give a shit if they were dead or alive. I have no intention of ever finding them. They are a painful memory, best forgotten, now deliberately hidden in the windmills of my mind.

I never told anybody about my rape. I didn't tell my friends or my family. It really fucked and messed with my head. It did have a detrimental effect on my life.

However I carried that pain, the hurt, the trauma for many years without any professional help. I mistakenly thought it was my fault, most victims do. Mentally, I blamed myself for what I had said to Kim, So was it my fault?

No! I wasn't asking for it.

There was no excuse for what they did. I was innocent.
However the damage of such an act, coupled with neurodiversity, would create a baggage of problems that would affect the rest of my life.

I was traumatised there was no doubt about that. I didn't speak about it. Didn't want to speak about it. I blocked it out, masked it. I hid that intense deep-rooted pain in trying to believe I'd actually been raped. I had read stories about rape. That unwarranted shame it caused to those poor innocent victims. But here I was, no different to those unfortunate victims, masking anger and shame.

Sadly, I too was a victim of rape, and like most others, did nothing about it.

I should have reported the crime, but I never did. Why didn't I? The truth be told, I was frightened, I really thought no one would believe me. Blamed myself as I always do, probably was asking for it, which I know is totally not true.

So I carried on and tried to be normal, unsure as to what normal really is.

I have PTSD, **post-traumatic stress disorder**, because I've spent years just masking trying to be normal. If there is ever a normal!

After this I never drank a drop of alcohol again. I've been teetotal all my life ever since this traumatic event. Not a bad decision, that's for sure.

Knowing what I know now about ADHD, people with neurodiversity tend to be quite erratic when it comes to drink and drugs. It appears, it was probably a wise decision all those years ago to abstain from alcohol. I've learned to live my life without it, so I don't miss it, I don't crave it. People do find it odd when they find out I'm teetotal. Sometimes people just can't believe I don't drink alcohol. I've even been accused of being pissed, when in fact it's just a natural ADHD dopamine high. It really baffles some. I've chosen to live my life as a teetotaler, I feel in control and I'm not missing out on anything...

Going back to Kim and dean..I did question why they did what they did? However, I believe in Karma.

Karma is an action, work, or deed, and its effect or consequences. In Indian religions, the term refers to a principle of cause and effect, often descriptively called the principle of karma, wherein intent and actions of an individual influence the future of that individual. Good intent and good deeds contribute to good karma while bad intent and bad deeds contribute to bad karma and bad.

I'm hopeful Karma has worked its magic with those two individuals. It can work in magical ways. I'm sure they've had their Karma for what they did. I sometimes wonder if they ever remember what they did to me. Was there any remorse? Did they ever feel guilty? I will never know and I guess I never want to know.

But, hopefully Karma got them...

I've always seen myself as a white witch, and believing in Karma, it's been a factor throughout my life, those people who cross me, tend to get their just deserts.

I'm not a sole, to hold grudges. A grudge, prolonged eventually creates unhappiness. I haven't got time for unhappiness. Life's too short for unhappiness. My brain can't cope with despair.

It's bad enough having to cope with ADHD!

We learn from our lessons; we will get hurt; we always want revenge...

Then we realise that actually, happiness and forgiving people is the best revenge....

Credit: Grimsby Evening Telegraph

CHAPTER FOUR

DON'T CRY FOR ME

With my traumas put aside, but far from forgotten, I set about planning my psychological and physical escape from all that had happened to me. This would include, leaving my beloved Grimsby. I focused my mind on a fresh start, a new beginning, somewhere else to live, a place where no one knew me or the shame I felt. No tears for me then...Be brave, move on!

Further work experience while taking my resit exams, saw me working in the Grimsby Telegraph's photographic department. I bought myself a Praktica 35mm camera and decided to explore the creative side of photography. A decision that would forever provide me with a lifelong passion for photography.

I shall always be grateful to Brian, a comrade at the Telegraph, for his encouragement. He told me I had a talent for taking pictures. So, with help and guidance, from him and the crew at the Newspaper, I explored and became an expert on photography.

My photographs of a local dance festival were published and well received. Those actual photographs can still be viewed, as I put them in one of my treasured scrap books.

After Google had paid me a licensing fee to publish, my seagull eating a chip photograph in 2021. Brian, my mentor at The Telegraph contacted me after all those years. He congratulated me for the achievement and again, reminded me how great a photographer I was and should have made it my career. I unfortunately never did make it my career. Believe it or not I lacked confidence in myself, never thought I was good enough, and so never persuaded it further.

A GCSE Photography assignment taken around Grimsby, early 90s, using black & white and sepia. Model: my friend Aaron.

However back then in the early 90's photography became my passion. I would get friends to do model assignments for me, and I'd experiment with an assortment of themes and techniques. Creating Madonna styled photographs, similar to the black & white photos I saw in Athena. My ADHD fixation on her, controlling my thinking. Incredible, black and white sepia tone pictures, resulted. Those amazing photographs that are still in my portfolio, along with various other modelling photographs of friends taken around Grimsby.

So my photography kept me occupied as well as my part time employment. I was praying I'd achieve the grades to enable me to get the Hell out of Grimsby and attend college. Meanwhile I would continue entertaining myself, by partying with my sister and her friends, this became a priority, and hopefully it would ease the pain and anguish I was inwardly hiding.

One thing I've never been afraid of, that's hard work. I've inherited this work ethic from my parents and Madonna. Work hard and you'll achieve success. So when I failed my GCSEs the first time round, I was so determined the second time round to do my absolute best on my results, and be rewarded with at least C grade GCSEs, or possibly higher.

Throughout my life, I've always aimed to be independent. Earning money, to enable me to buy my own things and not rely on anyone else but myself, was a priority. So while I waited to go to college I worked my socks off.

Just to add to my list of traumas, during my resitting of my GCSE's, my then art teacher exposed himself to me.
It took place in the darkroom, my pervert art teacher unzipping his flies and exposing himself. So much for trusting a teacher. I just screamed, and ran out of the darkroom.
Later, I did confront him, calling him 'gross'.' He just laughed sadly, I should have reported him, but I didn't.
They'd probably have said I was lying, and not believed me, so I kept it quiet.
I was horrified. That my teacher exposed himself to me in a dark room. What was he expecting me to do? You can imagine my dilemma.
I never did tell anyone about it, protecting this teacher's identity...
Fortunately not all, educationists, abuse their position.

I worked very hard in my GCSE resits, determined to achieve those grades I so needed. My super hyper fixation that's what made me so determined to achieve my dream. I had a dream and I made it my priority. Hoping it was going to change my life, for the better, I had made a plan that by September 1992, I was to move away from Grimsby, and start my new life in the West Midlands.
In the period before I went to college, I spent the time trying to keep myself busy, in a vain attempt to blot out the anguish of my traumas.

GCSE Photography black & white project.
Early 90s.

Model: My friend Edward Winfield

At the time I didn't really have a one particular best friend as such. I would continue to drift between Kelly and Helen.

In the past Helen and I had our differences, what with boyfriend issues and the like. But nothing could be as bad as the rape trauma I'd suffered, so I put a side to our differences and made friends.

I can recall going to Manchester on a train, with Helen. To experience the Mecca of Affleck's Palace and visit Eastern Bloc Records. At the time Affleck's was the mecca for alternative cultures, an emporium of eclecticism.

The atmosphere was amazing.

We meandered through a colourful maze of outrageous clothes and garments from every part of the world. Suede waistcoats, platform shoes, all sorts of unusual things. Right up my street it was, and I had a fabulous time.

Manchester impressed me, a Mecca of vibrant people, in their unique individual style of fashions. It was also the home of some of the great legendary musicians of the time in the 90's, The Stone Roses, Happy Mondays, The Charlatans, Morrissey to name just a few. I hoped, one day soon I would be living in this city.

I made it my ultimate dream to one day be living there. However, you've got to be careful what you wish for.....

Just to give you another crazy insight on how my neurodivergent impulsive brain works; Before my sixteenth birthday my National Insurance card arrived. At the time I was quite obsessed with the legendary DJ Sasha. Back then he was known for his DJ sets playing Acid House Music. So on impulse I wrote back to National Insurance and told them they had forgotten to include one of my middle names. That being Sasha! A few weeks later my new National Insurance card arrived, and guess what? They had added the name 'Sasha' into my middle name. No questions asked! It was only when I was getting married to Ed that it then caused complications. The registrar had to put on our wedding certificate, also known as 'Sasha.' You couldn't get away with that now in the modern digital world...

Great music has always influenced my life, especially Madonna's. On reflection, Madonna made sex look wonderful, so I guess that's why I was a bit confused with my sexual experiences, which, as you know, have been horrific!

I learned that Madonna too has been a victim of rape, so possibly through her music and art it's her way she expresses the hurt such abuse inflicts on one's mind. When you've been a victim of sexual trauma you find ways to block it from memory. However, the trauma is still there, waiting in the recess of your mind for the opportunity to raise its ugly head and return, triggered by the simplest of things. You learn to deal with it, cover up your embarrassment, not talk about it, and get on with your life.

I never laid the burden of disclosing my traumas to my family or friends. I didn't want them to be upset, or feel any blame. So why add extra worry about putting my traumas onto them.

I was however lashing out all over, holding onto my secrets. No one had any idea, I never told them.

So I kept myself to myself...by working hard.

Madonna was my life line... Through her music she kept me going...

So I put away the tears of destruction...Don't cry for me...Grimsby!

GCSE Photography portfolio.
Model: Arran

GCSE Photography model: Bilo

Credit: Daily Express Seagull article

64

CHAPTER FIVE

CONFESSIONS

I was now working full time at Bluecrest Fish Factory, packing fish. My evenings and weekends I spent working at Leon's Fish Restaurant, and on Saturdays I worked at Hobo, the trendy fashion boutique. Grimsby, my birthplace, the haven of my childhood, the place I felt safe, now shattered beyond repair. Ripped apart by traumas and educational failures. I no longer trusted anyone. I just wanted to get the hell out of the place.

At home, I'd argue, and became a destructively disobedient Pratt, to the point of not giving a fuck about anything for that matter. Inwardly, I raged, unable to emotionally get my shit together. Neither parent could handle my defiance. I was rebelling against a society I believed failed me. Having insulted Mum, Dad's retribution was to smash up my stereo system in my bedroom.

I thought no one can control me. I was a wild child, running amok and life at home descended into anarchy with me the instigator.

However, throughout all this chaos of my unhinged erratic emotions at home, my parents never failed or once gave up on me, when at times they could have quite easily had. I have always felt guilty about how I behaved towards my parents at that time. All I've ever wanted was them to be proud of me. I just wanted them to love me. But they always loved me unconditionally and still do, I just didn't know it at the time. This is a classic example of how neurodiversity can make me overthink everything, then I'm crippled with self-esteem issues...

So in August 1992 I got my GCSE resit results and guess what? I got the grades I needed to go college in the West Midlands to study Photography.

I really excelled in my resits, it took a while but I eventually did it, achieving a grade B in art, photography and English Literature and finally a grade C in English.

I'd need to be there in September, so I needed to urgently sort out student digs. Mum was brilliant and helped me obtain a student grant. Luckily I'd saved up a little money, when working, but would it be enough? I hadn't thought about paying rent, paying bills or anything like that. Not economic thoughts at all. My only thought was to get the fuck out of Grimsby and start a new life.

One thing I know about having ADHD is that we are impulsive and sometimes we do things without thinking. I hadn't really thought about how I was going to live, where I was going to stay and how I was to survive.

Fortunately mum was on the ball.

My sister was also going to Oxford University so my Mum was losing me and my sister. So Mum set about finding student digs for both of us. I'll always be grateful to my Mum. She really was very encouraging.

Throughout all the chaos at home, my parents were fantastically proud I was leaving home to further my education.

Mum was a fantastic artist and created incredible pieces of artwork. She still does. She was accepted into the Slade School of Arts, an incredible art college in London. One of the best in the country. However, her own Dad was very draconian and frowned upon women going to college. Women should concentrate on being housewives, not artists, and stopped her attending.

Women's Lib, unrecognised, frowned upon in Granddad's days, sadly.

I feel mum's dreams have always been thwarted due to caring for others or outdated ethos. Mum really does have a big heart, she's one of the kindest, caring people you ever would want to meet.

I would trust my Mum with my life, she's a very special person.

So mum organised everything for me to go to college.

Mum didn't want me initially to live independently in student digs. She thought I was still too immature. It was arranged for me to live in a house under the guidance of the college. The room would be rented from the owners of the house who would provide meals and washing facilities. I would share a bedroom with another student. The internet was none existent back then, so you relied on information given by the college about your allocated accommodation.

I was to be billeted in student digs in a council house owned by a very scruffy dirty lady called Maggie. She lived in the house with a young teenage lad called James. She lived in the heart of a town called Wednesbury, which is situated just off the M6 motorway. Not far from the first IKEA and Walsall.

Before I left, mum did a huge shop. She bought all my favourite foods, along with essentials, such as shampoo, toilet rolls, toothbrush and toothpaste, all the things I would never have thought of packing.

I left all my Madonna scrapbooks in my bedroom at home. I wasn't taking them, they were too precious. However I did take some Madonna posters hoping I could display them in my new bedroom.

Mum drove a huge estate car and we packed it to absolute capacity. And we set off. I was on my way out of Grimsby, at long last to start a new life and have a new destiny.

I left Grimsby in September 1992 to do an Ordinary National Diploma in Photography at College in the West Midlands. I wanted to escape Grimsby, for many reasons. I believed starting afresh, somewhere else, would give me status, and impress people. The crazy thing, as it turned out, was that I was running away from myself.

I really had no idea what the future held.

Looking back I was a naive, just turned seventeen year-old girl, moving away from home to live in a new town near Birmingham. I was a vulnerable, gullible, trusting young girl, about to be thrown into the insecurity of student life with all its pitfalls.

Now, knowing I am a neurodivergent, I can see why I naively trusted people, I literally believed everything people told me and I always reacted on impulse. I don't think ahead, I don't think of the consequences, and I just hope for the best.

Every day is a journey, my mind impulsively excited.

As we pulled away I felt relieved. I'd prayed for this day and now it was happening.

To be honest it felt surreal.

With Mum at the wheel, we were fearless and set off. Off into an unknown territory we ventured, with only our guile to guide us.

To boldly go to where none of us have gone before. Our journey was enhanced with the music of Seal, Tracy Chapman and Fleetwood Mac, my Mum's favourite artists. My Mum, in her 40s, drove us safely to the West Midlands. We found my student Digs and she dropped me off. She would undertake a similar journey with my Sister as she took her to Oxford, shortly after me.

The journey seemed forever. The motorway was busy and frantic with cars rushing everywhere. I hadn't really experienced this mayhem before. I wasn't really prepared for such a drive.

On arriving at my digs, mum's face said it all. She was mortified. We'd arrived at an old council house, and not a very nice one at that. I'd lived most of my life in a bungalow in a nice part of Grimsby. Now this? Mum, took on that Hyacinth Bucket face, from TVs Keeping up Appearances. You know the one I mean, that look of disgust, when walking into Onslow's council house.

Maggie was waiting for us with her son James.

It was like a scene from Little Britain. Maggie was four feet nine if she was an inch. She was dumpy and fat. Her hair was grey and platted and it hung all the way down her back. It looked like it had never been washed. She wore a scruffy old tabard piny. James, her son, stood beside her. He looked about fifteen. His hair was greasy and he wore a heavy-metal T-shirt.

I can remember thinking, what the actual fuck.
My Mum's face was a picture. You could tell she was horrified. She didn't say a word but I knew what she must be thinking.

What the fuck!
But no, my mother never swore, she was always polite, but I could tell she wasn't happy.
Maggie spoke, in a broad Black Country accent, and invited us into her house. She reassured mum, not to worry about me, I'd be safe in her care and they'd look after me. I could see mum was horrified, no doubt wondering whether putting me with this family had been the right decision.

The house was dirty and pretty small. I kept thinking, God this is not like being at home in Grimsby where I have privacy. Mum helped me unload the car and we inspected my bedroom. My bedroom was really dated and the look took me back to the 1970s. It was fusty, smelly and poorly decorated. Two single beds filled the room.
I could see Mum didn't really want to leave me here.

She wasn't happy.
Me, too. I was far from happy. I certainly didn't want to stay. I felt homesick, and could quite easily have got back in the car and gone back home.

I know now, with ADHD, when things go wrong, I get overwhelmed. You just want to be on your own. I can remember after Mum reluctantly left, I just wanted to be left alone in that horrid bedroom. I didn't want to socialise with Maggie and her son, James. I had no interest in getting to know them, they were just not my kind of people. Classic examples of sensory overload, I felt physically and mentally overwhelmed.

An hour or so later there was a knock on the door. I thought it was mum, come to rescue me, but it was my new housemate, well roommate. She was called Debbie and she'd come all the way from Yorkshire.

I was so grateful that Debbie was my roommate. We'd both moved away from home for the first time and like mum, her family were horrified at the prospect of having to leave their child with Maggie and James. Debbie, too, like me, was outraged at having to stay in such a dump.

Our first evening together was spent at the local pub. We chatted and got to know each other a little better. It was nice to have a companion to confide in and share our concerns about our digs, Maggie and James.

Maggie had rules and apparently, on our first night, we'd already broken most of them. Curfew time had us in at a certain time each night. Going to the pub was Taboo, and we had to report our comings and goings. It was worse than being at home. Maggie was very controlling, and coupled with her lack of personal hygiene not a pleasant person to be around.

Maggie was dirty, smelly, and somewhat grotesque and needed a bath. Someone to avoid at all costs.

I really didn't want to eat her food, especially when she used to leave her dirty knickers on the side, next to the washing machine, when preparing meals.

It was just repulsive. It made you feel sick...

The next day was enrollment day at the college, and we made our way to the campus to register ourselves. It was really exciting. Students were everywhere and we interacted with students from all over the country. Each had their own ideas of all sorts of things and we found our minds engaged in an assortment of subjects rather than that horrible house we were living in.

Money was our next concern. My parents were helping me, and along with my savings, I believed I could cope financially. I was entitled to a grant of about £300 per term, which came via a cheque, to be exchanged for cash at a bank. I think my weekly rent, to live in that horrible rat hole, was £25 a week.

I got by, like most students do, by hook or by crook.

Debbie and I were very uncomfortable living with Maggie and James. Looking back, they were strange people indeed. Imagine you're watching characters from TVs 'Little Britain,' that was Maggie and James, hard and dirty.

Back then, we used 'phone boxes' to ring home. No mobile phones when I went to college.

Imagine that now.

Maggie had a landline phone, but we were forbidden to use it. Should our parents need to contact us, they had to ring Maggie's landline.

Not much privacy and I was convinced Maggie listened in.

It was a miserable existence. Debbie and I hated living there... I told my parents how depressed I was becoming, whilst visiting them for a weekend away in Derby. I jumped on a train from New Street train station in Birmingham, and headed to Derby for the weekend to meet my parents. They were both staying there for the weekend...I just had to escape Maggie's house.

I hadn't showered for a few days as I feared I was being spied on by Maggie and her son. I remember feeling so relieved to see my parents in that hotel in Derby. I took a long hot bath and stayed in it until it got cold. I can remember feeling so upset having to say goodbye to them both. My college course, on the other hand, was fantastic. I loved it, so I took strength in that. My Mum, on hearing about mine and Debbie's concerns, complained bitterly to the college once she returned back to Grimsby from Derby.

Informing them that Debbie and I were living in disgustingly unhygienic conditions and the proprietor was unpleasant and unsanitary. Dirty clothing was left unhygienic and unwashed everywhere. Mum insisted that Debbie and I be moved to a more suitable accommodation.

Mum assisted in pursuing the request for new accommodation for us both, which was successful. On the day we moved, mum came up in her car, we loaded up the car with our belongings and made a daytime dash to our new digs in Tipton.

Mum was beyond amazing. She was fantastic. I recall she cried all the way home, that's how upset she was. She informed me she'd had sleepless nights ever since leaving me at Maggie's and had, along with Debbie's Mum, done everything they could to get us out of there.

Mum was a superstar back then, and still is. She saved me and Debbie from this horrific hell house. Words can't describe how horrid it was, it was vile. I never did see Maggie or James again, thank God for that.

Bolton Court was a thirteen story tower block of flats. Built in the 1960s. Similar to the flats demolished in Freeman Street in Grimsby. The bottom section of the flat was residential homes but the top section was predominantly for students.

The place was a hustle and bustle of student life. It was a hive of activity. It buzzed with students discussing photography. There were students on other courses doing television and sound engineering, talking about TV, art, design. It was an exciting hubbub of student culture, and I was loving it.

Debbie and I lodged on the twelfth floor of Bolton Court. I think we must have been two of the youngest there, as most were in their twenties.

I'll never forget it. It was a great time to be alive, I was in my element.

My new bedroom was huge and it had a balcony which I loved. From the balcony you could see all across to Birmingham. On a clear day, you could see the big BT Tower. Debbie had the little room next to mine and the third bedroom was occupied by a guy called Jim. He was from Norfolk. A really sound guy, who was on a business management course.

Like in most student accommodation, the kitchen was a mess. Unwashed pots piled up. No one seemed to take responsibility for washing up. It fell on the individual who wanted crockery to do his own. If we needed a plate we'd have to wash it ourselves. Our staple diet was shit, consisting mainly of toast and butter. Occasionally we'd eat baked beans. Plates and the like would again pile up, waiting to be washed, and the cycle complete.

Fuck it was fun! I loved it all.

I loved being a student. I could really be myself.
I didn't have a boyfriend at the time, still not really interested in all that again.
I was still recovering from the pain and suffering I'd endured from such encounters in Grimsby, so I steered clear.

I never told anyone about the traumas I'd suffered, back home. I just got on with being a student and did my own thing.

I suppose being a student, drinking becomes part of the culture and of course my student colleagues would entice me to go out drinking.

They found it strange, me being a teetotaller, and sadly some would be quite forceful in trying to make me drink alcohol. But I stuck to my guns and refused. At first this would evoke laughter and I'd be made fun of.
Some were quite forceful but I kept my composure and rode their ridicule.
I think, on reflection, on the odd occasion, I did probably buy half a pint just to be part of the gang, so to speak. Make it look like I was joining in, having a drink, just to appease. In truth, it was window dressing, I didn't really drink it. It was there for show. Something in my hand. Get the whingers of my back.

I can remember walking around Wednesbury town, looking through a window of a sandwich shop, with deliciously hot pork and stuffing sandwiches with apple sauce and thinking, wow, now I'm living the life as an independent student, I can do what I like.

I was out of Grimsby living an independent life and God, did I feel cool about it! So, there I was, sitting in a greasy spoon café, supping a large mug of tea. It tasted weird. So very different from the Yorkshire tea bags mum used to use.

God I've come a long way! I was so proud of that.

I didn't really cook for myself, not because I couldn't, I just couldn't be bothered. When it comes to food, most neurodivergent's are crap. Well I am, I just don't have the discipline, so just grab what's available.

I smoked a lot at college, most of us did. Cigarettes were cheap back then and despite them now having to carry health warning labels, I continued to smoke. I smoked Menthol flavoured ones, not the ordinary cigarettes, which were not to my liking.

It was the student thing to do. Mind I did start smoking at thirteen, so by the time I was seventeen I was quite addicted. But I did finally quit smoking in 2010 for good.

Debbie was on the HND course. The Higher National Diploma. A work related course that focused on learning by doing. The aim being, to give you specific work skills. There were probably only a handful of us girls at the college, the majority of students being boys.

We girls were lovely together.

Everybody was friendly, kind and sociable and I felt I was amongst people I could trust and rely on. I'd made the right decision to leave Grimsby and was now looking forward to life as a college student.

Unfortunately, that was not to be, but for now I was on a high and looked forward to my assignments. I enjoyed my assignments. I went to Porthmadog in Wales, loved the trip and bonded well with all the students.

Back at college, groups of students would go out to nightclubs, and I would tag myself along. We'd go to the 5th Nightclub in Walsall, which was quite unique, playing alternate music to the normal 70s stuff.

We'd go to Patrick's in Wednesbury, somewhat backward for the time, but boy was it fun. We'd venture into Wolverhampton or Birmingham.

We were warned never to drink in the Three Horseshoes Pub which was just outside Bolton Court. It had a bad past history. It was rumoured that students in the past had gone through its windows, so we never ventured there. However, great times, lots of fun, friendly attitudes and enjoyable times were had by all.

A few of the students had cars. So we would beg for lifts, to get about.

I didn't drive so when no lift was available, I'd catch the 310 bus, to college and back again to my digs in Tipton.

So I had a great start. I enjoyed college life, and was really into being a studious student. I liked my assignments and my projects were going well. My photographic knowledge was really coming along and I was learning lots of new skills. I was very lucky, to be in a generation, before everything went digital. I look upon that as a huge bonus. I was taught, old school, learnt the real skills of photography, hands-on, the coal face rudiments of photography, possibly not often taught in today's world. I learnt how to develop film properly, process my own photographs, work with 5x4 real cameras, and the like. The full works.

At Bolton Court, a few floors below was a telephone. You can imagine how long the queues were to use it.

E.T. Phone home!

It would ring day and night. Answering incoming calls was an art. Descending, or ascending flights of stairs, to answer it, then the same to find the student wanted on the phone.

No mobile phones in those days.

There was only one washing machine, for the whole of the building. Mums were not around to do your washing. So washing clothes became a chore, and you'd often go weeks wearing the same clothes.

So, I smelt, so what, I was a student, that's what students do.

I'm so grateful I got to experience being a proper student at a proper college. Those first few weeks were great. I had fun and made loads of different friends in Bolton Court.

Debbie had a boyfriend back in Yorkshire. He came to visit her regularly most weekends. He had a Jeep and took me and Debbie on many journeys. It was a convertible and being in it gave you a fantastic feeling. An exhilarating and exciting ride. We drove hard and fast, along the M6, my hair flying through the air.

Wow what a ride, and how loud we would laugh.

As time went on, I started to hang out with other people, other than Debbie. Friendships come and go with me as you know. My neurodiversity I get fixated on people, then I get bored. A weird pattern of behaviour, I know, but it's a very ADHD thing.

I befriended a wonderful girl called Rose. Rose was a new age hippy, very bohemian and very pretty.

Yeah man!

She loved to smoke a bit of the herb! She was pretty with natural curly hair and I'd describe her as a true Bohemian. The term "Bohemian" applies to people who live an unconventional lifestyle, often with few permanent ties, involving musical, artistic, or literary pursuits. The original "Bohemians" were travellers or refugees from central Europe. So that indeed described my new friend, Rose.

She hung around with a load of really cool guys. I was introduced to Craig.

I absolutely loved the ground he walked on, we became good platonic best friends for that first year, another dopamine buddy for me...

Craig loved music and was really into his Jungle and Drum & Bass genre of music. Jungle music is a genre of dance music that developed out of the UK rave scene. He had a set of technic 1210s decks just like my friend Mike.

Mike, if you recall, was a good friend back in Grimsby. I tried to keep in regular contact with him. Quite bizarre, considering my history of seeking pastures new. But, Mike was platonic, not a boyfriend. Boys can be friends, just like girls, and this works for me. I've probably had more male platonic friends than girls.

Rose wanted me to experiment new things, as we only live once. Her intentions were always good. She wanted me to hang out with her. She'd invited me to her house and I stayed overnight on the sofa.

Rose lived in a house with Craig and another guy from up north.

Being away from one's boy or girlfriend is usually a recipe for disaster. Especially if a student has a partner, and his girlfriend or boyfriend is back home.

Out of sight, out of mind.

Temptation is but a lie away, and you become easily seduced.

Sadly, cheating on their boyfriends or girlfriends at college has become the norm.

I, fortunately, had no such problem. Boyfriends during this first year were taboo. I was a free agent out to enjoy the vibe of being at college.

Rose invited me over to her house and we had fun listening to music on Craig's decks. Rose smoked her herb variety, while I stuck to my menthol cigarettes.

However peer pressure got the better of me, and against my better judgement, I tried smoking Rose's weed. Fortunately for me, it wasn't for me. I coughed and reacted quite adversely to it. It made me feel quite poorly and I had an allergic reaction. The smell really put me off.

I never smoked weed again.

While the others got high on weed, I smoked my cigarettes, listened to the great music, and chilled out.

Rose invited me to go with her to the legendary rave venue called Quest in Wolverhampton. It had live MCs and played Hard-core, Jungle, Drum n Bass music. It was rated the best club for Hard-core old skool ravers. Guest DJs would include the likes of the legend that is DJ Carl Cox, Grooverider, Fabio, Micky Finn and Ratpack.

Rose suggested I should experiment with Ecstasy, saying I'd love it. I took her up on her offer...

We stood outside waiting to go into Quest, I can remember being somewhat anxious. My heart raced and I was very nervous. I get apprehensive in crowds and feel I need to escape. It's a neurodiversity thing and I was near to panic. Rose handed me some Ecstasy and I took it, not knowing what the hell it was going to do to me. I need to be in control, as you know, and realised this drug might take away that control. I began to panic.

Inside Quest, I can remember seeing faces. They were everywhere. It was
very multicultural. I recall never having seen so many different nationalities together like this all at the same time. The place throbbed with the beat of the bass, and I could feel it pounding through my heart, pounding really hard. It was then I realised the Ecstasy was taking effect. I remember panicking, recalling the fact that a girl, called Leah Betts, had recently headlined the news having died on Ecstasy. The pounding continued, my heart racing. I became anxious, my heart pounded, the feeling rushing through my hair and into my head...I was coming up on an 'E'.

My confession to you is... I was overwhelmed with a feeling of love. I loved everyone, but my love of Ecstasy ended there...

CHAPTER SIX

LIVE TO TELL

So this was my first experience of taking ecstasy, E. It's known as the love drug, and don't I know it? I took it while at Quest in Wolverhampton. I was there with Rose and Craig and their friends. Everybody loving each other. Complete strangers, cuddling, hugging, and stroking each other...

It was bloody surreal, tingling sensations all up the back of my neck, strangers gurning and touching your hair.
Sweat pouring off the walls as the bass hit you deep in the heart... Thud Thud. Music was fast and 'Hard-core'...I danced and danced hard...Fruit of the loom cycle shorts, doing the running man, the shuffle, then little box big box.
My ears ringing, pupils dilated, and chewing gum as my mouth began chittering, just bloody bizarre. But I was off my tits...

As you know, I hate not being in control of my own actions. When confronted with the unexpected, I need to be able to handle it. Being in control is my way of avoiding trauma.

Ecstasy was indeed something quite unexpected. Its effect is very surreal...

Maybe that was psychological, knowing a sixth sense, that if I took more I'd get addicted. Like my personality it gets addicted, craving and wanting more. Luckily I said NO, and never did it anymore.

My first half a year at college was going absolutely brilliant. I'd forgotten all the trauma. Well, I thought I had, but my neurodiversity masked my trauma so well. Whether I was hyper fixated on this new adventure or not I was riding a high. Apart from a hiccup with Maggie and James, student life was great.

A dream that finally came true...

We became regular ravers at Quest... Afterwards we would all go back to Craig and Rose's house. A party was always held. Craig played Hard-core, Jungle, Drum & Bass music on his decks to the early morning, and everybody partied. I didn't even know half the people there. I would get so excited, ADHD getting the better of me creating dopamine, always showing off dancing to the Hard-core and Jungle baseline all night...

I once entertained a MC rapper from the nightclub Quest. His name was MC Thrill. He was a tall black guy with dreadlocks. He had a very thin face and looked a lot like Snoop Doggy Dog. I hadn't been with anyone, or really wished to be, since the trauma back in Grimsby. However, I took a shine to MC Thrill. I remember kissing him a few times, but nothing further happened. I don't think he really wanted to take matters further. I think he may have had a girlfriend. I don't know, I never asked. I was so used to seeing students off their heads on drugs and getting off with each other, it was difficult to know what one should do.

But this guy was different, so I thought. He was respectful. He took me, in his car, on a sightseeing tour of Birmingham. We had a few more dates like this, and I felt very safe being with him. We'd cuddle, kiss but that would be all.

My relationship with MC Thrill eventually fizzled out. It wasn't really a boyfriend, girlfriend thing, more of a companionship.
I then found out he had been sentenced to a short prison sentence, I wasn't expecting that news. I actually never asked him why he had to go to prison.

However he insisted I come and visit him. I remember one of my college buddies who had a car, who kindly agreed to drive me to the open prison to visit him. It was all a very surreal time, and I never questioned a thing. I liked the idea of having him as my friend. He was different. Sadly a short time after he got out of prison, he got killed tragically in a car crash. I can remember feeling really hurt and sad. He was a nice guy. Tragic! So, rest in peace MC Thrill.
Life really is short so I guess you've really got to live it while you can, and that's what I intended to do.
Live it, the best I can....

Students in Bolton Court were getting a bit concerned about me. I was spending most of my time at Rose and Craig's place. I was having a great time, Rose was like an old hippy mother hen. Despite introducing me to explore drugs, her intentions were good. I knew that, whatever happened, she would have my best interest at heart.
But I confess, she was a bad influence, this is another contradiction, as she taught me it's ok to be experimental, as you only live once!
The craziest thing being in July 2021, Ed and I took a summer holiday.

I knew Rose had moved near where we were holidaying, and we got a golden chance to meet up with each other after years of being apart.

She was just the same wonderful Rose. I've got a lot of time for Rose, she taught me a lot. Love you Rose xx

Back to my story...
I returned to Bolton Court, after virtually living with Rose and Craig.
I was enjoying my life as a student, but having a good time, now being prioritised over course work.
I'd just sleep for hours, my college assignments not done. I can remember the head of the course, seeking me out to try and find out why I wasn't attending college. My problem being hyper fixating on my life with Rose and Craig. ADHD taking control again.
I became ill. I was always a sickly kid, my immune system not the best.
I think experimenting with drugs and smoking too much was beginning to take its toll. I wasn't eating properly, either. All of which was affecting my health.
I looked thin and pale and developed a really bad chest infection. So severe were the conditions, I ended up in the hospital. Pleurisy was the diagnosis and I was given antibiotics to counteract the effects.

So dire was my condition that I ended up back in Grimsby with Mum looking after me. I'd been on a waiting list to have my tonsils removed.

The opportunity to have them removed came, they were like golf balls, and they were horrific. So I had them removed at the hospital in Grimsby.
I was so poorly, when I came home, I never ventured anywhere. Stayed home and let mum get me better again, she was great. After I got well again, I returned to college. I returned to college with a positive attitude. I was determined to get on with my coursework and catch up with the work I'd neglected to do.
Life repeated itself, and I found myself going round and round in circles.
The usual ADHD inflictions affected my identity and I found myself fixated and bored with everything.

I was blocking out traumas of yester years and found myself ringing up Mum, regularly. I probably spoke more to Mum on the phone than I did my dad. I would ask her to put money in my bank, as I'd probably over stretched my budget and spent most of my allowance on buying platform shoes or flares or something outrageous from the Bullring Centre.
I would wear the most outrageous outfits at the nightclubs, mainly to bring attention to myself. I wanted everybody to go, Wow! Look at her outfit, she looks amazing!

I remember having my nose pierced, originally trying to shock mum but again to attract attention. I was an idiot, it got infected!

I formed a new friendship with a really lovely girl who lived in the top floor flat above mine in Bolton Court. She was called Nicole and she lived there with a few other students. Nicole came from a town quite nearby, and as our friendship developed she invited me to stay with her and her family on weekends.
Nicole became my 'Twirl Twin', a very good friend, and at the end of the term, I would end up going to Ibiza on a club 18-30 holiday, with Nicole and her friends...Two Twirls please...

But that comes later... I hereby confess to you, "I have a tale to tell, and it really does get hard to write it so well"....

CHAPTER SEVEN

PRIDE

Whilst visiting Nicole, in her hometown, I visited my first gay nightclub.
I was in my absolute element.
Influenced by Madonna, I just wanted to be best friends with a gay man.
This new revolutionary step for me was fantastic.

I Loved it.
I was your typical fag hag.
A fag hag? A heterosexual woman who spends much of her time with gay
men. I can remember feeling very safe. Nobody judged you. A nightclub
full of freedom. Everyone dressed uniquely.

I was accepted, all misfits together, so to speak. No fear of
unwanted attention here in the gay scene, that's for sure. I felt relaxed,
and a great venue where I could express my true inner self with no
judgement.

Madonna's Vogue came to mind, copying her dance moves, Vogue
dancing...
Recalling outfits by designer Jean-Paul Gaultier who is renowned for
creating lots of Madonna's outfits especially the iconic pointed bra. I recall
she had walked the catwalk with Jean Paul, then controversially exposed
her breasts at the end of runway. The crowd went wild, all attention on
Madonna.
So why not, I heard my ADHD brain encouragingly.

So I did.
I jumped on the stage and exposed my breasts. I felt liberated and didn't
give a shit. The crowd roared with cheers at such exhibitionism. Everyone
for that moment in time loved me, for the first-time in my life I felt I'd
found my true audience of acceptance. I felt euphoric, images in my mind
of Madonna, so this is what Madonna must feel like. I was having the time
of my life.

Debbie moved out of our flat. I think she may have gone to live with somebody else but I really can't remember. I do remember, however, another lad moving in, he came from a posh family down south, a nice guy, I liked his company in a platonic flatmate way, we used to play video games on the Sega my favourite was road rash, I would spend hours mastering the art to get to the top levels, highly addictive.

My bedroom at Bolton Court got trashed one night. Somebody broke in and turned my room upside down, all my stuff all over the place. I can remember feeling violated. Why somebody would've done it, baffles me. However, I did hear someone was pissed off as they thought I had taken their washing out the only washing machine in the building, which was not me! Again I was an easy target for others to place the blame onto. Scary how vulnerable something like that has on someone like me, with ADHD.

Kelly's ex-boyfriend, Mike from Grimsby, used to send me old cassette mix tape recordings. They reminded me of home, and the great times we had at the airfield listening and dancing to music on Mike's 1210's decks. I even got mix tapes on CD many years later from his good friend Pete. Mike came to stay with me when I was in my second year at college, but more about that later. Mike was a great guy, a platonic friend, a bit wacky. I do remember when my Great Nanna died, she left an assortment of exclusive clothes, gold coats, and dresses.
Mike wasn't afraid to wear them, he was quite a unique individual, with a style all of his own.

Just a quick note, you may have noticed my vocabulary, and use of words are not wide-ranging. I constantly repeat what I say, and duplicate words. I struggle to express what I'm trying to say and how to write it. Unfortunately crippled with my ADHD and dyslexia I do struggle. You are reading this book in the authentic way I speak, so there will be my grammar mistakes but this is the whole point I want you to be on this journey of discovery with me. Well that's my excuse at any rate. I like to tell it as it is, and that's what you're getting. I'm sure the grammar police will pick up on my errors, even though I've proofread and edited my book about a 100 times over...

So where was I...? Oh yes college...

Around spring, Bolton Court had yet another new resident. We were very fortunate, a guy called Sam came to live in our flats. He possessed a VHS video camera. This allowed us residents to film on VHS cassettes on his video camera, we could then film our student life.

I fixated on filming student life.
These I still have on VHS. What a shame these VHS tapes are not converted over to a modern day format. They'd make a great documentary.

In the early 90s I documented student life. It was quite a revolutionary thing to do in those days. I was doing Big Brother before Big Brother did Big Brother. I thought at the time, 'Oh My God', I could get famous.

I filmed so much.

It's there, my documentary masterpiece, of life as a student in the 1990s, awaiting resurrection.

At college lots of students were Goths. The term Goths, originated from the name given to nomadic Germanic people, who fought against Roman rule in the late 300s and early 400s A.D. It was adopted in the 1980s by fans of Gothic Rock, an off-shoot of the punk music genre. It's a music based subculture with its own unique identity. Most Goths love dark colours, including black, purple, and red. They also enjoy using darker shades of lipstick and eyeshadow. Gothic fashion is often associated with death. It is also known for being heavily influenced by the macabre and morbid. Goths listen to a wide variety of music genres, including heavy metal, rock, and punk. Some prefer more obscure music, while others enjoy art. Often they are very creative when it comes to art.

I loved its culture, and could easily have become one. My sister was quite Gothic in her fashion, and listened to the likes of Siouxsie & the Banshees and the Cure.

I made a very good friend of a Goth girl called Ruth. Ruth was extremely good at art and photography. Her make-up and the way she applied it was outstanding. A professional make-up artist came to stay with her and I can honestly say I've never been so expertly made up the way she did it. It was superb. She used proper stage makeup like celebrities use, for their magazine photographs.

Ruth, taught me a lot about makeup. She had beautiful skin, and the way she applied her makeup was absolutely flawless.

I started hanging out with the Goths and had many a great night going out with them to nightclubs. One being the 5th in Walsall. We would go in convoy together from Bolton Court.

On these incredible nights I could discover more of the real me, and what life had to offer. I mixed with many differing cultures and interacted with all sorts of different people. I enjoyed, and danced to many musical genres. Wore my own unique far out fashion trend and mixed with the coolest of groups around. I'd fixate on a group, knowing that's where I wanted to be.

You see, being accepted and becoming part of their culture's lifestyle was important to me. I needed to feel part of something, be somebody, and this I tried to do.

Such was Madonna's philosophy, reinvent yourself. This I did. "If your joy is derived from what society thinks of you, you're always going to be disappointed"...

CHAPTER EIGHT

REINVENTION

So, I reinvented myself. No longer that damaged little girl, from Grimsby, who didn't do very well at school, who ran away from herself, hopefully, now reborn. Now with lots of friends around me, I ventured forward hopeful this was the beginning of a new me. I can remember, at the time, thinking best to have lots of friends rather than fixate on one.

I became very good friends with a girl called Jenny. She was my housemate, in my second year of college. She was incredibly good at art and on the same course as me. We decided to leave Bolton Court, and eventually in our 2nd year of college got a house share together in a big student house. We had to share a bed not in any weird sexual way purely because the room we were renting only had one bed in it.

There was about six other students who would share the house with us, one being Nicole, my other good friend from Bolton Court.

But, there I go again, getting ahead of myself. ADHD taking charge, as usual. So back to my first year at college.

The students on my course were all very creative, excellent at art and photography. I felt I was amongst friends and colleagues, with similar goals and desires to me. I needed to gain recognition, achieve proficiency in photography, and show the world I was back.

But it wasn't to be, well not yet anyway.

My ADHD side tracked those objectives. I got bored. Missed assignments. Became distracted by student life yet again, constant merry go round of distractions and began that all so familiar decline.

Jenny came to my rescue, which I will always be grateful for. She got me back on track, and I was thankful for that. She became my model, in a lighting assessment, I was far from completing. It was the beginning of a friendship that would help turn around my negative attitude and get on track again.

Again, I'm getting ahead of myself.

We girls used to help out on assignments by modelling for each other. When doing work experience for the Grimsby Telegraph in 1990, I offered to be 'The Model for the Day'.' I enjoyed it immensely. I got a full page spread.

Fame at last.

Crazy thing is, in my interview for the 'Model For the Day,' I exaggerated the truth slightly, suggesting my friend Mike, remember the DJ, was a record producer and I was a singer. Again, good old ADHD fixating on my dream to become a singer and Mike to become a producer.

I'd probably say I'm true to myself, and my love and fixation on Madonna is absolutely genuine. I've seen Madonna in concert many times. I've never sidestepped my passion for her.

In my second year at college, I began to fixate on Jenny.

Artistically she was attuned to, and wore, the latest fashion trends. She looked fabulous. Her understanding of art and design was exceptional, and no doubt, she was destined for greater things.

She was great fun to be with, and have around.

I had my first taste, and experience, of acid in the first year of college. The effects of 'tripping' can last for hours. I've tried ecstasy, as you know, and I'll never take it again. Weed? I hated it. It made me sick. Whizz, the street name for the drug speed, an amphetamine, bizarrely calmed me down. However in my later life, I was to discover that some of the treatments used for ADHD are bizarrely amphetamine based medication or stimulants.

When prescribed correctly they help treat ADHD as they create dopamine and help the brain, giving more clarity and focus.

I can remember dropping a few Acid tabs in Bolton Court, I felt safe, and in control there, it had been organised by a few of my friends that we were all going to drop acid together.

I've still got a few original funny VHS videos of us all, at Bolton Court, tripping out. We'd just sit there for hours, laughing together, watching the ceiling, swirl around in psychedelic colours. An incredible feeling. It opens your mind.

I didn't mind trying acid.

In a weird way, it would last for hours, possibly too long, and sometimes I'd wish it to stop.

I remember laying in my bath, and colours would swirl and swarm around in a kaleidoscope of colour. I guess this is an ideal way to describe how my ADHD mind worked, a little bit trippy, life viewed in an assortment of flickering colours and laughing at the stupidest of things.

Me and some of my college friends used to trip for hours. Acid tabs and bombs were taken regularly with chill-out music by ORB. Orb were an English electronic music group of the late 80s. It was known for its psychedelic sound, and developed a cult following among clubbers, "coming down" from drug-induced highs.

In college I mixed with artists, photographers, sound engineering and musicians. I fixated on becoming a recording star and wanted to record a song. That dream was realised in my second year at college and I got to sing and record my very first song in a recording studio.

However, to sum up my first year at college. I met up with loads of new friends, experienced differing cultures, and hung out with groups like Goths, alternatives, Hippies, Gays and the like...

I don't regret any of it... Life is for living, to be experienced, and to be experimental with... I always need to be in control, so I never let the drugs I experimented with take control of my life. Thus allowing me, as Madonna so perfectly confessed...

"Better to live one year as a tiger, than a hundred as a sheep."

CHAPTER NINE

GIRLS WANNA

I just want to talk about Ed for a moment.

If you remember his family and mine were neighbourhood friends. He sent me my first Valentine card when I was five. Ed went away to London, to get a Bachelor's Degree in sports science, the same year I went to the West Midlands. His Dad, at that time had allegedly been cheating on his Mum, with her then friend Brenda. The affair sent shock waves through the whole family. I can remember Mum calling me up at college, to tell me Ed's parents were splitting up, due to Ed's Dad's adultery.

It was a shock.

I was absolutely devastated. I'd always regarded Ed's parents as being the perfect couple, his wife, the classical, 'Stepford Wife,' attractive, dutiful, and subservient, an incredible cook. Ed's family were the first family I ever knew when growing up in the 1980s, to have a microwave and a VHS video recorder. Such revolutionary machines that paved the way for our future.

Ed's Mum was glamorous, Brenda, the woman he ran off with, the opposite, in many respects of Ed's Mum. No one could understand why he'd abandoned his wife for Brenda, but that's life.

Life can be cruel and unfair. We will never understand, sometimes in life you never will understand why?

Ed's Mum fell apart.

Mum, being the caring person she was, went to help Ed's Mum. I was at college when I found out the scandalous news. I can recall a song by Madonna that was ironically out at the time of the affair, the song was from the Erotica album, it was called 'Thief of Hearts'. About a woman stealing a man. Its lyrics are so poignant to Ed's Mum's predicament... I can remember playing this song over and over again. I had the album on a cassette tape, feeling really pissed off that Ed's dad cheated on his wife.

I felt really sorry for Ed and his brothers and I wanted to reach out and offer empathy, especially to Ed, who I'd heard, through the grapevine, had gone off the rails. The two families were inseparable. Grew up together, holidayed together, they were the best of friends; until this. Then, overnight, everything had changed. Ed's family was in tatters. Divorce threatened to destroy the family.

It was absolutely heart-breaking.

I got the impression, Ed's dad had waited until the boys had left home, before leaving his wife, but I didn't know that for sure. Nonetheless, I can remember being really shocked at their separation.

At the time, of all this upheaval, I was at college and recall, wondering how Ed was coping with the news. Dealing with disorder in one's life is the norm for me and I've employed many strategies over the years to cope with it. I wondered how he would deal with the upheavals he now faced. It appears, like me, he went off the rails for a time. I've been there too, so I could empathise with him.

I guess that's why Ed, and I have such a deep rooted connection. We've both experienced the pain of feeling broken in one way or another, the trauma of not being able to cope and the failure of self-respect.

I completed my first year at college and completed all my modules. I literally scraped through by the skin of my teeth, but what the hell, I passed. I could have done better, I know, but was too busy experimenting with life.

Mum and dad were delighted I'd passed my first year at college. I'd let them down, on so many occasions, it felt good to finally have achieved something they were proud of. That's all I've ever wanted in life, is to make them proud.

In that first year, I felt sad towards the end of the summer term. Knowing I'd be returning back to Grimsby. I would miss the companionship of all my new friends. Incidentally, some of those friendships still hold good today.

By reconnection through the power of social media.

During that first year, at college, I was healing, getting over the trauma, masking it, as we neurodivergents do so well. My friends at college knew nothing about it, yet, their friendship and support, unknowingly, helped me cope with it.

I was involved, being accepted, and having fun.
It wasn't actually about the college course itself, it was actually more about me, finding out who I was, making important friendships and learning about people.

I'd decided, in my second year at college, to live in a shared house with Jenny. It was a huge Victorian house that was just up the road from the college campus.

I came back to Grimsby in the summer, I enrolled on a student holiday shift pattern at Bluecrest, and at Leon's fish restaurant.

Life repeats itself.

Whilst at Leon's I renewed my friendship with Lisa, who currently is now an actor on Coronation Street.

Lisa is always great fun. She has always been into acting and drama. Her destiny to make it her full time career, and she now has so successfully achieved it.

Who would have believed that we used to work serving fish, chips, and cups of tea together in Leon's fish restaurant? Which at the time was one of the best fish and chip restaurants in Grimsby. I lost touch with her when I returned to college, but in recent years we've reconnected again.

Anyway, getting back on track, going off at a tangent as usual. Students, at Bluecrest, were not always welcomed with open arms. On the contrary, sometimes with hostilities. Full time, Bluecrest workers, for whatever reason, thought we students were snobs. We were just the same as they were but they just couldn't see it like that. I've always found in life, I can easily adapt to people. Whatever, their class, creed or occupation. I guess it's the way my personality works. I always have empathy for people. Try to see the best in people even when they've hurt me.

Another thing about friends and friendships. Out of sight out of mind. ADHD is the culprit here I'm afraid. I can go for weeks, sometimes years without contacting people. It's not because I don't like them or care about them, I just forget about them because my brain forgets about people. That goes for everybody, friends and family. I must admit, I'm lucky to now have friends who recognise my condition, and accept my lack of contact over long periods of time. Best friends are rare for me, but those who do understand my faults, we still remain the best of friends.

So during the summer, I worked really hard, and made lots of money. It was towards the end of the summer, Nicole, my friend from college, had planned to go to Ibiza on a club 18-30 Holiday. I of course had planned to go with her.

I had been abroad before. I went to Portugal with my parents, just before my dad got ill. It was my first holiday abroad on an aeroplane and it was special.

So going to Ibiza was the second time, to fly on an aeroplane. This time, however, I was actually going away with my friends. I had also just celebrated my eighteenth birthday. Holidays like this were all the rage back in the 90s, and targeted the younger teenage generations.

Not that it would be advertised as such, but such holidays were aimed at sex, drugs, drink and partying all night. Ibiza, back then had become notorious for a revolution in House Music, as well as various other genres of Dance Music. Ibiza back then was full of open air nightclubs, where top DJs played the latest Club Classic Ibiza Anthems. Fun loving people partied the day and nights away. At the time, it was the place to be, and still is today. It was the trendiest place in the whole world to visit. A gang of us girls, gathered at Birmingham Airport, preparing to fly to Ibiza. Four of us in all, Nicole and me, Kate and Kelly.

We arrived in Ibiza and were whisked to San Antonio by one of the holiday Reps who was immediately smitten by Kate.

It was so bloody hot, and having fair skin I became ill with heat stroke. I was very sick and had to stay in the hotel room on the first night, while the girls went out partying, and had a great time. The next day, I felt better so we pre-booked all the excursions including boat cruises and the lot. It was to be one big party after another...
We were loud, unforgettable and out for a good time.
Back then on the beach, nobody gave a stuff, if you sunbathed topless. I really didn't care. I was an exhibitionist, I admit, I was liberated, without judgement. However, having ADHD I do have self-esteem issues.
When I looked around at the bodies of the other girls I felt inadequate. Which is another contradiction as at the same time, I was happy to sunbathe topless for everyone to see. I know it's a weird conundrum. I've always had these bat shit crazy confidence issues, this was another of those occasions. However, as usual, I shielded those thoughts and successfully managed to mask my embarrassment. I came across to everyone I was super confident.

I wasn't looking for a man. All I wanted was a good time. To enjoy the ambiance of the music and to dance the night away in the legendary famous nightclubs in Ibiza. This I did. It knackered me and true to form ADHD got the better of me, I became totally hyperactive, I then crashed and burned.

A complete meltdown. Then went into a weird mental and physical paralysis.
Bearing in mind I'm teetotal and hadn't taken drugs, I literally was on a natural high on Coca-Cola, orange juice and water.

Our holiday was in full swing. Party on...

Us girls apart from Kate she was too busy all loved up with her holiday Rep. We went to the best club nights in Ibiza, one night we all got chatted up by a group of lads, we all eventually returned back to our two bedroomed apartment together.

I experienced my first encounter of a holiday one night stand. I'm sure we have all done and experienced it. We were liberated young ladies, free and single to do as we pleased.

The crazy thing is we could all hear each other, we all just burst out laughing.

Our holiday caused an uproar. We just laughed our heads off on hearing each other's made up moans. Hysterical scenes, to be savoured...

However my experience of a one night stand was that I felt like an empty vessel. The physical motion had no meaning, no feeling, no love, and no nothing. I was frightened to actually enjoy it, so I pretended I did. It made me feel somewhat guilty, it made me feel weird and dirty...

Flashbacks came back to haunt me, clearly I was still severely traumatised. Looking back, I should have gotten professional help sooner, to help overcome my post-traumatic stress.

A great holiday, it absolutely was. However I had my reservations, but as usual I put aside my concerns and got on with it, masking my true feelings that kept coming back to haunt me...

The streets of San Antonio bustled with an assortment of holiday makers. Nightclubs buzzed with musical excitement. They thronged to the musical beat of clubbers as they raved the night away. Amazing places like Café Del Mar, famous for watching the sunsets and sunrise. So many famous nightclubs in Ibiza to visit, with the best DJ's in the world, the mecca of dance music. Pacha, Space, Es Paradis, Privilege and Amnesia to name a few that are probably still famous today. The crazy foam parties, and not wearing much clothing, but remember with fondness those incredible Ibiza club nights. Legendary '1993' Ibiza Club Anthems created nostalgic memories from; Leftfield 'Open up', Energy 52 'Cafe Del Mar', Mory Kante 'Yeke Yeke', X -Press 2 'London X -Press'.
We were all good time girls just having holiday fun...

Things drastically went wrong, the last day of my holiday. It's how you pick yourself up that's the real challenge isn't it....

CHAPTER TEN

IBIZA

So on the last day of our club 18-30 holiday in San Antonio, we were all on the beach sunbathing. A group of army boys were close by. These lads had been on the same tours as us and were great fun. They were very loud and funny. I even posed topless in photographs with them... So maybe I was giving out the wrong impression, who knows...

However, the truth was, I didn't fancy any of them.

They were pals of Rob, our other holiday Rep... Rob was a big lad, loud, and very cock-sure of himself. I was sunbathing topless in my bikini bottoms like all the girls were on the beach. I didn't feel I was parading myself as a sex object.

I'd gone into the sea where lots of people were splashing around in the water. We had a pink lilo and we took turns to float about on it.

The sea was warm and beautifully calm. The latest Ibiza Club Anthems that we'd heard in the nightclubs were blaring out across the beach. I felt really happy and content.

I was having a great holiday with the girls...

I felt completely relaxed, floating on the lilo. I had drifted out a bit further into the sea, I was quite near to where the warning buoy was situated.

Chill out time... Feeling the warmth of the Ibiza sun on my face...

I could hear in the distance a load of cheering. It was the army guys, hysterical jeering; over what, I couldn't see. I'd no idea what was going on. I looked up and saw Rob splashing towards me...

Alarm bells should have rang, but they didn't. I was caught totally off guard.

I thought this was strange. What in the hell was going on? Before I knew it, Rob pulled me off the lilo. I could just about touch the ground on tiptoe, it wasn't shallow water.

I can honestly say I had no idea what the hell was happening. At first I thought it was a joke, Rob larking about. Rob was a big guy, over six feet and at least twenty stones. He was a strong powerful man, me, a small petite girl.

What he did next, brought back the trauma of an ordeal I thought I'd never have to face again.

How wrong was I? ...

He pulled my pink bikini bottoms and raped me. I was stranded completely immersed in the water. I couldn't move, the intense pain and paralysis with complete fear.

I went into some weird shock...

People stared, but maybe they didn't realise what was actually going on, as it was hidden by the water...

I was physically being raped in the sea, in full view of the whole beach.

Then the flashbacks flooded back to my mind of the trauma I had encountered with Kim and Dean.

I was in shock, I was frozen in fear. All I could hear in the distance was the army boys cheering, laughing and shouting as if it were a game. Like it was done for a bet or a dare.

Whatever! It was rape. In broad daylight, too. In Ibiza in San Antonio, with people all around.

How's that possible? How did people not know? Rob, our holiday Rep, who we trusted.

I've always questioned this? Did I ask for it?

No! There is no excuse...

I was loud, paraded myself topless, on an 18-30 Ibiza holiday, one of the girls I certainly was. What did I expect? Not to be raped, that's for sure.

But my holiday Rep did just that.

I had no intention of sleeping with him, not like my friend Kate who was having a fling with the other holiday Rep. Maybe he thought we were all up for it. I wasn't.

I went from being totally relaxed to feeling violated. I remember feeling trapped and vulnerable. I panicked, that claustrophobic dread of being imprisoned, of being helpless, scared, without a getaway, overtook me. Disorder in my life is bad enough. The need to be in control is paramount. But this guy was now in control. He was big and scary and the fact he was doing it in front of everybody, and getting away with it, gave him approval.

It was totally wrong.

My body was so sore, the sunburn adding to my discomfort. He'd obviously been egged on by the army guys and had gone through with it. They acted like animals, every last one of them, and they should feel ashamed of what they did.

Sadly, I doubt it.

For the guilty, it lasted but a couple of minutes, sadly much, much longer for me the victim. His actions alone made it a criminal assault. He then forcefully pushed me back into the water. Then with the cheers from the army lads, he went back onto the beach leaving me in a total state of shock.

I felt physically sick, and couldn't get my head round what had just happened. There were people around me in the water, and they just let it happen. Surely they must've known what he was doing to me, it was a crime. So why didn't they help?

I was angry.

Why I didn't scream I'll never know. I didn't even push him away.

Well I couldn't push him away, he was too big.

After he had gone, I managed to climb back onto the lilo and laid there in total shock and disbelief.

I lay there for what seemed hours, afraid to go back onto the beach, my confused state of mind not comprehending what had just happened.

I was in total shock, then my emotions kicked in, I felt humiliated, embarrassed and ashamed. Was it my fault?

Those army lads had tried to get off with me throughout the holiday, but I'd refused their advances. Was this the reason they singled me out? I shall never know. Eventually I went back to the beach and joined the girls sunbathing. I didn't mention a word about what had just happened to me with Rob.

The girls were actually totally oblivious to what had just gone on out in the sea. They obviously never saw anything. So maybe no one did see? So many questions that I will never know...

I was too embarrassed and ashamed to tell the girls about it, not wanting to cause a drama and ruin our fabulous holiday. So I kept quiet, I kept it my secret.

This is what I've always done all my life with trauma, I have built up a strategy to block it out, pretending it never happened. As always masking it, like it never happened or existed. I pulled up my big girl socks, and got on with life...

I told myself there was nothing that could have been done. The police probably wouldn't have believed me anyway. I really did think this at the time.

My neurodiversity mind started to blame and question myself. Not thinking logically like a normal neurological brain.

I kept having guilty thoughts. Blaming myself, thinking I shouldn't have posed topless for photographs with those army lads. Maybe I was giving out the wrong impression. Maybe I was asking for it! Causing my self-esteem to hit rock bottom. I was in a total state of denial and confusion. No it was not my fault!

To the outside world I played my part, no one would ever know. I would carry on trying to be normal. I would keep masking my trauma. I would keep smiling, I would keep carrying on with life. I had to erase it out of my mind. Like it never ever happened! I would need to gain back my self-control...

Eventually we all went back to the hotel, packed our suitcases, ready for the off, to fly back to Birmingham.
Before we left, our holiday Reps came to say goodbye. Rob stood before me, laughing and joking, as if what he did had never happened. He showed no remorse whatsoever... he got away with it...or did he? Karma works in magical ways, I'm sure his karma was eventually served...
We flew back to Birmingham and I tried to be as normal as possible. Not wanting to ruin the girls' holiday. Now that I understand my neurodiversity, it enabled me to mask the truth from the girls...

Just an important note;
If anything like this should happen to my daughter, I would be absolutely heartbroken. As a young girl you're prey to would be predators. Over protective mum, I might be, but experience has taught me to be very cautious. That word of warning is a must to all mums and daughters. Through my own traumatic experiences, I've confidently raised my daughter to have a wise understanding about would be predators. I've taught her to always have a strong voice, and never be silenced. I've educated her never to be a victim, to always speak out if anyone did any wrong doings to her. Through my own personal traumas, I'm very protective of my daughter. The lessons I've learned, I have taught her well. Through my strength, knowledge and wisdom, hopefully she will never have to experience such malice's.

...So I kept this incident in Ibiza, as a deep dark secret for many years, eventually causing more mental health traumas and post-traumatic stress.
When we eventually got back to Birmingham, I travelled back home to Grimsby.
To prepare myself for my second and final year at college...

Little did I know that this second year was going to be probably one of the hardest years emotionally and mentally in my life... I'm gonna close my body down...

CHAPTER ELEVEN

RESCUE ME

I believe that you can rescue me...

When we got back to Birmingham from Ibiza I felt really deflated. What should have been a once-in-a-lifetime holiday, brought only memories of yet another trauma. I still couldn't get my head round the fact it actually happened.

The girls didn't know, because I didn't tell them. So they were buzzing about the holiday. I tried my best to act the same and masked my true feelings.

But for me, the true reality thrust me into a dark hole. I was mentally scarred by what had happened to me on that last day, but as usual I masked it. Kept it to myself, and told no one. He'd used his authority to take advantage of a vulnerable girl and one wonders if I was his first, or one of many.

It should have been reported, but like what happened with Kim & Dean I let it go, and got on with my life...

I was due back, for my second year at college, in the first week of September 1993. I'd abandoned Bolton Court, for a student house share. I was excited and looked forward to my second year at college and all the new experiences I'd encounter.

Remember, I was going to be sharing a bedroom with Jenny who I'd formed a really good friendship with. She also was doing a photography course, she was a fantastic photographer and artist.

Jenny had a love for fashion and make-up. To me, she was a fantastic all-round human, and I will always be grateful to have shared a room with her. I was going through a lot of hidden trauma at this time, and Jenny, regrettably, would have to share the brunt of my troubles.

Thank God she was there for me.

Back home, in Grimsby, mum got the 'empty nest' syndrome, having had both of her daughters leave home. I was to learn much later, this had affected her quite badly. She'd been sad and unhappy, her motherly instincts, for the time being, apparently made redundant.

However, mother's support would soon be necessary.

My parents were preparing to go, on a once in a lifetime trip, to Australia. Mum was off to visit and be reunited with her sister. Her sister had moved out to Sydney in the 1960s and she'd not seen her since then. They'd planned to stay for over a month.

I was anxious for them, and for me, if the truth be told.

Going to Australia was a big deal for them. For me, it was a disaster. Even though I was living away from home, my parents were reassuringly, always at the end of a telephone. If I needed them they were just a phone call away. For a month they wouldn't be.

So I went back to college.

I can remember arriving at my new house to find Jenny waiting for me. We were excited, both looking forward to our new digs, and a new term at college.

I'd lost a bit of weight over the summer.

I hadn't been eating properly since my return home from Ibiza. I soon became severely anorexic and then it would develop into the nightmare of Bulimia. It dominated my life and affected my friendships and relationships as you will soon discover...

Going back to Jenny and our new student house. We both shared the house with about six or more students. We knew most of them from our first year studies. One being my 'Twirl Twin' friend Nicole, whom I had just returned back from Ibiza with.

So we lived in a house full of very creative people. Photographers, sound engineers and artists, all housed under one roof. Our prospects were exciting, and Jenny and I enthusiastically unpacked our belongings into a single wardrobe. We had to share a double bed which we didn't mind doing.

It was rather funny, sharing a bed, because we weren't lesbians.

Jenny had hand drawn some amazing artwork. They were quite psychedelic, their colours bright and attractive. We hung them, along the back wall of our room, to cover the disgusting brown wallpaper the last residents had put up. Jenny had bought her TV and VHS video recorder from home, we even had our own toaster.

She was well organised. All I bought was my clothes. But that's me, make do and hope for the best. So I was grateful for Jenny having brought these little luxuries. It was like home from home.

A couple of doors down, in another student house, lived a guy called Garry. Garry was on a sound engineering course. I knew Garry from the first year. He was great fun. He was heavily into the 'The Rave' scene, and went to Bowlers and Wigan Pier, northern rave venues.

Later Jenny and Garry got quite close, and ended up becoming boyfriend and girlfriend. So for a while Jenny used to go and stay at Garry's house. So I would sometimes be left alone in our room, which was not a problem for me. Music creating nostalgic memories at the time; Janet Jackson's 'That's The Way Love Goes' and Mary J Blige's Real Love.'

It was the opening night of Madonna's World Tour, 'The Girlie Show' at Wembley Stadium.

I went on my own...

I've always been kind of fearless in that way, unafraid to do anything. Acting on impulse I'd bought my ticket, got on a coach, and took myself down to London, to see my Madonna. I still feel honoured to have been present on the opening night of this tour. The next day, the press was all over it, and I collected every single newspaper clipping and cutting I could find.

The craziest thing was I'd booked a coach trip through Solid Entertainment, which was a Grimsby-based company, so I came back to Grimsby to get on the coach to London, then back again to Grimsby...Confusing to be sure.

On reflection I did it all the wrong way round. However, my parents always booked solid entertainment so I just thought I'd book it through them. No internet back then, so all bookings were done via the telephone.

It was easy. That's me. The simple solution every time, well it wasn't that simple, really was it? I had to make two journeys to Grimsby, when in hindsight I could have just gone direct to London from Birmingham, saving half the time travelling.

My collection of Madonna memorabilia remained at home, too precious a collection to take to college. I kept it in my bedroom in Grimsby in an old chest.

I'm very protective of my Madonna collection. So when I found pictures and articles of her at college, I'd post them back to my dad, for him to look after and put away safely in my Madonna chest.

They'll remain safe and protected, by my Dad.

Madonna, 'opened a door,' for me with her ultra-sexy song, 'Erotica.' She appeared on a revolving circular stage, wearing sequined hot pants and a sequined black top. She held a riding crop and wore PVC boots up to her knees, and had short cropped pixie bleach-blonde hair.

I was incredibly mesmerised by her, I wanted to be her. She was so sensational, so erotic, so sexy, and so me.

I recall, just standing there in awe, emotionally charged with unfaltering devotion; I imagined I was Madonna and I fixated upon her. She would take away my pain, without ever realising it.

We have never met personally, only viewed on a stage, from afar, but Madonna is my strength, my reinvention, the rock on which I stand.

My parents flew off to Australia on holiday, and their absence in my life did have a devastating impact on my mental health. The thought of not being able to contact them, messed me up psychologically. Some weird kind of attachment issue, from when I had my stomach pumped in hospital, and mum was not allowed to visit me, is believed to be the cause.

I can remember the day my eating disorder started.

I felt vulnerable. I doubted myself, didn't feel good about myself. Mentally I was not in a happy place.

I loathed being me.

The craziest thing was, I wasn't overweight, far from it as a matter of fact. But there I was questioning my ability to cope. Possibly if I'd have been a lot stronger I might not have succumbed, but I wasn't, my defences were down. I was in mental disharmony, thus triggering the start of my eating disorder.

Let me explain in more detail.

I was doing a bit of modelling for a lad on our course, when a comment from one of the students, whose name I forget, flippantly suggested I was overweight and needed to lose a few pounds.

I wasn't overweight.

It should have ended there but I took it to heart.

People really should be mindful of what they say, keep their opinions to themselves, because you never know how your vulnerable victim will react. With me, of course, it was part of the many reasons that triggered irreversible complications that would seriously affect my life and health. My self-esteem was at an all-time low.

From that day onwards, I took control of my life on what I ate. I quickly became a physical shadow of my former self. My food intake drastically reduced.

My anorexia began in October 1993 the same day I started a relationship with a lad from one of the sound engineering courses. His name was James and was also Garry's best friend, who was dating Jenny, my roommate.

To begin with, everything seemed pretty normal and we'd all hang out together, go night clubbing and enjoy each other's company. However, while this was going on, my anorexia took hold and I was getting worse.

I was losing weight quite quickly. I regimented what I ate.

Eating became tiresome and a time-consuming chore. However, control was essential, and I was determined nobody would stop me.

Understanding anorexia at this point in my story is paramount, as the condition was triggered by a random comment. I was told I looked overweight, by a student. Well that possibly was the catalyst that caused my anorexia. But crippled with severe self-esteem issues, an undiagnosed ADHD, post-traumatic stress, they were the actual real reasons why it all began.

Anorexia is a serious mental health eating disorder that can kill you.

My typical daily diet would consist of very minimum restricted calories. This, I told myself, was good. However, my calorie consumption during the day was very low. My college timetable had me finishing by 3 pm, and if I got home by 3:30pm I allowed myself half a Weight Watchers meal. If after that time, I wasn't home, I told myself I wasn't allowed. I'd fast during the night, and start all over again the following day.

That would be my daily intake of food until the following day and the cycle would repeat itself and eventually food consumptions would further dominate my logic. I was in control and nobody was going to stop me.

College commitments often made it impossible to get home in time for food.

It got to the point where I was not eating very much at all.

Calorie intake dropped even further.

I would drink only water. But every now and then, I'd allow myself half a cup of low sugar hot chocolate, with no milk. This my neurodiversity brain was telling me was all I needed.

My bones began to show through my body, and stick out on my hips. Sleep became uncomfortable as I could feel my hip bones. I was freezing cold.

My periods stopped.

My body no longer functioned normally. I was obsessed with always looking in the mirror. What I imagined I saw, looking back at me, were layers of ugly fat on a once attractive young girl.

I loathe myself and hit rock bottom.

I started using the sunbeds at the college gym. Had I known then, what I now know about the dangers of skin cancer, I probably would have had second thoughts about using one.

In 2018 I had Melanoma cancer removed from the back of my leg. If somebody, back then had said I was going to get skin cancer from using a sunbed, I'd have just laughed, and got suntanned.

So, I started to go to the gym every day and use the sunbeds. I went from somebody who hated exercise to a proper gym bunny. I loved the fact, I was burning calories. My body transformed.

Now when I looked in the mirror, there was no fat, just sinewy.
I was now looking very skinny and tanned. People were beginning to notice.
I was attracting attention. They were noticing my weight loss, this creating my ADHD brain dopamine.

At the time, Madonna was looking athletically fit, with her toned defined arms dominating my attention. As you are aware, I've always had a fascination for Madonna, and I could see I was getting arms like hers, which I was delighted with. This unwittingly would fuel my anorexia, being fixated on getting toned arms like Madonna, it actually took my mind off all the shit I was mentally going through.

I would be at the college campus, and have students come up to me, admiring my body, telling me I had an incredible figure, the best body in the college.

The sad reality of all this was, I was sick. Very sick indeed.
I had an eating disorder, and believed I was in control of the condition. I was starving myself, caning myself in the gym, and unwittingly lying on killer sunbeds, which unbeknown to me at the time, could be the reason I had skin cancer later in life.

James, my first real boyfriend, was on a sound engineering course. The first term being in the West Midlands, however, the second term was based in Manchester. So I knew, eventually James would leave the West Midlands in order to complete his course. If I was to stay with James, I would have to go to Manchester.

A quandary, I can remember feeling quite uneasy about, which was a contradiction as I always had dreamed of living in Manchester.
James was a huge comfort for me. We used to love watching Noel's House Party together, especially Mr Blobby. Mr Blobby with his bulbous pink head and yellow spots. I bought James for Christmas everything Mr Blobby. Even the Christmas number one of 1993 was Mr Blobby!

I was so thin, everything hurt and being obsessed with my anorexia, my neurodiversity was just taking over. A shame really, because James was a handsome young guy, with a girlfriend, more bothered about starving herself.

James unexpectedly asked me to marry him. I of course said yes! He'd bought me an engagement ring that cost him a bit of money...

Just before Christmas 1993, my parents returned back home from Australia. I was more than relieved, Mum came to pick me up and took me back to Grimsby.

I will never forget my Mum's face, on first seeing me, when I opened the door. She was shocked to see how thin and frail I had become. She just stood there and she was clearly very upset. What had become of her daughter, while she had been in Australia?

'What have you been doing? My Mum said, in total utter shock and disbelief.

Then I told her I was engaged to James. It was all too much for my Mum to take in.

My poor Mum, she had just come back from a holiday of a lifetime, she hadn't expected the bombshell, and now her daughter would be suffering with anorexia and was engaged...

However, at the time I saw no reason for her to be concerned. My anorexia was under my control. Not her concern...

I was gaining lots of attention from my weight loss, I was asked to do quite a bit of modelling work, which I loved. My ADHD exhibitionism is in full swing.

I was in complete denial.

Still in control. Unaware, what full blown anorexia was doing to me.

Christmas 1993 was a nightmare...

I broke my Mum's heart. I was refusing to eat. Christmas was far from jolly. Mum was begging me to eat. I just refused and I recall my Christmas dinner consisting of a few peas, a very tiny bit of turkey, looking very lonely on my Christmas plate. I played with it for a while, pushing it around my plate, reluctant to put the food in my mouth.

To please my Mum, I eventually ate a bit but felt so guilty. I felt I'd let myself down. Lost control of my actions so to speak. It felt wrong somehow, and I felt disappointed in myself.

To my own disgust, I found a carrier bag, put my fingers down my throat and expelled what little food I'd eaten. I remember the rush of acid rising up through my throat, a swollen neck and sore throat.

Not a very nice feeling at all. But, I was back in control again, unaware Bulimia was now in control of me.

Bulimia is a serious, potentially life-threatening eating disorder. You lose control over your eating and purge, in an uncontrollable urge to get rid of the extra calories in an unhealthy way.

As there was no gym at my parents' house. I'd fanatically run around the block and then workout with dumbbells trying to shed calories.

A quick flashback; Ed before I left Grimsby, had given me a set of dumbbells. To help me achieve those Madonna toned arms. I used those weights religiously every day, they reminded me of Ed, so in a way Ed was always with me. Those dumbbells went everywhere. However, in 2008 when we officially got together and rekindled our love, I gave his dumbbells back, with a happy ever after loving kiss...

I was getting too engrossed with my eating disorder, I now was purging food. Mum had begged me to get help, or at least see a doctor in the West Midlands.

I promised her I would, and I actually did listen.

I was very lucky to meet a lovely, understanding nurse, whose name escapes me, she lived locally with her family. She had never really dealt with somebody with an eating disorder before, but was willing to help. She took me under her wing and my therapy began. She wanted to help me reconnect with the stability of family life, so invited me to her home for a meal and to meet her family.

I soon realised I didn't really want to be helped, the intrusion would interfere with my control. With this in mind, I reluctantly agreed to go to her home.

I felt frustrated.

She was getting in the way of my control. Neurodivergents are prone to eating disorders, a mental health condition that can be triggered from trauma and my God, was I dealing with trauma.

I wasn't healing.

Quite the opposite in fact...

James had to move to Manchester to finish his course...

My course enabled me to find work placement within the photographic industry.

A great opportunity, I thought, to see James, and find work placement in a photographic studio in Manchester. I had always wanted to live in Manchester, so I thought, maybe this could be my next stepping stone.

When James moved to Manchester our relationship was clearly on the rocks.

No doubt about it...

I was totally self-consumed in my own eating disorder and personal problems to consider anything else. My undiagnosed ADHD, fuelling my disinterest in James, but fixating on my weight loss.

Out of sight out of mind. Can't be bothered.

Really bad, that, I know, he was my boyfriend after all.

We were arguing quite a lot, and it was getting kind of volatile between us.

I went to stay with James in Manchester for one week. I had successfully secured myself work placement in a photographic studio in Manchester, that dealt with commercial Photography.

I would have had a great time, but my eating disorder continued to take control of my life. A friendly, but harmless joke, made by one of the photographers about my weight, upset me.

I took it personally...That's how sensitive I was becoming.

I was getting extremely thin. Under six stone in weight, maybe less. Clothes were hanging off me. I looked ill and very poorly, and had serious self-esteem and self-loathing issues.

I had a feeling that things between James and I weren't as good as they once were. Quite the opposite I feared. I returned back to the West Midlands after staying with James, in Manchester for the week on my work placement.
My psychic vibes were telling me, all was not well, and I kind of knew that he was going to cheat on me. It's a psychic insight I believe I have.
And yes he did cheat on me, so my psychic abilities told me the truth.
I found out through a mutual college friend, who had the decency to inform me. James had gone on a night out to the Hacienda, Manchester's legendary nightclub. He met a girl on a one night stand, and the rest you can guess...
I confronted him and he confessed it was true...

I was gutted, I really was gutted. We were engaged and he cheated on me. Until James, I'd never had a full-time boyfriend, so to be cheated on, was the first time. It really did hurt.
Angrily, I refused to give him back the ring. He wanted to sell it and pay his parents back the money he'd borrowed to buy it, in the first place.
It was my ring, he gave it to me, and so no I wasn't giving it back.
He wasn't happy. Tough shit, he shouldn't have cheated on me.
I sold it on my return to Grimsby that summer to a jeweller.
We were young, eighteen year old students at college, where temptation is but a nightclub away. It was a college romance that I thought was important at the time. However I was reassured by my Mum, I was young, and had plenty of time to find other relationships and possibly find true love.
Yes it was a painful experience, but I was so consumed with my eating disorder.
I was so self-obsessed with exercise and tanning, I got over it quite quickly...
In my frame of mind at that time, I thought it a blessing he cheated on me, because now I could just control myself and not have to worry about him.

One thing I hadn't realised was I was actually causing problems for my roommate Jenny. I started to inflict self-doubt on her. She too had started to cut down on food, and began to question her body image. Thinking she wouldn't be good enough if she wasn't skinny thin. I certainly didn't intend for Jenny to feel like that. I never did it intentionally but we shared a room together. So when I reflected back at my eating disorder, it seriously was affecting Jenny. Without me even realising it, I was making Jenny very sick...

I never disclosed at the time to Jenny about my obsessive traits, or my eating disorders. It was a personal thing for me to deal with alone.

So when I discovered how my behaviour was affecting Jenny I was absolutely devastated. I really needed someone so desperately to rescue me...it's time to understand...

CHAPTER TWELVE

UNDERSTAND

Time to rewind back a little...

Fill in some gaps and profile some of the characters.

Mike, who I met in Grimsby, Kelly's boyfriend at the time, had separated from her.

I had formed a very good friendship with Mike. A platonic brother and sister type of relationship in fact. The best kind. No boyfriend, girlfriend complications. I never wanted anything more from Mike other than being his friend and he mine.

He was quite dark skinned and had little dreadlocks. He looked foreign and loved to wear unusual clothes. He wasn't afraid to express himself through fashion. He used to wear my Great Nannas gold Lorax jackets. He looked fantastic in it, really trendy. He wasn't a cross dresser, he just looked stylish, wearing anything. Mike was one of those guys.

A very unique person.

Mike loved music especially House Music and was an accomplished and talented DJ. Mike and I used to talk about him becoming a record producer, and me a singer.

Get out of Grimsby, make records, and become famous.

What dreams we both had.

I absolutely loved Mike to pieces in a brotherly way, even when he split up from Kelly, we still remained good friends.

Such a great guy.

I would probably class Mike as one of my first, best male platonic friends. Over the years I've tended to make platonic friendships with males more than females.

But that's probably ADHD guiding my judgments.

It's said you can't really have male friends without it spilling over into some kind of sexual encounter. I disagree because I've had plenty of male friends all platonic. Mike was one of them...

Mike came to stay with me, in the student house in Wednesbury.
However, it wasn't long before Mike had soon made some new friends. He had befriended a lad called Bill, who ironically was also from Grimsby. He was on the sound engineering course at our college. Quite a coincidence as it turned out.
Mike eventually moved in with Bill, in his student digs in Walsall...

Jenny and Mike had also formed a good friendship. They both were getting very concerned about my well-being, especially my eating disorder.

I recall going to Bill's house in Walsall, to visit Mike with Jenny. I wouldn't eat any food while there, only nibbling at a slice of watermelon. I felt so guilty about eating the watermelon, so I would start purging to bring it back up.

My eating disorder was getting worse, despite having seen a nurse, who tried her best to give me help. I still was not yet in recovery, my eating disorder roared at full throttle. Dominating my life...

Jenny unfortunately, was being badly affected by my eating disorder. I was so hyper fixated on myself, totally oblivious to the fact it was affecting Jenny. My neurodiversity aggravated my dilemma, the more I was in control, the more the fixation released dopamine, unable to understand what the hell was going on and how it was affecting those around me...

Eventually, Mike and Jenny made a decision and confronted me about my eating disorder. I didn't take it well at all. I went into denial and got upset with them both, for challenging me about it...

I had become a joke to some of the students, some even calling me 'Han-orexia'... I recall being at a student house party. I remember dancing away, lost in the music, minding my own business. When a few derogatory comments were made, regarding my non-existent breasts! Comments about them looking saggy, and how I needed to wear a better bra! You see, I had lost so much weight that my boobs had turned to sacks of excess skin. So when I danced, they still moved around, even though I was so thin. People can be cruel and judgemental. I was subjected to a torrent of cruel jibes and jokes. Yes the comments were insulting, but like water off a duck's back, I was very much in control of myself... So fuck them!
Well that's what I thought. But I was far from being in control...

So when Jenny and Mike challenged me about my eating disorder. I just locked up. Not interested. Didn't understand. Don't want to understand..

I was in complete denial...

I couldn't understand how something affecting me could possibly be affecting Jenny. I refused to accept it.

They were adamant I should listen...

When confronted with reality, I was shocked to discover my actions were impacting those around me.

It was an eye-opener. I'd been blind to the fact, embroiled in my own world, to have even considered what I might be doing to those close to me.

Over time I've learnt to understand and accept this.

But now, confronted with the truth, I had a massive learning curve to master.

Truth hurts. I felt guilty. Had I really done this to Jenny?

Yes. Unintentionally, but I had.

Imagine travelling down a long road and you come to a turn off, you turn into it, and find yourself stuck in a cul-de-sac. That's the analogy I faced.

Getting stuck, spinning around, and looking for the way to get back on that road again. That was my issue, I was so consumed in myself and my eating disorder that I was not open to what was going on around me.

Jenny had been that upset and messed up over my eating disorder, she'd confided in Mike. Mike had been shocked by it all, and literally was begging me to sort it out...but it wasn't as easy as that.

I knew deep down things had to change, but I couldn't make it stop. Whilst in control of my eating disorders, it helped me from all the hurt and pain I had endured. Deep routed traumas that no one knew the truth about. I masked myself, always trying to appear normal.

Jenny was truly devastated. I could see she was hurting. It was getting so bad that she just couldn't live in the same room with me anymore. My obsession with my eating disorder was ruining her life. I tried to explain that I wasn't deliberately trying to ruin her existence, but looking back, I probably was... Her life, living with me, was a nightmare...

I remember seeing Jenny crying her eyes out, and informing me that she and Garry had separated. James had cheated on me, remember... However, Garry hadn't cheated on Jenny, far from it...

What Jenny then told me, came as a bit of a shock. I always believed they were really very close. They were always cuddling, kissing and doing things together. They had similar interests in music and were great together.

The ideal couple...

What she told me, had really knocked her for six. It turned out Garry was a closeted homosexual, and wanted to come out of the closet and be honest with her. He hadn't cheated on her, in any way, but knew his desires were not directed to her, but to men. This absolutely destroyed Jenny. She just couldn't get her head around the fact, her Garry was a homosexual. Not that he was a homosexual, no problem with that, but that their relationship had been built upon a sham...

On top of Garry's confession, her roommate me, obsessed with an eating disorder, was manifesting even more distress. No wonder she was in a bad place.

A nightmare situation, I wouldn't wish on my worst enemy.

I could have done much better in my final year at College. I had the potential but unfortunately my eating disorder just took control. I really began to struggle with my coursework.

I had lost interest in most things, my eating disorder taking control for my dopamine fix. I was going to the gym, lying on sunbeds that sadly was becoming my objective. When you have ADHD, being in control is quite a task. ADHD creates the opposite and you have to build strategies on how to cope. With anorexia and Bulimia I was, I thought, in full control.

Well I thought I was.

I used to think, would this merry go round of eating and purging ever stop?

In the early 90s it was the generation of the 'Supermodel'.' Models were thin and lean, and that was the norm. I recall, promising myself never to be chubby again. So I fixated on staying thin and being in control for as long as I could.

I enjoyed the dopamine attention my eating disorder was giving me. If truth be told, at the time, I liked being skinny in some weird attention seeking way. I know now, it was a much fucked up philosophy, not healthy, and very dangerous...

By the summer of 1994 it was time to leave the West Midlands having finished my photographic course. However, I didn't like the idea of going back to Grimsby.

I had given some thought about the possibility of moving on to Manchester. So I wrote a letter to the same photographic studio, where I did my college work placement, based in Manchester. I wrote to ask, if they had any vacancies coming up, and hopefully consider me. I waited for their reply...

Jenny and I packed up all our belongings and left our student digs for the last time. It felt sad that the journey in the West Midlands was coming to an end...

An end of the era, so to speak. But an era that took me first away from Grimsby will never be forgotten.

My eating disorder continued....But not as strict as it was in the West Midlands but nonetheless, it was still there and still taking control.

Back in Grimsby I started using Ed's dumbbells more. I was still obsessed with tanning myself and hired a cheap canopy sunbed to go over my bed.

How irresponsible was that? But I was so obsessed with having a tan. I'd literally lay under the sunbed for about an hour a day. It was a recipe for disaster. Probably the reason for my skin cancer in my 40s.

When you're young you don't care do you? Despite being told to stop, you do it anyway. It's like telling someone to stop smoking. If you're going to smoke, you'll smoke. Getting tanned and going on a sunbed was like that with me. I was going to do it, whatever anyone said.

And I did.

I hyper fixated on getting a tan, on keeping my Madonna arms, and on my weight loss. As a result, I stopped eating red meat. I wouldn't eat bread, sweets, crisps, cakes in fact I wouldn't eat anything that I thought was unhealthy. I actually remained that strict discipline for many years after. My eating disorder was dominating and wasn't going away...

During that summer of 1994, I made plans, again I'd work at Grimsby's Bluecrest factory, packing fish, to earn money. I worked around the clock with overtime, accumulating as much money as possible. In the factory I reconnected with Amy, who I was friends with at Infant and Junior school. We formed a good friendship, and had lots of laughs packing fish together.

I still, when my neurodiversity remembers, communicate with Amy to this very day, mainly through the revolutionary social media.

However it's that out of sight out of mind, kind of a thing with me. Amy knows, not to take it personally, it's not a slight on her.

At the time, we both decided to go on summer holiday together. We would do this after we'd finished working our summer at Bluecrest. Student employment was only for certain summer months, so we'd be free to go on holiday somewhere. So we booked via Teletext, no internet back then, to go to a Greek Island for a week. We really had no idea where it was, but it was cheap, and affordable.

Hopefully, I'd be able to move on from the trauma of my last holiday in Ibiza.

I also made another friend at Bluecrest while working there. She was called Kerry. She lived with her boyfriend David, and I'd often go after work to their flat, to have tea. Years later I was sad to hear David had been in a road traffic accident and had been killed instantly. I was absolutely heartbroken, devastated by such a tragedy. They were such a lovely couple. I still keep in touch with Kerry when my ADHD allows me to remember. RIP David x

As I've always said, you've got to live your life to the fullest, you never know what's around the next corner, and that is what I intended to do, live my life to the fullest...

Prior to our departure to the Greek Island, I bumped into Ed in our local pub. He was with a girl, called Sally, this was a different one, to the one I remembered he was going out with when I was at college. Same name though but different face...

She was mousey and dowdy, actually quite spotty. Yes, I was being 'catty,' even judgemental. As I've said on many occasions, ADHD people say it as they see it. Worts and all...

I just kept thinking why is he with her? She's absolutely disgusting.

Putting to one aside my opinion of Sally I went and sat with them. It was obvious, the second I sat down, Sally didn't want me there. Ed started flirting with me outrageously, he was slightly intoxicated so his confidence was strong. We talked, joked and laughed about old times, our families, and the Valentine card he sent me when he was five. Sally, glared and squirmed uneasy, you could see she was getting embarrassingly annoyed.

It was really nice to see Ed laughing again, because I had concerns about how he was coping over his parent's separation. He said he'd moved on.

However, Ed certainly was drinking a lot more than I remember him doing, when I left Grimsby in 1992. He still looked like the Ed I knew, however his beautiful eyes were not as sparky as I remembered them. Those happy, sparky blue eyes now looked a little grey. He was definitely drinking more, and sadly smoking weed so we're the rumours that I was told true......

So Amy and I embarked on our holiday to the Greek Island. We flew first to Athens and it was all good fun, no issues. I didn't feel as stressful as I thought I might. I started to ease down off the gas a little with my eating disorder, but not fully over the major issues.

I wasn't in recovery just yet...

To get to the island you had to take a boat. 'Island hopping,' as it's called by the locals. It turned out the island we were staying on was mainly for the locals of Athens and not really a tourist place. When we arrived, there were no cars on this island, just horse drawn carriages. The harbour was awash with expensive boats no doubt from the very wealthy people of Athens. It was a very pretty place.

The holiday started off well up until my eating disorder raised its ugly head.

Amy got pissed off with me quite quickly, probably that's when the arguments started. I really cannot remember what the arguments were about? I just know, they got quite heated and quite vile. Insults were thrown, followed by name calling. It became intolerable, horrible and very uncomfortable.

I absolutely hate falling out with people. I hate arguments, it makes me feel poorly. I sometimes can't cope with conflict situations. Amy just couldn't cope with me, which was totally understandable. I don't think anyone could cope with me.

I just wanted to have a great time but my eating disorder took control again.

We both came back from that holiday, not really talking to each other, and we didn't keep in touch much after that. Well obviously not until years later....

In Amy's eyes, I was probably that thoughtless fickle friend that spoilt her holiday. She was, probably, in some respects, right about that, but in my eyes I wasn't. I was struggling with a very controlling eating disorder and with my neurodiversity urging me to take time out, I sort of isolated myself, and made no contact.

I mean, I know I shared a room with Jenny at college, but I did however have quite a bit of time on my own. Which I crave, I crave that alone time. Jenny was out a lot, at the time with Garry, so we were not on top of each other.

I must mention here, how bad my Bulimia was during the holiday. It can be very tiring, constantly sticking your fingers down your throat and purging. It's quite a disgusting thing to do, and afterwards you feel disgusted with yourself for doing it and exhausted. And once you start purging it's very difficult to stop. It's got control over you. My Bulimia did get severely bad, binge eating and purging constantly.

Not the easiest of tasks I can assure you. It's no wonder I ended up with acid reflux problems and stomach issues later in life. If only I knew then, what I know now, the damage I was inflicting on my body.

But I didn't.

So on holiday Amy was witness to all my maladies, and all my mental fuck ups. I guess, like I stressed out Jenny, I did the same to Amy.

Looking back it was quite horrific.

I actually needed help, proper professional help. Relationships were strained. My friends were wary and standoffish. It was a nightmare for me, and an even bigger one for my friends.

I was fucking up friendships as quickly as I was making them.

I pissed people off with my actions and outlandish behaviour traits.

Not on purpose, I must add, but a genuine sense of not thinking I'd done anything wrong. I was labelled, selfish, self-centred, and narcissistic and out only for myself.

On returning back home, after the holiday, I received a letter from the photographic studio in Manchester. They couldn't offer me a full-time job but they would be more than happy to give me work experience again.

It was the opportunity I'd been waiting for, to live in Manchester. I still had a little bit of money left from the holiday, not a lot, but enough.

Fate would now enter my life, and whisk me off to Manchester.
It came in the disguise of a girl called Cathy, I knew her from college. She called me randomly at my parent's house in Grimsby. After chatting for a while on the telephone, she informed me she was moving to Manchester in September and would I consider living with her. I jumped at the offer...absolutely YES!

She said she had secured a property in Manchester. It was a house share. She was dating a guy called Steve. He was on the same sound engineering course as my ex-boyfriend James, so, like James, he had moved to Manchester to complete his course. Another guy on the same course as Steve, called Andy, was also moving into the house. So Cathy, knowing I wanted to move to Manchester, had called me and asked me if I wanted to move in as well. This was like music to my ears. My dream was about to come true. I had secured full-time work experience at the photographic studio.

Okay, without pay. No problem...

I told mum I was moving to Manchester in September and asked her if she could drive me and all my belongings to my lodgings in Manchester.

This she did.
I was to lodge in a typical traditional Manchester terraced house. Its facade was built out of dark red bricks with a dominant big bay window facing the road.

I was in a downstairs bedroom, Cathy and Steve were upstairs and Andy had the use of a fantastic loft room.

Due to the excitement of finally living my dream in Manchester. I started to ease up on my eating disorder. My Bulimia appeared to wane a little. Dopamine was being created, as my new fixations were elsewhere.

However the never ending eating disorder merry go round, then changed to compulsive binge eating and I started putting on weight...

I really had no idea how I was going to pay the rent... I didn't really think that far ahead. I would cross that bridge when I got to Manchester.

So I decided to visit the landlord. He had an office at the end of the street. When I got there, I explained my dilemma, hoping he'd understand my situation.

Like Hell he did, he went absolutely ballistic. He was angry, because no one had told him I'd moved into his house. I guess, looking back on the situation, he had more than every cause to be angry. He threatened to kick me out. I pleaded for him to reconsider. I'd already unpacked my belongings and they were already in my room. I visualised being put out on the street, my belongings strewn around me.

I begged him again. I'd nowhere to live.

Not my problem, he replied, and lectured me further. I felt like a little girl, being chastised for some misdemeanour she'd no idea she'd made. I felt stupid, but this is how my brain works sometimes. It doesn't think before it speaks.

I act on impulse. Not logic. We compromised, found a solution...

It was nice to have my own bedroom at last, it was a lot nicer than my old digs in Wednesbury. Years later I found out that the landlord of my old lodgings in Wednesbury was on a TV show called 'Rogue Landlords'. It was quite crazy to think that I lived in one of the worst shit holes in the West Midlands owned by one of the worst landlords in the UK. This rented house in Manchester wasn't the best, I admit, but it was nicer than what I'd been used to...

Okay, I survived... Always trying to learn lessons of life. Always trying to understand my erratic behaviour, and why I behave the way I do.....But moving on, the future's looking bright...Manchester MADchester here I come....

CHAPTER THIRTEEN

FUTURE

So my life in Manchester started in September 1994.
As a teenager I'd dreamt of moving there, the dream now a reality. I was looking forward to experiencing its vibrant music and dance scenes, and going to the legendary Hacienda nightclub. A decade prior in 1984, Madonna performed her first UK live debut for the TV show 'The Tube' at the Hacienda, so I couldn't wait to visit.

I wanted to become a singer, a dream more than achievable, here in Manchester. So I wrote a letter to 808 State, a Mancunian band. They pioneered Electronic Music, they were a prominent influence on the UKs burgeoning Acid House scene. With classics like 'Pacific State.' I wanted to be a singer and if they wanted me to sing on their 'Mother Dance' tracks, to contact me on my mum's landline. My mum's phone never rang...

So, at last, here I was in Manchester, my dream city. Here I planned to grow up fast. But can I grow up? Not sure my ADHD brain will allow it. I fear I will forever be that young girl with a twelve year old brain. I think even when I'm in my 70s it'll still be like that.

So I'm here in Manchester, in my own bedroom. Living with my college chums, Cathy, Andy and Steve. I can remember putting posters on my bedroom wall of Madonna and then getting fixated on 'Take That.' I first saw Take That, when they performed at my school sports hall in Grimsby, they weren't famous then.

Now they were, so I went around bragging that I'd met them, hoping to impress everyone. Again the fixation thing on,' Take That.'

The house was cold, damp and very outdated. Andy had the best bedroom.
He was an incredible sound engineer, destined to have a remarkable career in music. Very eccentric though.

He helped form a music band in our kitchen. His band was a genre of Electronic Music, that was influenced by Trip Hop, Drum and Bass, Jazz and Folk.

Andy was confident and set in his ways. He was more like a Bohemian. He slept in a hammock, and loved Trip Hop music. He enjoyed moon dancing parties in Thailand.

Today, he's still highly successful in the music business. Producing for the likes of top recording artists and more recently producing sound tracks for huge box office films in Hollywood.

Steve on the other hand eventually gave up on doing sound engineering and got a job in retail. He moved into high street fashion and forgot all about sound engineering.

Cathy's parents funded her daughter's stay in Manchester. She was pretty, cute, but boy could she be a feisty bitch if she wanted to be.

And of course there was me. A complex, yet to be diagnosed neurodivergent with attitude...

So that was me and my housemates. A powder keg of destruction, waiting for the fuse to be lit. It was only a matter of time before arguments and fall outs would destroy our happy home.

I started work placement at the photographic studio as arranged. Things had changed. It was different and initially I became an unpaid skivvy, a dogsbody, a gopher.

I hated it.

Technology was now in control of photography. I was doing all this for free. My main source of income was the Dole.

Cash opens doors, not the Dole. Being a skivvy was untenable. I was at the mercy of all the studios employers, viewed only as an apprentice. I'd start from the bottom, and work myself up. That's how it was done. In addition, was I to make the tea, and be their gopher?

Not for me, I'm afraid.

I was better than that. I'd got my OND and wanted to be a photographer. But, to achieve that, it looked like I had to be skivvy first.

No way! I felt like shit on the management's shoe.

I was trying to recover from my eating disorder. In rain or shine I'd walk to work. Possibly walking a couple of miles a day. However, I did start to gain weight. I wasn't big, quite tiny, really, but because I'd gone so thin any weight I put on showed quite quickly. I didn't like the weight gain. I felt out of control.

People started to notice my weight gain. As usual they were cruel. You're getting fat! Chubby! Came the jibes...

It was a vicious circle, a real head fuck, especially with someone like me, who had a dysfunctional brain disorder. I was desperately trying to recover from my eating disorder, and people made fun of me.

If only those, insensitive bastards, had engaged their brains, first, before belittling me. But sadly, people like that don't.

I know that's a bit rich coming from me, because I'm one of them. True! I don't think before I speak, but I've got an excuse. Those who mocked, hadn't ADHD had they?

No excuses to be rude.

More reason than to engage your brain before speaking.

I had no income. My work experience placement paid me nothing, so I had no alternative but to keep signing on the dole. Not my idea of control. I've always earned my monies, by working for it. Claiming Dole was against all my principles.

So desperate to get extra income, I went to look for a paid job. While walking home, I passed Ethel Austin's, a clothing retailer. They sold baby clothes, underwear and ladies fashion.

They wanted an assistant. I applied and got the job. I was to start immediately which would clash, with my voluntary, unpaid position at the photographic studio.

I had a decision to make. Paid work, or unpaid work? A no brainer. I hated being on the Dole.

So I embarked on a full-time job at Ethel Austin's...

The uniform was vile but compulsory. I hated it, but was forced to wear it? I looked like a middle-aged lady. Ugh! I looked hell of a mess.

I wanted to fit in with my housemates, who appeared cool, outgoing, trendsetters. I wanted to be more like them, but I just couldn't.

Andy had a wicked and cruel sense of humour.

He cruelly announced, to my face, I'd never be anything, but a shelf-stacker. Hateful, words I'd heard before, words that have haunted me for years.

No one knows how painful that one simple statement hurts me.

I literally take things said as literal...

In 2019 Ed and I went to see Andy in Sheffield. He was on tour with his band. We met up and were invited back to stage. We reminisced about college and our time in Manchester together. Calling me a 'shelf-stacker' cropped up, and Andy was genuinely mortified to think he'd said that to me. He hadn't realised how it had plagued me for years and the detrimental effect it had had on me. He apologised and he really genuinely couldn't remember making that statement. I know he didn't mean it, so all is now forgiven.

Now knowing I have ADHD, flippant comments are taken literally, the shelf-stacking comment an example.

I took it literally, and with it, all those years of resentment. Absolutely crazy isn't it? Anyway, let's get back to the story. Again, you've just witnessed my ADHD in action.

I go off on tangents.

So where was I?

Oh that's right, I'm back in Ethel Austin's in my really disgusting work uniform. One evening, after work, it was rumoured, The Stone Roses, were using the building behind the shop to practise. I could hear them. The rumours were true.

Only in Manchester could this happen. The Stone Roses were playing, right behind where I worked.

How exciting was that?

The following night, at a nearby kebab shop, standing in the queue, in front of me, was the legendary Ian Brown, Stone Roses lead singer. He looked exactly as photographed in magazines, and music videos. There he was, in front of me, I was embarrassed, looking like a dork, in my 'Nunty Nora,' outfit I was forced to wear.

How embarrassing was that?

Suddenly, he turned around and asked me in a broad Mancunian accent, 'you alright love?' 'Am I all right, love?'

What the, Fuck! "Am I all right, love?'

I wasn't! But, who in their right mind, suffering from ADHD, could answer such a complex question? I've never ever been in my right mind.

But what the Hell? It was the singer from Stone Roses. Course I was alright. I was talking to Ian Brown. I was over the moon. A musical star asked me a question.

Hell, that doesn't happen every day, I just unashamedly melted, like a chunk of chocolate in an admirer's hand.

I was speechless.

Life became dull, drab and boring. Dopamine levels dropped. I was working a 9-to-5 job at Ethel Austin's and hating it. It was as dull as dishwater. As dull as dishwater, summed up my life at that moment in time.

However it didn't matter. I was living in Manchester, and that's what mattered to me. I was living my dream.

I fixated on Andy, because I was bored. He was getting recognised in the Manchester music scene, producing tracks and becoming famous with his female vocalist Viv. She was also a professional photographer, drop dead gorgeous she was.

She knew all the celebrities, and took photographs of everybody. Those photos appeared in an underground magazine called ID. The publication was dedicated to fashion, music, art, and youth culture.

I fixated on Viv, at the time. She had, in my ADHD mind, the perfect career in photography. She sang, with a very unusual folk-pop singing voice that was new and unique. A different talent destined for greater things.

Viv's connections got Andy recognized and opened the opportunity for a huge record deal with his band.

They were both living the life I wanted to live. Andy never wanted to record a song with me. I did ask him if Viv would allow me to come with her, as her assistant photographer, when I wasn't working at the shop.

So, to my utter amazement, and delight, she agreed.

I went with Viv to be her assistant photographer for the day... she photographed the group 'Boo Radley's,' an alternative rock band, they were just releasing a massive song 'Wake Up,' which was a massive hit. I sensed a vibe that Viv didn't like me all that much. Probably too Loud and boisterous for her. But that's me. Loud and boisterous. Not the sort of person she wanted to hang out with. Was I jealous? You're dead right I was. She was everything I wanted to be. Of course I was envious, she was living the perfect life. A life I wanted...

We had to move house. Andy's bedroom ceiling collapsed, fortunately with him not in it. So we moved to the house next door. Our landlord owned both properties.

Andy was hardly ever at home, making and producing records. Cathy got a job in retail, in Manchester city centre and she gained a load of new friends, friends that would also become my friends too.

Manchester was an exciting, one-stop party central. Its nightclubs were legendary and the Hacienda became my favourite place to party, that and the gay village.

I didn't have a boyfriend. I really wasn't at all bothered about dating. What with James cheating on me, I didn't want any of that again.

So boyfriends were out.

I was still recovering from all the mental health shit, which was really creating havoc with my mind set. On top of that madness, I had an eating disorder to deal with. So, boyfriends were out...

It was me against an unforgiving public. They knew nothing about my condition. Uncaring individuals who thought only of their own welfare.

So the Hacienda, nonjudgmentally, became my solace.

That's all I wanted. To have a good time on my terms. However, I did wonder whether I would be 'left on the shelf,' but for God's sake, I was only nineteen, plenty of time yet.

I worried about my periods. My mum had read about polycystic ovaries, and wondered if I was suffering similar symptoms. Polycystic ovary syndrome, or PCOS, is the most common endocrine disorder in women of reproductive age. It affects the way your ovaries work. It's all to do with the hormones in the body not working properly. My GP seemed to think it was actually my stomach and not my ovaries. He referred me to the local hospital where I had my bowels investigated. I remember, a cold silver instrument was inserted into my bottom. After which I was told I had IBS, irritated bowel syndrome.

My anxiety went through the roof. I had mistreated my body with an eating disorder, so I kind of understood IBS. However, my hormones were all over the place. I was growing hair on my upper lip and out of my belly button.

A scary development.

I again thought of PCOS. If indeed you are suffering from polycystic ovary syndrome, your ovaries, produce an abnormal amount of androgens, male sex hormones.

So, was I, a woman, turning into a man? No of course not, but it was worrying?   Later, in life, I was diagnosed with PCOS, so I felt somewhat let down by that GP who misdiagnosed my condition.

A chance, innocent encounter, with a man on a train, when visiting my parents in Grimsby, caused scary repercussions. He asked for my phone number. Again that ADHD of mine, innocently took control, and I gave him my parents' number.

This guy turned out to be a bit of a nutter.

He kept calling me up at my parent's house, so I gave him my number in Manchester to get rid of him.

Another ADHD mistake.

As it turned out, he was having affairs in Grimsby and Manchester all at the same time and was looking to me for another.

It turned out he was a nut job!

He came to my house in Manchester, with photographs, claiming he photographed models.

A stalker, or what?

He told me his name was Phil. He called, and visited, me constantly.

He was a weirdo, not quite right in the head. But it wasn't to end there, oh no there was more to come, much more.

I'd just returned home from work in Manchester. I was alone in the house, when there was a banging on the front door. Loud, manic thumping. I opened the door, and there was this bloke Phil, with a baseball bat in his hand.

Fucking Hell, a baseball bat!

Believe it or not, I remained calm. I found out later in life that people with ADHD remain calm in traumatic situations. In front of me was a crazy Phil, wheeling a baseball bat around his head, shouting, 'where is he?' 'Where is he?'

'Where is who?' I asked.

'Andy! You know Andy, where is he?'

I felt I was in some weird nightmare, proper crazy bat-shit stuff! My head, being fried by his craziness.

Andy? How did this crazy person know Andy? As far as I was aware, they'd never met. As it turned out, this Phil nutter, who believed Andy, had told his Manchester girlfriend about meeting me, and he was out to get Andy for telling her.

How, or why remained a mystery.

So a guy I randomly met on the train going to Grimsby, was in front of me with a baseball bat in his hand.

What a fuck head.

Looking back, I think this Phil guy had ADHD worse than me. Whatever, he wasn't a full shilling that was for sure.

A very dangerous individual, in fact.

The next thing I knew, his girlfriend was at the house, swinging punches at me. I was still acting cool, dodging her punches.

What madness, just crazy.

Barmy Phil, with a baseball bat, and his girlfriend, were in the house, looking for Andy. Phil's girlfriend was trying to punch me, while Phil was trying to stop her.

It was just bedlam.

I remember, thinking, what the fuck was going on. I'd just come home from Ethel Austin, still wearing that horrible uniform, bad enough having to wear the flaming thing, and now all this.

I remember getting out of the house, away from this', baseball bat, wheeling Tasmanian devil and his manic sidekick, but no they followed me out. She rushed past me, back to a car parked in the street. And would you believe there was another one? Phil's mate was sitting in the car.

Curiouser and curiouser, said I, as I tumbled further down this never-ending rabbit hole. What next I thought, a March hare wheeling a machete?

No! No March hare, but much more curious than that. They all started to laugh.

Laugh for fuck sake.

I certainly wasn't laughing, I can tell you that, for a fact.

It was all a joke, insisted Phil, hysterically admitting, he'd done it for a laugh.

They then tried to convince me it was all a prank. A prank? No way. My mind raced through memories of my traumas. I certainly wasn't laughing!

My, mind was in fucking chaos

I warned him off me, telling him I never wanted to see him again. Stay away from me, this house, you pervert, I told him, or else I'd call the police.

They left. I just wanted this nutcase gone out of my life forever.

But no such luck.

He tried again to contact me, years later. I was working at a job in Manchester city centre. He'd somehow found out where I worked and started stalking me, but I'll come to that incident later.

Somehow, my personality attracts crazy bat-shit people, who, like vampires, want to drain the life out of me. My individuality is very unique to others. Outwardly I look permanently happy, whatever my situation I always have a smile on my face.

That's what ADHD people do.

Sophie, a girl who worked at the photographic studio, informed me that FX Labs, close by, was looking for a sales rep and thought of me. She arranged an interview.

I'm forever grateful to Sophie for doing that.

Sophie was a bubbly, full of life character, who with her boyfriend were into network marketing with a company called Amway. An American multi-level marketing company that sold health, beauty, and home care products. Inspired by their marketing claims of getting rich quick, they recruited a lot of people, who started pedalling cleaning products, at twice the price to their unsuspecting friends and neighbours.

I'm sure it works and I'm sure people have been very successful with it but to me it was my idea of hell. I'm loud and boisterous, on the outside, the ideal personality for recruiting people, the centre of attention, a boom box of energy.

But inside, I'm not at all like that.

I don't really like dealing with a lot of people. I can't really cope. So, with a sign of relief, I declined Amway.

I was sure 1995 was going to be my year. I was living with Cathy and Andy. Cathy's boyfriend Steve, I believed was no longer on the scene, they'd split up and he'd moved out. With my ADHD in control, I was too fixated on the success of Andy and Viv, to be bothered about Steve and Cathy.

So in February 1995, I secured an interview at FX Labs, one of the North's biggest photographic laboratories. It processed film and photographs for commercial companies. At the time, they were experimenting very successfully, with digital technology, printing both traditionally and digitally.

For my interview, I dyed my hair bleach blonde, and arched my eyebrows, colouring them dark.

A new look, similar to Madonna's. I wanted to look my best...

My work experiences, and other work placements put me in good stead.

I didn't have a CV. So, in the interview, I waffled on, 'wax lyrical,' so to speak, in my bubbly, enthusiastic way, telling them who I was, what I did and why I wanted the job.

Did I get the job?

Yes! My car awaited me.

What? My car? Panic!

I didn't have a driving licence! So, we compromised, the job was mine on the condition I passed my driving test.

My parents didn't learn to drive until they were in their 40s. They'd wished they had done it years before. It gives you more opportunities in life, more freedom, insisted my parents.

I hadn't given it much thought when I was seventeen, at the time most of my friends were taking lessons. I was too busy trying to accumulate enough money, in the hope of getting the hell out of Grimsby.

I remember calling my parents on a pay phone, telling them the great news but I would need to learn to drive to do the job I was offered. Financially I wasn't in a position to fund driving lessons.

Dad agreed to pay for driving lessons. I'm so lucky to have understanding parents. I guess Dad saw it as an investment for my future.

So I embarked on a crash course of lessons. I drove every day for about three weeks. My driving instructor was a woman who lived locally in Middleton.

She had a strong Manchester accent.

I recall my first lesson. She pulled up outside my house. I can remember feeling very scared. I was excited but nervous. As usual I fixated on the need to pass my driving test to keep my job at FX Labs.

So for three weeks I had intense driving lessons with my lady driving instructor. With neurodiversity you may recall, you fixate on things. The fact she was smoking a cigarette all the time, and wasn't the most encouraging of instructors, was most unpleasant. She wore American tan tights, her car smelly full of dog hairs.

She basically said, I was crap and was wasting her time as I would never pass the driving test.

I mean I don't know if this was some kind of weird psychology or she actually genuinely meant it, I really don't know. Dad paid £300 for this and according to this woman, I wasn't going to pass.

I felt horrible at the time. Had dad wasted his money?

Three weeks driving with her every day took its toll. I was beginning to hate her, and I'm sure she didn't like me. She was always shouting at me!

But we tolerated each other.

I took my driving test at a Manchester test centre. My examiner was a lady as well.

Against all odds, I passed my test for the first time.

My parents were absolutely delighted and in March 1995 I started work for FX Labs as their sales representative. I'll never forget, being given a brand-new white Vauxhall Corsa. Time to Celebrate, So I drove off into the future to come....

CHAPTER FOURTEEN

CELEBRATION

So, to celebrate my first day at work, I drove my brand new shiny white Vauxhall Corsa into a bollard...

As you know my brain often interprets things differently to that of a normal person. Take the number plate on my new car as an example. To me it spelt out the name of a place in which a horrific disaster took place. Probably inappropriate to think like that, but that's my logic.

I just see things differently.

I don't mean to offend, but to the uninitiated, I do. My neurodivergent brain sees things a bit weird.

I'll never forget, looking at that number plate, and thinking, 'disaster.' It was a word that best described my relationship with that car, disastrous!

They gave me the keys and I went to a small compound at the back of the building where it was parked. I noticed a small CCTV camera kept a watchful eye over the area.

I saw the car, and immediately thought, how in hell am I going to get it out? It was so tightly squeezed in, beside a huge concrete bollard. Barely enough room to climb in it, not to mention, drive it out.

Well, I tried, and hit that blasted concrete bollard. An inevitable disaster, just waiting for me.

I crushed and dented the whole of the passenger side, from front to back. I caused £800 worth of damage on my very first day.

I went back inside, to tell my bosses what I'd done, expecting an absolute rollicking. I could hear laughter. Everyone in the office was looking at a video of me crashing into the bollard. The CCTV camera had recorded all of it. They kept rewinding, and howling with laughter.

So what was a disaster for me, turned out to be a standing joke for my workmates? I drove that car, like that, everywhere. They refused to get it fixed. I'd probably damage it again so why bother repairing it? Any rate they'll save £800.

Not much faith in my driving then, was there?

True to form, my second accident was with a cyclist. We collided, the cyclist ending up, holding on to the car's windscreen wipers. I'll never forget that terrified look on his face. I accidentally put my foot on the accelerator before realising it should have been the brake. I braked and the now traumatised cyclist went flying off.

Blame was never really established. Luckily, he was unhurt and I simply checked to see everything was okay with him.

I was to cover inner and Greater Manchester, Bolton, Chorley, and certain parts of Lancashire. I even went as far as Macclesfield, Cheshire and Alderley Edge. I'm a skilful map reader so I used a road map to find my way around.

No Sat Navs then, remember they were a luxury.

I worked for a short while with a sexist grumpy old guy called Barry. He hated the fact I was a young girl doing the same job as him, and had a company car.

It really stuck in his throat and he used to make a lot of detrimental comments about me. He was a belligerent, bigoted creep, who was well out of order. Over the years, I've met a few like him, and they just make your stomach churn.

Don't they?

He did mine. Glad they eventually got rid of him, he deserved it...

His son, on the other hand, Dave, was just the opposite. A really nice guy. I would end up being a lodger in his house, but that comes later...

So I started earning money, and spending it. I remember as a child I wore Asda Zooms, so I fixated on buying Nikes! Spend! Spend! Spend! Along came store card after store card, and again Spend! Spend! Spend!

With ADHD you crave the next dopamine fix, mine at the time was, shopping. I was like an addict needing yet another fix, the thrill of shopping for an overpowering drug and I shopped, and shopped and shopped. They say money won't buy you happiness. It bloody well did in my eyes, bought me a whole load of happiness and my freedom.

I'm sure you've guessed what happened next. Yes! I got into debt. Pay Peter to pay Paul, my store card debt syndrome.

My mind had taken over my principles which were, if you can't afford something, you save up for it, that's what Dad had always told me.

Not with store cards you don't. Buy it now! Pay later.

So store card debt mounted up and I was forced to take a night time job to earn extra cash to pay for my fixation.

I started working in the evenings as a barmaid, in Manchester city centre.

I was a good barmaid. My friendly, pleasant attitude, a hit with the punters. It was tiring though, and I drained quite quickly.

I'm a teetotaller as you know, and have learnt, very successfully, to live my life without alcohol. So in environments where there is alcohol, I tend to, try to fit in, by acting a little bit drunk.

A lot of people can't get their heads round that, and ask me why I don't drink.

There are many reasons, but for the uninitiated, I lie, and tell them I don't like the taste of the alcohol.

We had regulars. Hurricane Higgins, the snooker player, was one. He liked his drink. He was always pissed, and often found slumped at the bottom of the stairs. Back then the Square Albert attracted a lot of drinkers, who'd come to the square, for a fun, good time, and get absolutely hammered.

Oh! What good old days they were!

Back to my life in our house. Steve had moved out.

Andy was going on a mission in Thailand with a journalist woman, and busy recording music with Viv. So he moved out as well.

Cathy and I moved out as well. We went to live in an upstairs flat further down the street. So this was our third property we'd occupied. Now there were just us two girls living together.

I had my car. I could drive around. Life for a short while was good fun.

I befriended a girl I met at the gym called Becky. I got the feeling she was a little envious, because of my car. So I gave her lifts to and from her home. An ADHD moment? Possibly.

It took over two hours, and I was late getting home every night. It became a chore, so I stopped it.

She wasn't very pleased.

People like me, with ADHD are often taken advantage of. People pleasers, we're too good natured, for our own sake. Very obliging and trusting. We avoid conflict, so we rarely complain.

But giving Becky a lift every day was too much. I felt I was being used. Maybe I was. So I stopped with the lifts.

However, we kind of stayed friends, and went night clubbing a few times in Manchester. However my teetotal approach to alcohol and drugs, didn't go down too well with her. Becky used to get very drunk and of course, I was her free taxi home. I became her designated driver, each and every night we went out.

Yet again, was I being taken advantage of?

I met Alex, who ran a phone shop, selling mobile phones. Mobile phones in those days, were a new, not yet the must have phone, they are today. I'd fixated on his beautiful brand-new Mercedes with a private plate. He had seen me admiring his car, and came over to me, he then started chatting me up. He was a well-spoken, dark skinned guy, a bit smooth, slightly sleazy, but ever so shifty.

I agreed to meet him, and he came to the house, in his Merc, to pick me up.

Mobile phones were the future, he insisted, and persuaded me to get one. They were quite big in those days, not like the thin, slim things of today. He convinced me to take out a contract and get a phone. Back then, mobile phones were extremely expensive and the tariffs were extortionate.

Now, signing up to a contract is the worst thing, anyone could suggest I did. Having ADHD means my boundary lines were stretched. The concept of being regularly billed for a service is not a good idea for someone who has money management problems.

It was inevitable, I'd drift very quickly, into trouble, and true to my affliction, and I got into debt. I got a Bailiff's letter and tried to pay the bill, with a maxed out credit card.

Not a good idea.

To get out of jail free, I was allowed to set up a payment plan, of a fiver a month, a five year commitment, that would seem to last forever.

It turned out, according to smooth talking Alex, he was also a musical talent scout. If to believe, he said he had discovered Gabriel, who, at the time, had achieved the number one spot, in the charts with the song 'Dreams,'

Um? Not sure I believed that at the time, but I gave him the benefit of the doubt.

However, my original, sleazy, characterisation of Alex proved to be accurate. I found out, he had children and often cheated on his partner. As far as being a talent scout was concerned, well no doubt that was a lie as well.

A pathological liar, and philosopher if ever there was one.

God do I attract the weirdos...

So true to form, when Alex got what he wanted, he dumped me. The usual, maladies, came to mind. That feeling of being used and taken for granted,

After Alex, I fixated on only going out with only dark skinned men.

With ADHD you're always looking for that new fix, that new toy, that new experience. The thought excited the brain, and there I was fancying men with dark skin, and of course a Merc.

Richard was a car trader I met at the Greyhound track in Manchester. He too had a Mercedes Benz, and met my other fixation of being dark skinned. So off I went again, my dopamine fix taking control. My head absolutely crazed with this new fascination.

I loved it.

But it wasn't to last.

Like Alex, this sleaze bag dumped me as well. It must be me, or my ADHD that attracts such sleazy douche bags.

Why do such men, with big flashy cars, and vast egos, think they can pick up pretty naive girls, in this fashion, use them and move on.

Fortunately not all men are like those two sleazy creeps. There are men out there who do care.

Thank God.

So was this the pattern, me attracting untrustworthy men, to pray on my naivety? Why couldn't I get a regular boyfriend? But, if truth be told, life lessons were being learnt. Lessons, all girls should be aware of and I certainly was learning by my mistakes.

Mistakes! God I've made a few but learned a lot...

Cathy had a friend, living in London, called Abby who was going through a mental breakdown.

Abby reached out to Cathy and asked if she could come and stay with her in Manchester, to hopefully recover and get back on her feet.

When Abby arrived at our house in Manchester, we instantly formed a lasting friendship. We both had the same outlook on life, and personality wise, we were very similar, Abby, possibly a little mellower than me. Other than that, we bonded well. Abby was very intelligent, in fact, had excellent writing skills.

I'd planned to ask her to help me write a book I was eager to write, but sadly it never materialised. That's usually the case with ADHD, we have these fantastic ideas but never get round to fulfilling them.

However, that dream of writing my book, has finally materialised. You're reading the proof.

I actually managed to do it.

I'm going off on a tangent again, but by now, you'll be used to that.

I'm sure, if Abby gets to read my book, she'd be really proud of me. We'd discussed its content; what themes to include, what to put in it, what to leave out. It wouldn't be a diary but segments of my life. My life in Manchester was all there for the writing. An exciting, chronological account of the stories that had influenced my life.

But it wasn't to be. Not then at any rate. I would have to wait until well into my forties, to realise that dream of another year.

Abby was an exotic looking, young lady, with beautiful soft olive skin. Skin with the nicest of textures I'd ever seen. She had beautiful dark black hair with contrasting dark blue eyes.

The moment we met, we were fixated on each other. Both of us felt the same attraction. Cathy was a little jealous of our relationship, after all Abby was Cathy's friend, but Abby and I just hit it off, like we were lifelong friends.

Both Abby and I had a love for dark skinned men. She was fun, we laughed, and had a crazy mad time together, every day.
Everything was always excitingly cool.
Even though the pair of us were a bit unhinged, what with Abby's mental health problems, and me with my undiagnosed ADHD, we had fun together. I believe our psyches had arranged for our paths to cross.

I'd found out much later Abby had been heartbroken over a guy, resulting in her attempt to take her own life and ending up in hospital.
Abby was so happy, here in Manchester and wanted to stay. At the start she slept on the sofa in our small living room. But before I knew it, she was sharing my bed. It wasn't a lesbian thing, just two girly friends sharing a bed. I'd been used to sharing my bed at other lodgings, so it came rather natural to me. It felt right, and we used to cuddle and give each other a tic or in other words a tickle.

Nothing wrong with that.

Abby and I used to go cruising around Manchester in my little Vauxhall Corsa. This used to piss Cathy off. Cathy distanced herself from our activities and I felt she was somewhat jealous of my developing friendship with her friend.

Abby and I used to have Snoop Doggy Dog blaring out from a cassette recorder in the car. 'Rollin down the street, sippin on gin n juice', laid back, came the lyrics.

We pretended to be all sorts of people. Pop stars, recording artists, even film stars, to name a few. We had great fun, putting the seats in my car, right back like gangsters do, with me driving one handed. We listened and sang, Snoop Doggy Dog blaring out, and we drove along, ultra, ultra, cool.

Abby, like me, was a very spiritual person. We both thought ourselves psychics and I told her about my experiences as a child, growing up in a haunted bedroom. She too had her own ghostly experiences, so we had this psychic connection.

They say poltergeists feed off negative energy or the energy of people that are unbalanced or troubled. The film, 'The Exorcist,' featured a troubled girl, possessed by an evil spirit. An example of where I'm heading with this. I believe Abby too was a troubled person, along with my own, fucked up troubles, and so could possibly have attracted such entities.

We created some very bizarre energy together, so possibly unwittingly manifested some weird spirit entity between us.

Let me explain. I can remember strange things were happening to us both. Abby felt a spirit had possessed her. Holding her back, interfering with her life. She even felt it was crushing her in her sleep.

That used to freak Abby and me out. Our connection was so strong we could feel each other's experiences.

For instance, one night Abby woke up screaming, she was terrified, telling me, a weird spirit had manifested itself and had tried to physically assault her.

To a non-believer, the spirit world must look like the figment of a believer's imagination. Someone who doesn't understand such phenomena would see such sightings, which has far-fetched nonsense.

Maybe it is, but I'm a believer in such things and to me it was real.

Abby was traumatised, and I believe she did experience it.

I stand witness to this spirit, having had it physically touch me. You'd know, when it was around. It was as if it were breathing on you, the hairs on your arms would stand up, and you'd feel an icy chill, a shiver through your body. You'd feel its presence, as if it was watching you. I believed it to be the spirit of a man.

Whatever it was, we had to get rid of it.

We'd be out in the car and feel its presence. I'm convinced, our joint psyches, physically created this haunting. It was as real as we were. We'd somehow summoned up this poltergeist thing with our energy.

I know there'll be doubters out there, doubting our every word, thinking us to be bat shit crazy. I understand that. But take my word on it, it was real.

Abby and I both possessed a sixth-sense. We kind of knew what each of us was going to say, or were thinking.

A bizarre connection that bonded us together.

Abby will always have a special place in my heart. We have that very special, spiritual connection.

I do believe a greater force, yet to be discovered, brought us together. I celebrate its interjection into both our lives..."So here's my story, no risk, no glory"

CHAPTER FIFTEEN

TAKE CARE

Abby and myself loved fashion and bought the craziest of outfits to go to the Hacienda nightclub and gay village in. Buying multi-coloured nail polishes from the Arndale Market, that would take hours to dry. We lived for the nightlife culture.

Garry, Jenny's ex-boyfriend, now a homosexual, came to visit at our flat.

Fantastic to see him again.

Garry absolutely loved dance music so we all went out regularly to Manchester night clubs.

My dopamine levels were high and I was having the time of my life.

Things were great, and for the first time, in a long time, I was genuinely very happy. The heartache, and tragedies, that had affected my life, in Grimsby and the West Midlands, slowly fading away.

Things were easy and there was no stress.

Reflecting, the fact that Garry had re-entered my life, and my obsession with Madonna, and Gay men, he reminded me of the song he'd written for me back when we were in college together.

I'm off at a tangent again, aren't I? I forgot to tell you, when in the West Midlands, I recorded a song, foolishly thinking it would get me a recording contract.

It was a dance track with a great melody and inspiring lyrics

You should take more care of who you trust
Because you can't see through those eyes of lust
You give your love away too easily
Now you want some respect...

Nothing came of it, other than I had the opportunity of recording my very first song. Which is such a shame because it was such a catchy tune. Garry played a significant role in my life, allowing me to sing and record a song he wrote.

Thank you Garry.

I once drove back home to Grimsby, to see the sights and introduce Garry to my parents. It was an enjoyable break from the routine.

To be honest life in Manchester was absolutely fabulous. I couldn't ask for a better life. Abby encouraged my fixation, and we lived life on the wild side, on the dance floors in all of Manchester's nightclubs.

Absolutely insane. But we loved it.

Now as you know I don't drink and I wasn't taking drugs. So I was living off my natural energy. I was high on natural dopamine, and loving it. Abby used to feed my ego by calling me Madonna.

My birth sign is Leo. Leo's are show-offs if you believe in that sort of stuff. Abby said I looked like a lioness with my big blond hair, she was the Brown Cow. Such were our affectionate names for each other.

Life was good, full of laughter, jokes and pranks. I'd party all night long with very little sleep. ADHD people survive on very little sleep and because I was young in those days, I had an insane amount of vitality.

Burning the candle at both ends will eventually lead to disaster. I crashed and burned, and trust me when I crash, I crash hard. I was so physically exhausted I couldn't move.

It was as if I was paralysed. Not a pleasant experience.

So I would have these huge highs, become euphoric, intoxicated by my natural energy and then crash and burn.

I really didn't look after myself properly, which certainly aggravated my recovery. My eating disorder was ebbing somewhat, but I was still not eating properly. Abby also, in her past, had an eating disorder, so between us we weren't into cooking meals. So between us we lived on diet coke, cigarettes, lots of chocolate and snack crap.

It was not a very healthy life, that's for sure.

So, here we all are, living the best lives, vibrating off each other's energy.

Who could ask for a better existence?? Not me, it was wonderful.

Cathy's parents had a timeshare apartment in Spain and Cathy asked Abby and the rest of us to go on holiday with her.

Cathy and I were still living in the upstairs flat and Abby was still dossing with me in my bedroom. Cathy was clearly jealous of my close friendship with Abby. She hadn't intended for me and Abby to become the best of friends.

However, she'd invited us girls to go to her parents' apartment in Spain so we all agreed. A girl called Maz came along to.

So we all went on holiday with Cathy.

It all seemed so perfect. The flights to Spain were pretty cheap. We were staying in Cathy's parent's timeshare apartment for free. What more could we ask for?

What could possibly go wrong?

We landed in Spain at night, it was dark and when we arrived at Cathy's parents' apartment there was no electricity. Cathy was frantically trying to call her parents and get this rectified.

So you can imagine the drama.

Abby and I saw the funny side of it, laughing, fuelling Cathy's anger. Maz really didn't give a shit, in fact, she just fucked off out of the apartment, and went off, on her own, to explore.

We didn't see Maz for quite a few days. I remember getting concerned. However, we needn't be worried. Spanish nightlife had been her sanctuary. She was a party girl, so had gone to a nearby bar to explore the nightlife, and met new friends there.

Eventually we got the electricity on, and selected our bedrooms. Selfishly Cathy took the bedroom, without consultation, leaving us a sofa, a chair and a single bed to sleep on.

The next day, the weather was cloudy, but warm. The sun's rays were deceivingly strong, and Cathy, who'd spent most of the day sunbathing, got sunburnt. She'd not put on sun cream, so now looked like a cooked lobster. She literally was burnt, all over her body, and she was not at all happy.

She was in so much pain she had to lay on her bed with Aloe Vera all over her sunburned body. It turned out she had a sunstroke and was lucky not to have ended up in hospital.

She was quite ill with it, and flew back home to Manchester.

Without Cathy around Abby and I had a whale of a time.

One day, whilst sunbathing topless, a jeep pulled up, and out got a man. He looked local and had a beard. He looked at us, and proceeded. He unzipped his fly and started pleasuring himself.

So was typical of the local males around here? We hoped not.

We retaliated, shouting at him. Called him a pervert and told him to fuck off! He took the hint, zipped up his fly, got in his jeep and fucked off

As he drove off, Abby and I burst out laughing. The thought of this weird pervert, wanking himself, while we sunbathing, was hysterical.

However, on reflection, maybe we should have reported him. He was a dirty old man, preying on young girls. A dangerous pervert who needed locking up.

But we didn't report it, put it down to experience, and got on with our holiday.

Our friendship strengthened. We'd dress up, to the nines, full make-up, glamorous dresses, and go to town, clubbing. We'd wander around the nightlife, enjoying the spectacle and having fun. We'd talk in American accents, and pretend to be Americans, from Detroit.

Madonna's from Detroit, Michigan. So I hit on the idea of impersonating her. I gave it full work, telling everybody I was from Detroit. Abby openly encouraged me.

It was absolutely hilarious.

On our second to last day of our stay, much to our relief, Maz returned. She didn't know about Cathy, so we had to explain to her that Cathy had got sunstroke and had returned home.

I suspected, on my return to Manchester, Cathy would be a little annoyed with me. Clearly she didn't like my friendship with her friend Abby, so I was expecting a lot of flak.

Cathy was not going to make life easy for either of us on our return, I was certain of that.

Maz took a different flight home, she was going to the West Midlands.

On the flight home, we had bat-shit fun again, pretending to be Americans. We fooled most of the passengers we were from Detroit.

Hilarious!

We arrived in the early hours and drove back to the flat in Manchester. My key, for some strange reason, wouldn't open the door. Abby somehow managed to unpick the lock with a hair grip and open the door. On inspection, we discovered the lock had been changed. It appeared Cathy had changed the locks, without my permission, which according to our tenancy agreement, she needed.

What was she playing at, surely she can't be that pissed off with me, she's locked me out of my own flat?

Once inside the flat, we saw Cathy. She said nothing. Clearly she was annoyed to see we'd got inside the flat. Both Abby and I knew our relationship with Cathy had reached rock bottom, and sensed our time in the flat together was coming to an end.

Things got pretty shitty between Cathy, me and Abby and we knew it was time to move out of the flat and look for a new place to live. My work colleague, Dave, had a two bedroomed house in East Manchester. He said we could rent one of the rooms.

It wasn't big, but it was ours if we wanted it.

It meant us still sharing a bed together but what the Hell. It wasn't perfect, but the rent was cheap. So we went for it.

Dave was a nice guy, very safe, very stable, should I say boring, but nice with it. I was very grateful, he allowed me and Abby to move into his home.

I was still working on weekends, as a barmaid at the pub. The manager asked me if I'd be interested in becoming a barmaid, as well, at 'Holy City Zoo'.' A new nightclub, due to open in the summer of 1995.

I always act on impulse and always suffer the consequences. My ADHD got the better of me.

Why not, I told myself. It'll be exciting, being involved with the launch of a brand-new night club. A new dance scene to rival the Hacienda.

It'll be fun.

It was pitched as the new Hacienda of Manchester. The mecca for top dance DJs. People came from all over the country, just to listen to the DJs and dance to the music.

One evening while working at the pub, I met a Mancunian talent scout, who told me he was a talent scout for musicians and singers. So, with confidence, I told him I was the next Madonna, had a great singing voice and had recorded a demo. I pleaded for him to give me a break. This he did, and gave me the name of a recording studio and for me to meet him there. He was looking for a new vocal talent to sing on his dance records.

Would I be that singing voice? I really thought this was it. That moment in my life I'd dreamed forever to happen.

I was going to be the next Madonna, after all. My desire to be a singer.

I can remember turning up at the studio. Everyone was cool. Chilled. I could smell marijuana. Someone smoked a spliff. If I'm honest I had no idea what was expected of me. I'd not done anything quite like this before. Yes, with Garry, but this was way out different.

Then my nerves got the better of me, and I started to bottle it. I remember feeling clammy, that wave of uncertainty drifted over me. All of a sudden I lost all my confidence.

ADHD can do this. It can disable you. Within minutes you can go from being ultra-confident to a pathetic, blob of jabbering jelly.

I recall, going into a room, entering a vocal booth and putting on headphones. Sound engineers were in an adjacent room. I was told all I needed to do was to listen to the music, sing and they would overlay my vocals on top of the music and record it.

The music started, coming through my headphones, I heard but my mind went blank. Again, typical of ADHD I was suddenly overwhelmed with it all.

I just couldn't get the words out of my mouth. Just couldn't sing.

I, the girl that knows every note and all the words to just about every Madonna's song, was struck dumb!

Here was I, with the chance of a lifetime, and I fluffed it. I'm in a studio in Manchester with a talent scout and I just couldn't do it.
I can remember the musicians and the talent scout, encouraging me to try again.

I was frozen solid as a stalagmite.
I just stood there, looking blank, utterly confused, and unable to get my voice to sing. My brain was unable to coordinate my voice to the melody. I froze, wanting the ground to open up, and swallow me. It was the most embarrassing thing I've ever endured. I felt humiliated. I just wanted to get the Hell out of there, as fast as I could.

I'd been given the opportunity to record a song, an opportunity to work with musicians, the opportunity to become a recording artist, make a record and be famous and I just couldn't do it.

In the end after many attempts to record, the talent scout stepped in calling it a day, and my session came to an end.

So I never became the Madonna I so wanted to be.

It was stage fright.

A meltdown. Pure ADHD brain fog.
A problem I've experienced, and lived with throughout my life.
It hinders my progress, deflated by that feeling of not being good enough.
My failure in the record studio, reminded me of my educational failures in the classroom. Those remedial classes they condemned me to.

You see, I just can't do things properly.
Or can I? Or is that, my neurodiversity talking?

Deep down, I know I can do things. I need to be given a chance, possibly a second chance, even a third if necessary. So you need to be patient with me. Because I can do it!

So I left the studios utterly defeated, deflated. I'd hit rock bottom, my self-esteem totally shredded, my ADHD brain, frazzled. I was reminded of that defamatory comment my English teacher had once said when I was at school all those years ago.

You'll never get anywhere in life, you'll be nothing more than a girl who works in a stacking shelves. Hurtful, damming words that came back to haunt me. But, I'm not one for lying down. I will never give up! Maybe my dreams for that moment were shattered, licking my wounds but I'd fight back, get over it, and as Arnold Schwarzenegger so profoundly puts it, "I'll be back.'

I was determined to make it in the music industry. How? Well somehow. But I will be back. So as the lyrics of my song suggest, 'You should take more care of who you trust.' And go forward with your own convictions...

141

CHAPTER SIXTEEN

HOLY CITY

My fixation on becoming a singer continued. I was determined to get a second shot at becoming a star and met up with one or two guys claiming to be musical talent scouts or agents.

I met this huge dark skinned guy, who lived in Moss Side, Manchester. He reminded me of the Notorious B.I.G.

This so-called talent scout was friendly enough and I thought him the genuine article, my ADHD blinding me to the truth. As it turned out, he was a fake, and only wanted to get into my knickers.
Desperate to make an impression, I wasn't being honest myself. I gave him a CD, which was actually recorded by Andy and Viv. Then I proceeded to say it was me singing it, a complete white lie.

What possessed me to do that I don't know, let's blame it on ADHD influence shall we. Lack of confidence, who knows why I did that and thought I'd get away with it. I recall, feeling a little guilty, my self-esteem low, and then making out that Andy's group was actually me. That's how desperate I was to be given another opportunity of cutting a record. To find that someone, who would take me under their wing, nurture my singing career and make me a superstar, like Madonna.

So I invited this guy round to Dave's house one evening. I remember Dave going out for the night, giving me the opportunity to talk about music, impress him with my musical knowledge, and get him to help me.

I genuinely thought, this guy had an interest in making me a singer. You know me, what with my trusting nature, my good heart, and all that naive bull shit.

So I threw caution to the wind and became yet again vulnerable.

Experience, from earlier trauma, should have warned me to be cautious, but stardom glistened in my eyes. I should have paid more attention to Shakespeare, who wrote, in 'The Merchant of Venice', 'All that glisters, is not gold.'

It certainly wasn't.

My starry visions of stardom became the eyes of concern. I had that uneasy feeling his eyes were undressing me. Foreplay for what he expected to do next.

The next thing I know he literally launched himself at me, bearing in mind he was a big guy. I thought what the hell is happening?" It was terribly painful. He was fat, heavy, repulsive and grotesque. He was pushing his mouth and tongue so hard onto my face it was painful.

I was taken completely off guard, I didn't know what the hell to do next.

The next thing I knew his hands were all over my body and he's making these weird groaning noises. He was violently violating me. Somehow, I managed to get myself off the sofa and push him away. I stood up, he was still on the sofa, sweating, huffing and puffing like an overweight kid struggling for breath in a sweetshop.

My Ibiza trauma, in the sea at San Antonio, along with flashbacks of Kim and Dean rushed to my mind. Yet again I was being violated. I know how far-fetched that sounds, but I am a very vulnerable human being. Too trusting for my own safety. It's a disability, linked to my ADHD.

I had only one serious relationship in my life up to that point in my life and that was with James, and what did he do? Cheat on me. As usual, I questioned whether this man, mis read my intentions, and assumed I wanted to have sex.

I didn't. He attacked me, and in my eyes, that's attempted rape.

In those days, I was a young naive girl, dreaming of wanting to be the next Madonna, wanting to be famous, wanting everybody to love and admire me.

This guy, like certain others, took full advantage of my naiveté. He had no intention of helping me. No intention at all of making my dreams come true. He just took it upon himself to take what he wanted, and that was my body, sexually.

However, there's one thing he didn't take, and that was to my soul.

Having been a victim of rape, not once, but on multiple occasions, I've learnt to numb the pain of such horrendous acts. Deep down, it still hurts the violation and trauma I went through.

I told him to get the Hell out. Angrily, he got up and left.

Thank God, I never saw him again.

Feeling violated, I showered, washing every inch of my body, to rid myself of this abusive pervert's smell. I was in pain where his hands had violated me and remember looking in the mirror at my red and swollen mouth, now chaffed as if rubbed by rough sandpaper.

I'd been viscously violated and all I wanted to do was to go to bed, sleep and never wake up.

I took time off work. I told Dave that I had a cold, a fever. It was all lies but while Dave was at work I just wanted to stay in the house, alone. Abby was hardly ever there now, as she was romancing her new love.

It was a lonely time for me. I didn't tell Dave, I didn't tell Abby. In fact I didn't tell anybody what happened to me that night.

I was yet again the victim of trauma. Who would believe me anyway? It seemed so farfetched that, then at such a young age I had been raped as many times as I had. Maybe it was myself to blame, I thought it was all my fault.

It left me confused and doubting myself creating trauma that was not healing. I never wanted to tell my parents, I was feeling too ashamed and embarrassed about such traumatic events.

I didn't want them to be upset, my parents are wonderful people and they didn't deserve this added trauma adding to their lives. I had already been 'a pain in the arse' as a teenager, it was not fair to add any more upset and heartache on them. So I kept it a secret never to be told, until now.

However, I'm not the one to wallow in self-pity. I pulled myself together and went back to work...

I'm not a victim, I'm a survivor. I love life and whatever it throws at me, I face it head on. No one can take my soul. I will always fight to the end.

I might have self-doubt and low self-esteem issues but I'm strong in mind and spirit. Unbreakable, that's me. People might take advantage of my naivety, but can never take my soul...

Madonna had taught me through her music to stand up for myself and be strong. So all my pain and traumas, I had to push them back, to the very back of my mind. To keep fighting for what I believed in...keep smiling, keep masking the pain.

So I went back to work.

Abby decided to come back home and stay a few nights a week, which was lovely for me.

'Holy City Zoo,' a new nightclub soon to be launched in Manchester. It would mean me having two night time jobs as well as my day job.

What the Hell. Go for it I thought

So I pulled up outside the nightclub and was introduced to Wayne, who I thought was the doorman.

Wayne took my breath away. I was infatuated with him, from the very moment I saw him. I walked up to him full of confidence and told him how handsome I thought he was. He looked at me as if I was some kind of freak. He smiled and tried to be polite, saying he was single but not looking for a girlfriend.

I was to discover, Wayne wasn't the club's doorman, his brother Ted was.

Wayne was there to support his brother.

Although Wayne wasn't looking for a girlfriend, I, on the other hand, was creating dopamine and Wayne was my next fixation, he became my mission. Rejection the greatest aphrodisiac.

So the opening night of 'Holy City Zoo' nightclub came. It was a spectacular event, just as I imagined it would be. Everything was incredible, revolutionary for the Manchester club scene. Two well-known transvestites, called Coco and Angel, opened the show, they were both absolutely gorgeous. The building had everything a modern nightclub of that day should have. A swanky long bar full of glass fridges offering a variety of different alcoholic beverages for its customers, dance podiums and wrought iron cages, you name it, and it had it. Incredible lighting, with a state of the art DJ booth.

My confidence returned.

Not only was I one of the barmaids working there, but one of the dancers on the podiums. I worked late and danced insanely into the early hours of the morning.

I attracted attention. Sweat poured off me, punters coming up to me to comment on my amazing dancing skills.

It might have been superficial ego pleasing, but it's what I needed. Especially when my self-esteem had earlier hit rock bottom due to the trauma I'd recently encountered.

'Take That', The Manchester boy band, had been on a UK tour, they had been performing at the local arena.

Their management had arranged a late night party at the nightclub.

I was, at one point, absolutely obsessed with 'Take that', and here they were potentially going to be partying, at the nightclub I was a barmaid at. The original line-up featured Gary Barlow, Howard Donald, Mark Owen, Jason Orange and Robbie Williams. I think only Jason and Howard actually turned up at the party, I remember being quite gutted that Mark wasn't there as he was my favourite. They had PR and security people protecting them, I didn't get a chance to talk or mingle with them. However, in the hope of attracting their attention, I recall, dancing insanely crazily on one of the dance podiums.

Never was sure if they saw me, but I gave them one hell of a show, if they did.

I was working my day job at FX Labs, being the barmaid at the pub and now at, 'Holy City Zoo'.' nightclub.

I was working seven days a week with no day off. Inevitably it took its toll and unfortunately my daytime job would bear the brunt.

I had no choice, but to occasionally skive off for a bit during my daytime job. My night-time work was simply taking its toll on me, I'd taken on far too much, and that I just couldn't cope.

I would tell my bosses I was visiting clients out of the area, and then secretly pop back home, for a half hour nap, as I was beyond exhausted. I was surviving on as little as 3 hours sleep a night.

I was burned out and I couldn't stop myself from doing the work.

I was mentally and physically exhausted. Burning the candle at both ends, not eating properly and losing lots of weight.

Crash and burn time again.

Dave, my landlord and also my work colleague, grew suspicious, so questioned me about work. Neighbours had told Dave they'd seen me at home during the day. I made up some bullshit story, but I don't think he believed me. However, he let sleeping dogs lie, and said nothing. But Dave knew I was literally overdoing it, working all hours around the clock. Eventually it would take its toll...

While working at, 'Holy City Zoo,' I do recall meeting a lovely guy called Zipparah.

He was, much later, to become famous for being on Britain's Got Talent in 2012 with his very catchy RAP anthem, 'Where's my keys, Where's my phone?'

He had a larger than life personality with a genuine heart of gold and he took a shining to me. I was desperate to break into the music business and I'd explained I had not much luck by one so-called talent scout and my failed studio fiasco. He'd listened with interest, how I wanted to be the next Madonna and how determined I was, to find a producer, record a demo, and promote it.

He'd seemed keen to let me do vocals, on a rapping track he was developing, and invited me over to his house in Manchester to record it. Unlike my last studio failure, I was more prepared this time. Abby, my partner in crime, helped me out with the lyrics that were inspired by the song 'Everybody' by Madonna. We personalised the lyrics to make it my own. It reminded me of Madonna's struggles to get noticed...

'Everybody come on and dance with me,
Everybody come on, set me free.
Move the way that you want to move... Everybody'...

Madonna used to pester DJs, constantly, asking them to play her demos. The demo of her song, 'Everybody,' was awesome and the world took notice. It went global and everyone went wild dancing to it. It worked brilliantly. Zipparah added his own unique rap and complemented perfectly with my vocals. Based on the music melody of 'Respect Me,' by an American female singer called Adeva, recorded in 1989. It worked out brilliantly. I included a different twist on Madonna's original lyrics, 'Everybody dance and sing,' using my own vocals with my lyric variations.

I must admit I had great fun recording it and welcomed the fact that no one this time was trying to take advantage over me. It was a genuine attempt by Zipparah to give a young desperate girl achieve her dreams.

Sadly, nothing ever became of that track, like most things in my life, projects half abandoned and shelved, and forgotten about, such a shame as it was brilliant.

Hey you never know, one day, it may get listened to due to the interest in Zipparah and Madonna.

I still wasn't rich, but still wanted to be famous....

It wasn't long before the Manchester gang wars spilled over into the, 'Holy City Zoo,' nightclub. The gangs fought each other over the drugs trade and control of Manchester's club scene. The rivalry was largely taken over by younger members of each gang, and developed into a war over reputation and respect in the city. The gang's rivalry with Moss Side often spilled into city centre bars and clubs. I remember watching intimidating young men hanging about the club. It was obvious they were gang members keeping an eye on their territorial claims. It wouldn't be long before there would be a drive-by shooting at the club door. So the Cheetham Hill, Salford, Gooch gangs rivalled each other to take control of the night club.

Lots of clubs and bars closed down in Manchester because of the gangland hostilities. I was 20 years old when I worked at Holy City Zoo. I was independent and having the best of times.

Gangland conflicts intensified.

I remember walking past the manager's glass-fronted office and seeing a huge dark skinned guy, who I believed to be a gang member of Cheetham Hill. They were arguing, the manager looking fearfully afraid and threatened.

Things at the club went from bad to worse and I could see it was only a matter of time before the club closed for good. The club was becoming a frightening 'no holds barred' gangland meeting place. It was free for all, no restraints or restrictions. You were fearful, afraid of what might happen next. Working and dancing there was no longer fun. 'Holy City Zoo,' was no longer the nightclub it had been, but now a gangland refuge to be avoided.

I needed to get out, this was not for me.

I was partying in Canal Street, in the gay village. I was with Ted, the door man from 'Holy City Zoo,' and his brother Wayne. In one of the bars was the same Cheetham Hill gangster that threatened our nightclub manager.

What happened next took me by surprise.

Ted stood up. The gangster, for whatever reason, squared up to him, and hit Ted in the face.

Ted fell to the floor and was knocked out.

The next thing I knew Wayne was squaring up to the guy who'd just knocked his brother out.

I stupidly stepped in and separated them. The Cheetham Hill gang member could have had a gun or a knife I just didn't think. I pulled Wayne away and the gang member silently disappeared into the night.

Ted came too, and was clearly shook up. He just wanted to get the hell out of there so I drove both of them to their Mums.

I exchanged my phone number with Wayne and arranged to meet up again.

Finally I'd got my man, and Wayne and I were officially soon after became girlfriend and boyfriend from then on.

On one of many notorious nights, I was working at the club bar, a dark skinned guy from the Gooch gang and his gangster moll barged their way to the front of the bar. He asked for a certain bottle of champagne. I told him that we didn't have that brand. On hearing that he pulled a gun out of his pocket and waved in my face.

I didn't panic, ADHD remembers, fight or flight and I remained calm and quite chilled. Probably he pulled out the gun to impress his girlfriend.

I don't know.

He didn't frighten me. I didn't know what this guy expected me to do. Magically conjure one up? I had no idea whether the gun was loaded or not. I just stood and looked him dead in the eye. I repeated we didn't have the champagne he wanted.

Silence! More Silence.

A Mexican, 'Stand Off!'

He could have pulled the trigger, but he didn't. He started to laugh.

Laughed his head off! Showing off to his gangster moll, I bet.

But, I wasn't laughing. Nothing funny in putting a gun in the face of an unsuspected twenty year old barmaid. For all I knew I faced death.

It was an insane situation. It made my life in the West Midlands and Grimsby seem pretty tame, compared to this place. I came face to face with a gangland gangster with a gun.

It was surreal. But never again.

Time, I realised, to terminate this impossible job, and leave 'Holy City Zoo' nightclub and move on.

The final straw for me was the night Wayne came into the club to see his brother Ted and myself. I left the club with Wayne and somehow a random gangland member who aggressively approached us and insisted I took him home.

It was obvious, by his behaviour he was off his head on some form of narcotics.

At first instance I thought Wayne knew this guy, so reluctantly, he got inside the car with us. Once in the car, it was clear, Wayne didn't really know him.

The intruder in my car demanded I take him home. I went into auto pilot with no idea where I was going or how this nightmare would end.

From the backseat, my gangland trespasser started shouting instructions at me.

Go left, right, left again, he ordered, this nightmare had no end. I'm not very good at organising left and right. I did my best, my dyslexia creating even further distress. I kept on thinking, "Oh my God, I hope I'm going the right way.

The next thing I knew his arms were wrapped around my neck and his knee in the back of my seat. He grabbed my face even though I was still driving. He told me my life wouldn't be worth living if I didn't comply with his instructions.

That shocked and frightened me and I honestly believed he would have carried out his threat had I not complied.

Wayne was sitting in the passenger seat next to me. He didn't say a word. I had no idea what he was thinking or how he'd react should our situation worsen.

Eventually we got to a house near Salford. Menacingly our passenger kept shouting, stop and drive on. Repeating the order over and over again. I obeyed completely at this gangster thug's mercy.

Eventually we did come to a stop and this hoodlum angrily pushed my seat forward, banging my head on the steering wheel. I came over dizzy, felt sick, I thought I was going to pass out.

That's when Wayne eventually intervened, telling him to stop it. The thug retaliated, angrily telling Wayne to shut it. The verbal abuse continued, our passenger demanding Wayne take control of me. I was told I was out of control and should be told to shut up.

What? Me? What the Hell had I done? Clearly he was off his fucking head. Eventually the guy got out of the car. I quickly closed and locked the door. My head hurt from where he'd banged it against the steering wheel.

I still felt sick and dizzy.

To this day I still have no idea what the hell that was all about. All I know is that it was scary and would never wish that on anyone. It finally made up my mind to leave that awful place. 'Holy City Zoo,' was no longer that fun loving nightclub I loved, it had turned into a cesspit of villainy run by gangsters, and I wanted nothing more to do with it.

I thank God, Wayne, stepped in, for God knows what that hoodlum would have done to me if he hadn't. Looking back, I don't know why Wayne didn't intervene sooner, maybe scared the gangster could have pulled a weapon, and then I'd never have been here revealing all my secrets to you. Who knows? It will always remain a mystery.

So I knew from that day forward I had no choice but to quit my barmaid's job at the 'Holy City Zoo,' nightclub. Such a shame because it once was a fantastic club. Now it was just too dangerous. I wasn't going to put myself in danger any more. First a gun, then having my head bashed in. I valued my life far too much to put up with any more of that shit.

So I handed in my notice.

Eventually, 'Holy City Zoo,' closed.

Madonna's spirit always guides me through her music... I still wasn't rich, but I still wanted to be so desperately famous....I just wanted to prove myself to the world...

CHAPTER SEVENTEEN

LESSONS TO LEARN

I was now dating Wayne. One more chance for happiness.

Abby spent most of her time with her new boyfriend, so we'd only meet occasionally at Dave's house and go out for a McTucky's in Manchester's Gay Village.

At first, my relationship with Wayne wasn't as I'd expected it to be. Something, at the back of my mind, niggled me, but couldn't quite put my finger on what it was.

For one thing he was older than me. Twenty six I believe he told me he was. He lived with his Mother and Brother in South Manchester. He hadn't a car and worked down King Street, in Manchester.

What attracted me to him the first time was his handsome good looks. His hair, platted into little funky dreads, those cute little dimples, his stylish eyebrows and those big smiley teeth. He dressed smartly, and had that athletic body most women would crave for in a man, yet here I was, feeling a little uneasy about our relationship.

His Mum Liz, had come over from Jamaica in the 1960s and made a life for herself in Manchester. She was a larger-than-life lady with a lovely smile who worked at the local hospital. She introduced me to Jamaican Soul food, for which I shall ever be grateful. His parents had divorced. His Father was of Jamaican and Scottish descent and had moved over with his Mum from Jamaica in the 1960s but separated and lived separately.

On the surface, it appeared to be a lovely family and I was more than happy to become part of it. However, Wayne was to warn me from getting too involved. His reasoning, family politics.

I didn't really understand what he meant at the time. But I soon found out.

Wayne was very different to most boys. He acted rather strangely to me, like he wasn't bothered. I was his first white girlfriend so that might be the reason. I've even questioned was he Gay?

But I wasn't sure.

Maybe he felt he was betraying his family, by dating a white girl. Family tradition, and all that. I just didn't know. All I knew was that his family welcomed me into their home with open arms.

Sadly I did get the vibes, that Wayne himself, was a little embarrassed to be seen with me.

I told my parents about Wayne and they were very much looking forward to meeting him. However, Wayne was apprehensive. I got the impression he just didn't want to meet my parents.

That I couldn't understand. Alarm bells started to ring.

Well, to be honest, I did chase after him, having fixated on him. I was adamant in making him my boyfriend.

Was that wrong?

Not in my ADHD eyes it wasn't? My undiagnosed ADHD driving this obsession

At times I felt Wayne didn't even want to be with me. He'd often said we should just be friends, nothing more than friends. Move on he'd tell me, find someone else, but I just couldn't do that.

I just couldn't understand what his intentions were. Were we boyfriend and girlfriend or not? It was a frustrating situation, a strange relationship that wasn't fanning out as I'd imagined it would.

I just couldn't get my head around it.

I was to discover, Wayne's Mum hated Wayne's friends.

She hated them, telling me they were ruining Wayne's life.

I, of course, had no idea what the hell was going on. Clearly there was some dark secret not being disclosed to me.

It turned out that Wayne was on bail, on remand, for an armed robbery, and was awaiting his day in court.

Wayne had been arrested for attempted armed robbery.

At the time, I knew nothing of the details, other than Wayne had been named, and arrested, as the perpetrator of the crime.

Now, I knew why his Mum so hated his friends. They'd used him as a patsy and he was paying the price for their crime.

In the cold light of day, I really believe my Wayne was innocent, but being in love with him at the time, you would expect me to say that, wouldn't you.

According to Wayne's Mum, these criminals had set him up, hence her vendetta against them. The scam had backfired, leaving Wayne as the only suspect.

I never fully understood the full story, other than Wayne was on remand, and faced prison. So possibly, that's why Wayne had been acting strangely and didn't want to embark on a lasting relationship with me. If he went to prison, he'd not want to cause me further upset, so thought it best, we parted and went about a different path in life. I couldn't, and stayed by his side.

Before his appearance, at court, I did take Wayne to Grimsby to meet my parents, despite him not wanting to go.
He was liked by all my family. He met Nanna, my Dad's Mum.
I took him to Grimsby Town centre, to explore the not so famous sites of Grimsby and its surrounding areas.

Being close to Wayne's family was fortunate. I was to learn all about their life in Jamaica, its culture, its history, its traditions, and Jamaican Soul cuisine, a delicacy famous around the world. I was to be given a VIP tour of all that was Jamaican and loved it.
Loved it to the point of fixation. I wasn't a Jamaican, but I so wanted to be.
Wayne was probably my second proper relationship. James, probably was my first, but he ruined that by cheating on me.

I still worked at the pub on weekends, I remember one night Wayne came into the pub, wanting to borrow my car. I initially refused, explaining, it wasn't mine to lend.
I sensed something was wrong, wasn't sure what, but said nothing. My spiritual voices warn me of a pending disaster, forecasting unpleasant things to come.
My supernatural vibes were rarely wrong.
I knew, allowing Wayne to take the Corsa was wrong and very risky. He wasn't insured and if he crashed the car, there'd be hell to pay.
However, Wayne insisted I should lend him the car, and against my spiritual warnings, I handed him the keys to the Corsa, hoping my spiritual guardians were wrong.
They weren't.
Time elapsed. Suddenly the pub's phone rang. It was Wayne asking for me.
His voice was shaky and he told me, he's sorry, but my car's upside down on Cheetham Hill Road.
I panicked.
I hurried out of the pub, leaving Karen to tend the bar, while I ordered a taxi. The taxi arrived, the driver refusing to take me anywhere until he'd seen the colour of my money.

I flashed a twenty pound note in his face, and we drove off, to where

Wayne had crashed my car. I arrived at the scene, my precious Corsa, upside down on its roof in the middle of the street. All my personal belongings were all over the road including the mix cassette tapes my friends Mike and Pete had given me.

I was devastated.

Not only were my tapes destroyed but also the car. Oh my God, I thought, I'm going to lose my job.

Wayne wandered over to me and asked me, if I was going to ask him, if he was okay.

Okay? I shouted angrily. You're walking around aren't you? Course you're okay, you're not dead are you?

No! But I was. How in Hell was I going to explain this to my bosses? Wayne hadn't insurance, shouldn't have been driving the car, and most likely going to prison, for attempted armed robbery.

My head was in a complete ADHD meltdown. I couldn't think straight

What a fuck up.

Wayne was clearly upset with me, that I hadn't asked about his welfare first, I to him seemed more bothered about my damaged mix tapes.

That wasn't true. I just went into a weird shock head was just a mass of brain fog. I called Dave and told him what had happened. He said it sounded serious, but leave it with him, he'd see what he could do. Later on that evening, I got a phone call from one of the bosses who told me I hadn't to go to work until further notice. They would need to investigate further.

I was scared.

Worried what would happen. I was sure I was going to be sacked, after all it was my fault, I shouldn't have given Wayne the keys.

My boss later rang me. Enquiring as to what had happened. I panicked and began gibbering a story that wasn't making any sense, my brain was a whirl I felt physically sick.

I told my boss, Wayne had taken the keys without permission. This of course added further complications, as Wayne in their eyes, was now a thief.

One thing I've always been taught is that honesty is the best policy. I'd lied to my bosses, out of sheer panic. I'd not been thinking clearly. I'd gone into survival mode, and had sacrificed Wayne.

After the accident Wayne had gone into shock and had hibernated to his bedroom. He'd stayed there, in the dark without daring to open the blinds.

Depression had set in. He became anxious, worried about how all this would affect his court case?

In empathy with Wayne, and his family too, we were all very concerned that he was severely depressed.

This wasn't fair. It was my fault and I realised I had to own up to my part in all this conspiracy.

I told my boss the truth. I felt somewhat relieved. Honesty after all was the best policy.

I hate lying, part of having ADHD is that we are not good liars.

I waited expecting the sword of Damocles to fall upon my head.

In Greek mythology, the courtier Damocles was forced to sit beneath a sword suspended by a single hair to emphasise the instability of a king's fortunes.

Like Damocles, I was convinced something bad was most likely to happen to me.

Although I feared reprisal, I felt better for telling the truth. Honesty is the best policy, my parents had taught me.

And they were right!

Much to my surprise, me being honest, must have struck a chord with my bosses, for they decided not to take action, against me or Wayne. I kept my job and would you believe it, waiting for me on my return to work was another white Vauxhall Corsa. Honesty pays off, and an important lesson is learnt.

Wayne's court appearance fast approached, but I told no one, not even my parents.

It was our little secret. I didn't want any of our friends pre-judging him.

Wayne had secured himself a housing association flat in Moss Side.

It had been modernised, with a little Kitchenette and a bedroom. I started to spend more time with Wayne at his flat. Abby had now moved out of Dave's house and had her own little flat somewhere in Manchester. My friendship with Abby didn't end but our nightclubbing nights had dried up.

I no longer wanted to work at the pub and handed in my notice.

My ADHD behaviour of burning the candle at both ends, hopefully un-fixated.

I stayed at FX Labs thankful I still had a job.

The day I'd been dreaded arrived and Wayne went to court. He didn't want me to go. I had a set of keys for his flat, and said, if he went into prison, could I look after the flat for him, until he came out.

He didn't really want that, but I insisted. He also suggested we should call it a day, and each go our separate ways. I refused, saying whatever happens, even if he did go to prison, I'd still be there for him.

I told Dave I was moving out of the house. He was genuinely concerned about my relationship with Wayne citing his accident in the company's car. I didn't tell him I was moving into Wayne's flat as I'm sure he'd have frowned upon such a decision.

I told no one about the court case, or that I was moving into Wayne's flat.

Wayne was found guilty, and sentenced to serve six months in prison.

His final two months to be served in an open prison somewhere out of town.

My twenty-first birthday was coming up in the summer of 1996, and I had a boyfriend in prison.

I didn't want to inform my parents that Wayne was in prison. I didn't want them to think badly of him.

I wrestled with my decision to stay with Wayne reflecting upon the life I'd had in Grimsby and my upbringing. I felt distanced from the moral backgrounds, my childhood education had taught me.

So there I was, 'Between a rock and a hard place,' faced with a choice between two unsatisfactory options.

I was reminded by the saying,
"Love is not about how many times you say I love you, but how many times you prove that it's true."

I was in love with a man in prison, and nothing could change that. So I was going to stick by him.

Love overcomes all obstacles.

Absolutely insane.

Every week, I received a visitor's pass, enabling me to go and see Wayne in prison.

I was paying Wayne's rent, and working hard to keep everything as normal as possible for him. I wrote letters and sent photographs hoping to cheer him up and make him happy.

My ADHD is going overboard in an attempt to help make his imprisonment less stressful.

So every week, I'd visit Wayne in prison telling FX Labs I was visiting clients in the same area as the prison. Technically, I was skiving off work, but the end justifies the means, in other words, I felt it justified, the final result being something good. So, I didn't think I was doing anything wrong. Acting on impulse fulfilling a role I believed was right.

Again my ADHD behaviour creating, erratic irrational, non-logical impetuousness.

So each week, I would take it in turn, to take different members of Wayne's family to see him.

I did this, for every, single week, of Wayne's incarceration.

I'd always had a vision, my twenty-first birthday party would be fantastic.
I remember my sister's, she had lots of friends and it was just brilliant. I wished for something similar, but much grander.
A new bar named 'Barca', opened in Manchester. It was a very trendy place to hang out and owned by Mick Hucknall of 'Simply Red.'
This would make the ideal venue for my twenty-first.
I made an inquiry to see if I could hire an upstairs room for my party. With financial help from my parents I booked the room. I'd be given free food if a certain number of partygoers attended my party. My parents were going to come over to Manchester and stay in a nearby hotel.
So the invites went out...

My parents still didn't know that Wayne was in prison or I was living in his flat. Dad had paid for and booked for two hundred people to attend my party. He enquired, did I know two hundred people.

Yes, exaggerating the truth.

I don't really have many close friends. So I invited everybody I could possibly invite. I literally looked through my little black diary book and rang all and sundry, inviting them all to come to my party.

Sadly, on the night, hardly anybody turned up. Just a handful of friends that I knew from, 'Holy City Zoo', the pub, and FX Labs.

I ended up dragging, coaxing, random customers from downstairs in Barça to come up to my party. Dad was quite amused, the truth being, I didn't really have that many friends.

Nowhere near had the two hundred I said.

However for those invited, friends, that did turn up, and for those I dragged in from the club downstairs, we all had a great night. There was, of course, tons of food and we gorged ourselves like kings and queens. The highlight of the night was the actor Simon Gregson, who plays Steve McDonald in Coronation Street. He was downstairs in the bar and I persuaded him to come up to my party. I've a great photograph of me with him.

FX Labs regularly had social nights out and they'd organised one of those nights to coincide with my twenty-first, so I had an extra birthday with my colleagues from work.
So that was my twenty-first, not what I'd envisaged but nevertheless memorable for my Coronation street star guest.

Wayne's incarceration encouraged my friendship with Abby to be re-established. Abby had recently split from her boyfriend and she was struggling with this.
I was struggling with loneliness.
So together we would console ourselves, and keep each other company.

She visited the flat on many occasions, and on such occasions we decided to paint the flat.

So we set about re-painting the flat from boring magnolia. We decorated the flat in Wayne's favourite colours of blue and yellow.

IKEA provided further decor and the flat was transformed.

It was a difficult and confusing time for me. I was struggling to come to terms with Wayne being in prison.

You see, I wasn't quite sure if we'd stay a couple.

Confusing times indeed for me.

I was risking my job, by taking Wayne's family to see him in prison during work time. Should FX Labs find out, they'd be Hell to pay but I wasn't really bothered?

Should I be? But I wasn't. With ADHD you have no boundaries. I was young and carefree with no consequences to consider. I was now twenty one, young and reckless, and didn't give a shit.

Abby and I went out a few times partying, but it wasn't the same. Manchester could be a scary place, not like it had been in 'Holy City Zoo's,' hay day.

'The times they were changing,' once prophesied Bob Dylan. Manchester's night club scene was indeed changing, its decline openly visible.

I spent a lot of time with Wayne's family during these troubled times. Wayne's Mum used to take me to their Soul Nights. Soul Nights were the funkiest, dance and drinking joints in Manchester mainly for Jamaican and Caribbean clients. You could drink and dance till dawn. Then all you had to do was take it easy, like a Sunday morning, and get ready to start the whole thing over again the next night.

Often I was the only white girl there, but that didn't bother me in the slightest. I was in my element.

The older generation of Jamaicans, who were there, would look on, laugh and say, 'My God that girl with the white car, can certainly dance.' I became a part of Wayne's family and joined in with their customs and ate their soul food. It became part of my culture at the time, and embraced it.

I loved it.

The time spent waiting for Wayne to serve his sentence dragged dreadfully slow for me. Even with Abby around and the laughs we had, it didn't make it easier.

Time passed slowly.

I really missed Wayne. I can't deny that. I really wanted him home. I wanted him to see his flat that Abby and I had decorated for his return. I needed Wayne to still want me as his girlfriend, but an uneasy feeling about that, caused concern.

I wanted him to be proud of me.

I saw him every week for the six months he was in prison, but never alone. I always had someone with me, so on reflection, we'd never had time together, alone.

Whilst in prison, his family would never have seen Wayne, if I hadn't driven them to the prison. None of them could drive and travelling was impossible. I put Wayne and his family, before anything else, and made sure he saw his family as regularly as possible.

But would Wayne understand what I'd done for him? Would he still want me for his girlfriend?

I didn't know.

It was Christmas 1996.

The year Madonna had given birth to her daughter Lola and the Spice Girls were launching their new careers.

I was twenty one years old, living by myself in a flat in Moss Side waiting for my jailbird boyfriend to come out of prison. I was literally counting down the days to Wayne's release.

The day soon came for Wayne to come out of prison, just in time for Christmas of 1996.

So yet again, one more chance for happiness...inspired through Madonna's wisdom of words always supporting me... "You play with fire and you'll get burned...Here is the lesson that I've learned"...

CHAPTER EIGHTEEN

JOY MACHINE

I went to pick up Wayne from prison. It was a strange meeting. Wayne wasn't himself. I'd heard inmates can become institutionalised and somewhat disoriented on release.

Clearly Wayne's mind was elsewhere, and I realised settling back into society for Wayne would be a hard transition.

I honestly thought Wayne would be over the moon, to be back home, and all over me like a rash, proclaiming his undying love for me.

That never happened. He never did.

However, I don't think Wayne ever once said he loved me, it wasn't his style. So maybe I was expecting too much from him.

In prison, Wayne had studied the Koran and told me he needed to change his understanding of life, so he planned for a new future.

I felt redundant. It appeared, I wasn't high in Wayne's plans. He wanted to be an actor, so enrolled himself on a drama course at College.

What was that all about, I asked myself? I felt deflated. I'd done so much for him in prison and it now appeared that, had meant nothing to him.

If I'm totally honest with you I felt used.

To add insult to injury, it appeared Wayne has been claiming housing benefit for his flat, and there was me paying full rent on it.

That pissed me off.

I was eventually awarded the excess money paid in rent back, but it was given directly to Wayne, who refused to give it back to me.

This was the beginning of many disputes with Wayne.

Money issues continued to create further disharmony. Wayne wanted me to support him, because as he put it, I was financially independent, so should be responsible for our financial outgoings. Wayne kept saying I should give him a squeeze, meaning I should financially help him.

I don't think so.

I might have a job, but the wages were crap. Not enough to support him as well. How selfish of him. He had all the rent refund money and he expected me to give him more.

What the Hell was happening to him?

What the Hell was happening to us?

Mentally, he certainly wasn't the same man who went to prison, that's a fact. So had prison changed him?

If so, for the better or for the worse?

Bearing in mind what I'd done for him, and how I'd put my job at risk, by lying to my work colleagues, in order to help his family visit him, every week for six months, yes, I was certainly conned. .

Fucking used if you want the truth.

It's like Wayne took advantage of me. Used my trusting and caring nature to his own advantage.

I literally would do anything and everything for him, desperate to get noticed and attract his approval.

True, I chased after him. Embarrassing that now, on reflection, especially how things were turning out. But that's what I did, I chased after him.

Sadly I was beginning to question that fixation.

The Christmas of 1996, was not brilliant.

Wayne wanted only to concentrate on studying to be an actor at college, and nothing was more important to him than that. I just wanted to be his full-time girlfriend but it was obvious he didn't feel the same.

It was now becoming a one-sided love affair.

Sadly, Wayne was fast drifting away from me.

I booked a holiday in Turkey hoping it could rekindle our relationship. I paid for the whole trip, Wayne, again taking advantage of my generosity refusing to put his hand in his pocket, to help out.

Again, I'm the fucking Cash Machine.

I'm not saying life is all about money, on the contrary, life is a world full of experiences money can't buy.

That's my outlook on life.

Family values saw my Dad provide the funds for family finances, and I inherited that spirit. However, circumstances may not always allow this, so I was willing to overlook Wayne's reluctance to take any financial responsibilities.

Sadly, his attitude worsened and I started to question my relationship with him.

Again ADHD people are so trusting, we'll do anything for anybody. No fuss, no drama, just the thought, we're doing something good, gives us that adrenaline rush. Sadly, the men I got involved in, either used me, cheated on me, sexually assaulted me, or raped me. I just didn't have much luck with men, did I? I was hoping Wayne wouldn't be one of those men.

So I went to Turkey with Wayne. A disaster waiting to unfold.
Trick, suckered in by our holiday rep, into taking every extra trip on offer. We saw turtles, bathed in salt water lakes, even had mud baths, and I paid for the lot, leaving me with little or no money left to buy food and essentials.
Wayne paid for nothing, his hands deeply buried in his pockets.
So we had a bit of an issue. No money.
So I phoned my Mum, all the way from Turkey, and she came to my rescue. She wired money via Western Union to the hotel we were staying at. It took some time for the transaction to go through, so we were actually penniless for some time. Luckily the tours we were on included dinner and some local shops had free apple tea to sample.
So for a while that's what we ate and drank. What a cock up
I can remember having a Turkish bath on one of the tours and slipping on the tiles slicing my foot. Blood went everywhere. Wayne just stood there, not really giving a shit. Despite Wayne not giving a shit, I did have good experiences in Turkey, so I guess that was some consolation.

One of Wayne's sisters owned a house and after much persuading I agreed to leave the flat and move in with her. I was young and naive and took everything literally. I trusted everyone, not realising even his sister was using me, grooming me, to help her pay for her mortgage and possibly buy the house from her.

So I moved out of Wayne's flat and moved in with his sister at her house. Wayne I guess was planning to ditch me, but didn't have the nerve to do it straight away. I suspected his sister and him had planned this house fiasco to enable him to let me down easy, as they say.

Any rate, not sure. But either way, I ended up getting a mortgage for the house in 1997

So at the age of twenty two, I was the proud owner of my very first property.

Buying the house was not as easy as I'd imagined it to be, so Mum found a mortgage advisor in Grimsby, who sorted everything for me. No quibbles, no hassles. Papers were signed very quickly and before I knew it his sister moved out and I was the owner of my own little house.

Buying the house went smoothly, but not so with Wayne and me. I'd done everything for him. Paid for his flat, stayed true to him whilst in prison, took his family to see him while he was in jail, now he wanted out?

Why?

However, looking back to those early days of our relationship, I did fixate on him being my boyfriend, and he'd reluctantly gone along with it, so I can possibly understand now, why he wanted out.

But it still hurt, and I felt resentful. I did everything for him, and he'd repaid me with, well nothing.

I gave and he took.

Lesson learnt, I'm afraid.

In life you don't always get rewarded for the good you do, often it's the opposite. Wayne was about to end our relationship.

Some reward then, for all I did for him.

Life is a journey along many different roads. Destiny and fate deciding which road you take. I guess the road I was travelling along was not destined to be one Wayne would take.

Yes, our paths crossed briefly, but fate would take us in different directions.

Sadly, another's path would cross Wayne's and fate would lead us on different pathways.

I wanted to watch Wayne, in his first production, at his college.

Wayne didn't want me to go, which I found really unusual. We were still together at the time, so why wouldn't he want his girlfriend to see his first acting debut?

My intuition kicked in and I knew trouble was brewing.

Alarm bells should have rang. Something was amiss. But trustworthy I heard no such warning.

Well that's me isn't it? You should know by now. Gullible me! I put my trust in everyone hoping for the best. However, that trust was to be shattered by someone, I trusted most in all of this world, Wayne.

It was during Wayne's first drama production at college that I witnessed, an on stage attraction, between Wayne and a fellow girl student. Later I learned her name was Laura.

It was so obvious, Wayne had the hots for her.

Laura was of Chinese origins, sexily slim, with dark shiny glossy hair dangling down her back. She wore a crop top with a perfectly toned stomach and I'll never forget that belly button ring.

Dead right! I'll never forget that bellybutton jewel she paraded with erotic pride. To me it personified an animated aphrodisiac that would attract any male.

Wayne for one.

My ADHD fixated straight away on that ring's intoxication and I became obsessed with that bloody belly button obscenity.

That's what we do when you have ADHD. We fixate and react instinctively. But, please, remember, at the time, I had no idea I was suffering from such a fixation. So I reacted instinctively.

Was this Laura character trying to take Wayne away from me? Yes she was, so I reacted accordingly.

To a normal person such an obsession is madness, but not me. I was fixating on that bloody ring, and it made me feel uneasy. Wayne was mine and no belly button strumpet was going to take him away from me.

Was he having an affair with Laura?

Of course he was, I reasoned, but I elected to keep that fact from my brain. So I challenged him, but he of course denied it.

I've been gas-lighted, and emotionally manipulated by many people, on many occasions, even to the point of doubting my own sanity.

But not this time!

Was I being conned? Probably, but I needed my relationship with Wayne to continue.

My sixth sense has never let me down and I knew Wayne wasn't being honest with me. I was convinced, despite my emotional ADHD creating doubts, that Laura and Wayne were having an affair.

Wayne was becoming more and more distant. I was living in my newly bought property but Wayne didn't want to move in with me.

Wayne was happy on his own living in his flat in Moss Side. He would blank me out, leaving me hanging about unsure as to what the Hell I was to do. He refused to say our relationship was over.

I was confused.

Looking back over my relationship with Wayne, it's clear now how one-sided it had been. Wayne really hadn't wanted to commit himself to me. It was me who encouraged and nurtured our relationship. Which, on reflection, didn't really work.

If the truth be told, Wayne was weird, somewhat clinical, un-experimental and very unnatural when it came down to the bedroom side of things.

Maybe I was craving a loving companionship and someone to love me.

So I'd fixated on Wayne, hoping he was that person.

That now was up for debate...

I had the key to Wayne's flat but was too scared to confront the consequences. However it was time to confront my fears and face the truth. So I decided to tackle those fears head on. Knowing what my sixth sense had warned me to expect, I went over to Wayne's flat and let myself in.

There she was, as bold as brass, her bloody belly button ring sparkling in the light. I just wanted to rip that bloody jewel out of her stomach.

I hated her for what she'd done. I was shaking with anger and she wouldn't look me in the eye.

I challenged her to look me in the fucking eye and face me. She looked away, her shame clearly visible. I could have punched her in the face, but thought better of it. I rightly accused her of fucking my boyfriend in my flat, a flat I'd paid rent on for six months.

She said nothing

It was obvious I was angry. Calm but furious. She knew it too. She stood there and said nothing. The pain in my heart was heavy. A pain I'd never experienced before.

Truly, I was distraught. My life again was in ruins.

Wayne, who I thought was the love of my life, had cheated on me, with this strumpet. James had cheated on me in the West Midlands but I didn't feel this kind of pain, I was now experiencing.

I fucking hated this woman for what she'd done.

She hurriedly tried to collect her belongings, in an abortive attempt to leave.

No way! She would answer to me for her infidelity. So with a mouth full of profanity I verbally stopped her leaving the flat.

We were in the kitchen, and I noticed Wayne had cooked her a meal. He'd never done that for me. Cosy meal for two, I screamed.

That made me even angrier.

I noticed a used condom in the bin which I retrieved, and in my anger, emptied its contents over Wayne's bed.

I was fuming, and called Laura a Bitch.

I stormed out of the room, ranting and raving like a lunatic, telling her I was going to have it out with Wayne at his place of work.

I'm usually calm and collective in difficult situations, but once pushed beyond my placid stage, there's no stopping me.

This woman more than angered me and I was ready to blow my top. I told her I was going to see Wayne at his works and she was coming along with me.

She didn't object.

Whether she felt guilty or not, I was unsure, I doubt it though. The Bitch had seduced Wayne, and would answer for her infidelity.

But had she? Or was it Wayne to blame??

I didn't care, at this stage, I was in an angry state of confusion and dragged Laura to my car.

I drove like a madwoman. The traffic was heavy and it took ages.

Beside me sat Laura in utter silence.

I wasn't feeling too well at this stage. I ranted on Laura, who just ignored me.

The air was blue with my swearing, and Laura just sat there and said nothing. I finally pulled up outside his workplace, where Wayne worked, and dragged Laura out the car.

I found Wayne, amongst his workmates, and when he saw me with Laura his face fell to the floor.

I manhandled, Laura, in front of him telling him, "Here's your fucking whore, you're welcomed to each other.

The situation was awkward, no one was sure what to do next. So I left unsure as to where this confrontation would lead me next.

It would resolve itself later in the day.

I left Wayne's works, got into my car, drove back to the flat, collected my clothes, and closed the door on the pair of them for ever, or so I hoped.

However, the affair took its toll on me and I had to take time off work.

I just couldn't cope.

I'd just experienced my first proper heartbreak and I was absolutely devastated. I was heartbroken, my mind wrestling with why Wayne had done this to me? Why would he want to hurt me so horribly? All I ever wanted from him was for him to love me. It now appeared he didn't!

So there I was, emotionally drained and unable to physically function. I became irrational and started doing erratic things. I'd drive past his flat every night to see if I could catch them together.

I'd hoped he'd feel guilty, for what he'd done to me, considering what I'd done for him whilst in prison.

No chance! He didn't!

I was hoping against hope.

Finally curiosity got the better of me and I gathered enough courage to go to Wayne's flat, to return the keys and collect the remainder of my belongings.

A big mistake!

Arriving at the flat I inserted and turned the key. I opened the door to find Wayne blocked my way in. He was angry, and if looks could kill, I'd have died on the spot. There was hatred in those once beautiful eyes now they looked evil and full of hate. I could tell he loathed me.

I asked for my belongings back and he told me to wait at the door and he'd go and get them. The Hell I was going to wait at the door, the flat was as much mine as his, so I hustled my way in.

She was there, sat down, wearing a little red outfit, her bare stomach, displaying that fucking bellybutton ring, adding insult to injury.

She then had the cheek to tell me I was no longer Wayne's girlfriend, and for me to go. Well that was like waving a red flag to a bull.

I went absolutely ballistic, and became an uncontrollable nut job. I screamed insults at her, at the top of my voice, while Wayne stepped in and tried to throw me out of the flat.

That's when it happened!

I thought it was a heart attack. I just couldn't get my breath. I couldn't breathe. My chest felt like it was crushing in on me.

In fact I was having a panic attack due to the emotional trauma I'd driven myself into, but at the time I had no idea what the Hell was going on with me.

I panicked and found myself on the floor of the flat struggling to breathe.

Scary time.

It had been so scary, Wayne called for an ambulance.

So there I was, a tragic heartbroken figure lying on the floor of a soon to be ex-boyfriend's flat, having a panic attack, in front of his new girlfriend.

Not the nicest of places to be in.

In the chaos that was erupting around me, Laura decided to go, leaving Wayne to tend to me. Too much drama, I expect for a future drama queen.

Exit stage left. No encore for such a poor performance.

Reluctantly, Wayne stayed with me. He wasn't exactly caring and I suspect he thought I was making all this up. I wasn't but he wasn't prepared to accept my honesty.

Shame on him!

Again I was the victim, but as usual no one seemed to recognise that.

The ambulance men arrived, and they were wonderful. In private they'd asked me what had happened. I explained what had happened and they were satisfied no violence had taken place, and we were free to go our own way.

When you have ADHD you're like a dog with a bone. You hang on to everything. So despite Wayne's infidelity I had to move on.

There would be others.

I regained my composure, and set about proving my worth.

I was twenty two years old, owned a house in Manchester, and worked full time.

I had a positive outlook on life, so everything looked encouraging for the future.

Also I had my Joy Machine.

So what the hell is a joy machine you are asking yourselves?

Christmas 1997 my mum bought me a brown faux moleskin Filofax.

She bought me it because she thought it would be good for me to have some kind of organisation in my life. I literally was crap at timekeeping and somewhat disorganised. However, I was very much in control of my life but not very organised, so mum's present made sense.

So the Filofax became my bible. It had days of the week in little squares, and each day I would write what I'd done or what I had to do in the appropriate squares. Not only did I do all that, but highlighted everything in Nautical coloured fluorescent pens.

I filled in my Filofax sheets every day, to the point of hyper fixation.

That dopamine fix, a symptom of ADHD, kicking into my psyche. I got to love writing diaries. I'd write down everything; what I ate; what I drank; what I did for exercise. Just about everything I thought was interesting, went into my diary.

My fixation didn't end there. Oh no! To augment my Filofax I bought another diary to help coordinate my Filofax diary, and bought a notebook to list what I needed to do each day.

I became very proficient, super organised. My method of keeping a diary and colour coding its content worked. I was so delighted with the system my friend Abby affectionately called it my joy machine.

I used to put all my diaries in a bag with all my coloured pens and Biro pens, and the bag would accompany me on my travels.

Wherever I went the diaries would go.

I'd have to fill in the diaries every day. It became a compelling habit. I still do to this day before I go to bed. I get very frustrated and upset if my diaries are not filled in. I feel like I'm not coping well. Feel my life is falling apart if they're not correctly filled in with the appropriate colour-codes.

The joy machine is even mentioned in my ADHD assessment report, for my official diagnosis of ADHD.

If you saw my joy machine bag, you'd probably think me bat shit crazy. It's stacked full, with collections of diaries and pens. To an outsider, unaware of my condition, you'd question my mental health.

But that's ADHD you see.

Also my passion for keeping diaries and the like has rolled over into my new career. My boss informs me I'm the most organised sales person on the team.

My condition has led me to build a coping strategy, to survive. Hence the paper diary system and colour coding everything in fluorescent pens.

The joy machine gives me so much pleasure. I cannot imagine life without doing my joy machine. Sometimes I'm too tired to fill in the diaries but I make the effort. I've even been known to watch a film at home filling in the diaries because, for me, it's relaxing.

I love making lists and crossing things off lists.

It's a coping mechanism that I've developed, and is a workable strategy that has helped organise my life.

So from Christmas 1997 I started to record most of my activities. Prior to that it's a case of starting from the beginning and working myself forward, trying to remember life stories.

So there you go, that's my joy machine. It works for me. Keeps my life in control. I sometimes wonder when I'm a little old lady will I still be doing my joy machine? Of course I will, material for my future books....

The affair had left me with catastrophic complications both with my mental and physical health. My undiagnosed ADHD must have added to my distress and when recalling the incident, I often wonder, had I understood my condition at the time, I might have dealt with it less aggressively, taken a more stable approach.

But I didn't and ended up mentally and physically scared by the episode.

The affair with Wayne and Laura affected my mental wellbeing and bought back those physical conditions I thought I'd overcome.

I lost weight, and my anorexia returned. I was out of control and I envisaged the return of those unhappy times that have so haunted my life.

I needed to bounce back quickly and overcome this heartbreak ordeal.

People with ADHD can be high achievers, but some find it hard to start tasks no matter how hard the difficulty.

To achieve success in life, you're told, to work hard and concentrate on the tasks ahead. But the ADHD brains don't always function like that, and we often find ourselves struggling with our mental capacity on a daily basis.

Wayne cheating on me definitely took its toll and I found myself spiralling downhill out of control, fast. I could feel myself fixating on the split with Wayne to the point of obsession. It was causing my ADHD to go in overdrive. Such a horrid emotion and sensation that's difficult to control.

So, I needed to stop this decline and found looking at the positive achievements in my life helped my recovery.

So, at the age of twenty two, I literally had it all. A house with a mortgage, a job with a car and a bright and successful future lay ahead of me.

So I'd better not cock it up, have I?

I thought of those, doubting Thomas of my youth. If they could only see me now. I'd make them eat their words.

'Destined to be a shelf stacker,' I believe my teacher once told me. Well, eat your words, Mr Willis my old English teacher and hopefully, you'll choke on them too.

I'm a success!

I was beginning to believe in myself again. I could see now how successful I'd become, when compared with those teenage failures of my youth.

I was no longer a failure, but a successful young woman with the world at her feet.

I really had achieved all of this solely on my own with no help, just pure determination and hard work.

I felt important, a pick you tonic if I needed one.

However, there was a negative to my positivity. I was still wrapped up in pain, grief and anxiety from Wayne's desertion. I still was hurting, thinking of everything I'd done for him while he was in prison, and the monies I paid out to keep his flat alive, ready for his return from jail. The man who crashed my company car and forced me to be his chauffeur, had used me. He didn't give a shit, what I'd done for him. That's me afraid. ADHD being my unknown accomplice.

So after all I did for Wayne, he goes and cheats on me.

However I'm no one to keep holding a grudge..? You have to let things go...
I forgive but I never forget...there is no doubt about that. Inspired by the lyrics of the girls in TLC who expertly put it..."I don't want no Scrub...always talking about what he wants and just sits on his broken ass"...

CHAPTER NINETEEN

NAIVETY

Looking back, what the Hell was I doing, chasing after Wayne?
He treated me like shit and at the time ripped my heart to pieces...

Many years later, Wayne made contact with me to inform me that his Mum Liz had sadly passed away, and had invited me to her funeral.
Wayne apologised for all the heartache he had put me through many years ago.
I'm not one to hold a grudge, I will always forgive, but I will never forget how it made me feel. Wayne taught me a huge lesson in life, and that is I can survive...

It's that long ago now, and I've moved on so much in my life, that it no longer hurts.
I am so lucky that eventually I found real love with Ed, a man who truly loves me.

Just to Recap; So with the heartache and pain of Wayne, emotionally affecting my health and happiness, at that time. I plucked up the courage to go and visit my GP for medical help and support.
Depression and anxiety had taken control. So Prozac antidepressant pills were prescribed...

In addition I asked for counselling, and was put on a waiting list.
No one knew the traumatic events that I'd endured in the past, or what I'd gone through with Wayne.
No one would! I kept it to myself.
So would pouring out my predicaments to an unknown councillor be the answer?
I didn't know. I was desperate for help so considered all possibilities.

I rarely did discuss my fears with anyone.

I've spent a good deal of my life chasing after some goal or other. I certainly gave everything I had to achieve them. Some didn't work out sadly, but I gave them a bloody good try. I'm not one to give up.

I chased after love and that at the time appeared out of my grasp. I only wanted someone to love me, help take the pain away.

My family gave me unconditional love, but at the time, my young naive brain didn't see it like that. So off I went, seeking what was always right there.

I was holding onto so many deep rooted secrets and trauma, I just didn't want to burden my family with them.

Wayne continued to see Laura and obviously both were in the throes of a honeymoon period. He was, by all accounts, obsessed with her and I revengefully hoped, like what Wayne did to me, she would drop him like a hot potato.

Revenge is a dish best served cold. Eventually Laura was to dump him...

My work at FX Labs suffered, their bubbly, go lucky salesperson had turned into a bit of a misery. It's a fact, someone like me with neurodiversity, coupled with depression, will eventually take its toll. Sleeping became erratic and nights were long and very wakeful. Facing an early alarm clock, not recommended.

Which my work asked me to do.

I was asked by work to go to Liverpool every morning. It was a very early start and with my history, I didn't stand a chance.

So for months I travelled back and forth from Manchester to Liverpool. It wasn't much fun, getting up extremely early, and driving through heavy traffic and getting stuck in traffic jams. I was tired, sleepy and getting very bored.

And true to ADHD form, I was rapidly losing interest in my job.

With reservations, I attended counseling that I had requested.

Surprisingly, I found it very rewarding to start with. I was able to offload a lot of worrying hang-ups that were supposedly giving me grief, according to my councillor.

However, I wanted my councillor to reassure me, all would be well again with Wayne, and we'd get back together.

This he couldn't do, he was there to listen, not to judge or solve my problems, and offer expertise.

The healing would be down to me and sharing my problems with him was a way to recovery. So, I went to a few more counselling sessions. I talked, they listened but I'd then decided I'd had enough. I felt I wasn't really getting anywhere with it anymore, so I stopped attending.

I couldn't get Wayne out of my mind. I was still obsessed with him.

I tried to get my life back in order, and started going out with Abby again, but I found myself fixating on Wayne, hoping against hope I'd meet up with him. I couldn't shake off this feeling of loneliness and him abandoning me.

Life got more boring. Nothing exciting was happening.

I was plodding along, in a pointless existence, getting nowhere. I was working 9-to-5 in a job that now had me more as a delivery driver, driving back and forth, back and forth, from Manchester to Liverpool.

Life moves on and I was becoming disillusioned with my job.

Tragic events leave lasting memories and often one can recall exactly where one was or what they were doing when such events take place.

I remember Lady Diana being killed in Paris, and watching the news coverage of it on TV in the house I bought. There were also the Manchester bombings that destroyed most of Manchester City's centre.

I think myself very fortunate I'd decided to go back to Grimsby the weekend of the bombings. Had I been in Manchester, most probably, I would have gone to the pub, where I had worked and been caught up in the bombings. Fate stepped in again and saved me...

Manchester was changing rapidly and a new generation of Mancunians were bringing about evolutionary changes to the city. In all honesty, I didn't recognise the place when Ed and I, recently revisited the city, on a nostalgic visit to my old hangouts. It wasn't the city I remembered back in the 1990s.

So, where was I in my story? Yes, going up and down the motorway to Liverpool.

See what ADHD does to you, off I go again at a tangent. Anyway, I'm back now. So, this driving drag was literally the highlight of my day, and the reality of it was, I was getting bored, bored out my skull. I craved for a change, something to take me out of this monotonous merry go round, I was enduring every day.

Fate stepped in and I was to fixate on yet another project to achieve stardom.

Everything did change, but not in the way I was expecting.

What happened next was to have a detrimental effect on my life and cause my friends and comrades to judge me inappropriately.

I'd just got back from my Liverpool run and was asked to drop off some film, next door, to a glamour photographer called Nik. His studio was next to us, in Manchester City centre.
Little did I know, my meeting with Nik, in his studio, that day, would result in me making the craziest impulsive decisions I've ever made in my life.

At the time, I got a huge dopamine fix that overturned any cause for concern.

I'm an impulsive female, with ADHD and I do things on impulse. My brain, if you recall, doesn't work logically. My lower dopamine levels make me seek out more dopamine, in order for me to feel better.

It's a process called under stimulation.

In other words my brain is not getting enough stimulation to keep me focused on what I'm trying to do. So I needed to engage in situations that excited me, interested me, in order to produce those higher levels of dopamine that I craved for.

Ross's offer did just that. I was very tempted and highly interested in what he was to offer me.

So let me explain what happened in Nik's studio in greater detail.

I can remember walking up the stairs to Nik's studio and knocking on the door. I was told to come in and as I entered I was faced with a lot of people milling around. I assumed some were makeup artists, as on a chair, in front of me, I could see an assortment of makeup items.

I assume this was for, as yet, an unseen model.

Nik popped his head round the corner. A dirty rolled cigarette dangled from his mouth and he spoke in a pure Mancunian accent. He was thin with scraggy rock band hair. He wore a leather waistcoat, with tight leather pants held up with a big impressive belt.

In that distinctive Mancunian accent he introduced himself and asked me if I'd got his film. I said I had.

By now curiosity was getting the better of me. What on earth was going on in here I asked myself?
Sensing my inquisitiveness Nik asked me if I wanted to stay and watch, I said yes.

A decision, I now know, was a bad one.
However, I needed that dopamine rush, and my intrigue was feeding that urge.

What I was to witness was totally unexpected, they were making a porn film.

I entered what was clearly a set. There was a cameraman, lights, make-up artists, all milling around or sitting on a sofa in a kind of a waiting room area. Enter a naked guy and a tall slim naked blonde girl and they started making out.

No one battered an eyelid, it was as if watching these two having sex in front of them was normal. I was cool as a cucumber...

I just sat down staring unbelievably at these two having sex with each other. A make-up girl distracted me, and asked me if I wanted a cup of tea. I was really engrossed with what I was seeing and nodded my head.

It was a very surreal moment, and I was unsure whether I should be watching this. Was I shocked at what I was watching?

Should I be?

I was confused. It was all crazy and I was unsure what to think. I guess, because I followed Madonna's career, and in 1992 when she launched a book called, 'Sex.' An X-rated adult book with very explicit photos, similar to what I was watching here in this studio, I was ready to accept this as an acceptable art form.

Sex being glamorised as a form of erotic art.

So yes, I went along with it.

OK I'd seen bits of a porn film on the night I lost my virginity to Ben and the night I got raped by Kim and Dean. I thought, at the time, watching the porn films had encouraged my abusers.

However, watching it live, here in the studio, it was evolving into a legitimate art form and not the 'dirty,' obscenity I'd believed it to be.

Here I was, a sales rep from next door, sitting having a cup of tea on a sofa watching a porn film being made.

.   The cameraman ordered a break and filming stopped. It was all very staged and professional in a weird amateur professional kind of way.

Ross, the naked male porn star, made a beeline for me. He was literally stark bollock naked, so grabbed a towel to put round his waist. He asked me my name and what I was doing there. I explained I worked next door as a sales rep and was delivering Nik's film.

After learning how much I was earning as a sales rep, he suggested I could earn far more working as a model, for his girlfriend, Debbie who ran a glamour model agency in London

Now to a young impulsive naive girl like myself, who had neurological problems this sounded like a good deal.

So without even thinking about the consequences, I latched onto his offer. He gave me his girlfriend's business card and I fixated on becoming a glamour girl.

How naive can one stupid girl get?

Ross went on to tell me that Debbie, his girlfriend, had a flat in London where girls from all over the country could stay, and she would find them work in the glamour industry.

With that, the female porn star came over to me and introduced herself. Her name was Sam and she too was working for Debbie.

Nik came over, and I got the feeling I was being manoeuvred by them all, into accepting Ross's invitation. He informed me of his work and how he'd famously been featured in Playboy magazine. I innocently thought that was an achievement, and he went on to inform me, he'd take great pleasure in the future working with me.

The reality of that statement escaped me at the time, and I congratulated him on his success.

Naivety can easily overrule facing the truth, and had my inexperience, understood the reality of what I was getting myself into, I would probably never have gone to London.

However, I left Nik's pornographic studios, with a dopamine rush that needed enriching. I went back to work, lost in the possibility of improving my status, and becoming the next Madonna.

I needed to change direction. Leave my job and seek new pastures. I'd hoped, playing an active role in the glamour industry, would be the stepping stone I so desperately needed to get into the music business.

I was converted. A decision that would cause me chaos, upset and misunderstanding from others for a huge part of my life.

So I called Debbie......

She sounded lovely on the phone. Her sweet, well-educated posh accent, luring me into a sense of false security.

Ross; remember him, that naked porn star. Well, true to his word, he'd rang Debbie and told her all about me.

I was invited to Debbie's flat in London.

So okay, maybe this'll work. Madonna used sex to get where she is today, so why not I? I had nothing to lose, I was still upset over Wayne, and my dopamine levels needed a boost.

Anticipating excitement I drove to London to meet Debbie.

I really had no idea what to expect. It was a new adventure, something better than moping about Wayne, and driving back and forth to Liverpool every day.

I was feeding my dopamine fix and enjoying every minute of it...

I arrived safely in London and parked up outside Debbie's flat.
I phoned Debbie on my mobile phone, to let her know I had arrived. And sat nervously in the car and waited for her... She arrived in a sports car.

She had a pretty face, she dressed seductively, but a bit trashy for me. She invited me up to her flat, and I followed. I could see, on first impressions, she was disappointed in the way I looked. I wasn't what she expected at all. I was wearing combat trousers, a puffa jacket with buffalo 'Spice Girl' platform trainers. Not the typical glamour girl she was probably expecting.

I can remember thinking I wasn't pretty enough. Self esteem was low.

Once inside her flat she immediately told me to take my clothes off. I took a moment to assess my situation. What the fuck was I doing here? Did I really want to do this? Here I was, with a woman I barely knew, and stripping off for her.

I should have left there and then, but stupid me didn't.

I was hoping to become a glamour model, and if that meant parading starkers in front of her, then let it be.

So, I took all my clothes off and stood naked in front of her.

She produced a camera and started taking snaps of me. Again I assumed it to be normal practice. She confirmed that by explaining she needed a file to show potential clients. I'd got a good figure and big boobs, she informed me, and so I should get tons and tons of work.

After the photo session, she found me a sexy outfit to wear and proceeded to make up my face with trashy make-up.

Things were moving far too fast for me to comprehend. She hurriedly gave me the address on a piece of paper and said I should go there immediately, as he was waiting for me.

What? Who? Where? Waiting for me, to do what I enquired.

Don't worry it's really easy, she added, and take the money.

Then as quickly as she arrived, she left giving me the instruction to ring her when I'd finished the job.

I can remember thinking what the hell have I got myself into?

A normal brain would probably have told its owner to get the hell out of this place and go home.

That's what I should have done, but my ADHD brain had other instructions.

I thought well, she seems nice, maybe this is what I've got to do, to break into the glamour business.

I was so naive, totally oblivious to where it was taking me. If this is what you've got to do, to become a 'glamour girl,' then what the Hell, bring it on.

I was still taking Prozac, my dopamine levels higher than normal. Nothing could be worse than Wayne cheating on me.

I felt like shit.

So what the fuck, let's do it, my ADHD brain conning this naive misfit into believing it was her destined, to find fame, by going and fulfilling this task.

So I headed back out and drove myself to the address supplied.
Then the reality of what I was going to do kicked in.
I started to cry hysterically. I came to London to be a glamour model, seek fame, not be a second hand whore, I was told to be.
I can't go through with it, I reasoned. Just can't do it!
However, despite this inner conflict, I didn't go home. I continued on to the address that Debbie had given me.
I was only there a short while and with that he then handed me a load of money, told me to have a safe journey back to the flat.
I left, got back in my car and drove off.
My mind raced with confusion. What had I just done? The more I thought about it, the closer to the truth my thoughts led me.
Basically I'd been a prostitute, I had just been pimped out! Debbie was a madam.
I messaged Debbie to let her know I'd finished. She said I should get back to the flat and get some sleep, because tomorrow she'd need me bright eyed and bushy tailed.
She'd got me another job.
Tomorrow I was to star in a porn film.
My heart raced, what had I got myself into? Too late now and wondered what the morning would bring. I got back to the flat utterly exhausted, and mentally and physically drained. I felt as if I'd had a complete meltdown, unable to take into account what I'd actually done and what the Hell was happening to me.
I went to bed and of course didn't sleep very well...

CHAPTER TWENTY

SECRET

What had I just done?

I was riddled with my own disgust. I couldn't claim it was sexual abuse because I was responsible.

That's my problem.

I'm susceptible to persuasion. Too naive and trusting. A weakness in my character that I've had to deal with all my life. I'm too vulnerable at times for my own safety. I look normal, and try to hide the fact I'm struggling with a hidden disability that affects my thought processes. I overcompensate issues, in order to appear to be in control, masking the fact I have a brain disorder.

Debbie's flat was,' twee,' with all the necessary essentials. However, the decor, gave the impression it was a boudoir, I'd even go far and say, a brothel.

However, I tried to get to sleep, hoping all this had been a nightmare and I'd wake up in Manchester, and return to my 9 to 5 life.

The following morning I was woken abruptly, by a very fussy Debbie. It must have been very early because it was still dusk outside. I'm afraid I wasn't in Manchester, but still in Debbie's flat in London.

So this nightmare was for real.

Debbie ordered me out of bed. She had arranged for me to go to Harley Street and have an HIV test.

An HIV test? What's that all about, I thought?

I know Madonna was a huge campaigner for HIV and had performed in concerts promoting it. But why did I need to have an HIV test? What had I got myself into?

I do things on impulse, and don't think things through. I messed up over Wayne and now look where it's got me.

Am I a glamour model, a porn star or an Escort? I was confused.

At the back of my mind my dream of being the next Madonna, and wanting to be famous was still a goal.

Would what I'm doing now, secure that objective? Maybe.

I went with Debbie in her car to the walk-in clinic on Harley Street. On the way we discussed the money her client had given me and she took her commission. What was left was mine. I was to pay for the test myself out of what was left of the clients' money.

Subserviently, I obeyed. I had no say in what was happening, other than to listen and conform.

I sat and waited for my turn.

I was examined, paid my fee and was handed a certificate to say I was negative.

Debbie looked pleased with the result and we headed off to Surrey. Why Surrey? I asked and was told that's where the filming was to take place. I said nothing just sat there, my mind comfortably empty of any thought. I'd no idea what was expected of me or what I was supposed to do.

I could guess but drove such thoughts from my mind.

Debbie interrupted my defensive silence and told me I'd be working with Ross, her partner, the one I'd met in Manchester. She was so matter of fact about it too. The fact I was about to make a porn film with her boyfriend didn't worry her at all.

It worried me though.

We arrived at the location. It looked very posh.

Debbie said it was a privately owned home and they'd rented it for the day.

There were a lot of cars in the driveway and when inside we'd walk up a spiral stairway to the room at the top of the building.

I was met by a girl make-up artist who proceeded to give me a makeover. I felt important, glamorous in fact. People were fussing around me, which I quite enjoyed. I loved the attention.

Debbie came into the room with the outfit I was to wear.

There were a few guys milling around, who I believed were cameramen, but I wasn't paying much attention to what was going on around me. My mind was fixated on what the hell I was about to do.

I was transfixed, a puppet to be played with, my puppeteers pulling my strings. I didn't ask any questions I just obeyed, Debbie, telling me what to do and pulling my strings.

While still, in make-up, Ross came to see me. We exchanged polite conversation.

Apparently, filming was to take place in one of the rooms, and my name would be made up. I was a bored housewife, wanting a bit of fun in her life.

That was the plot, the script to be made up as the story unfolded.

So that was my part. I'd be an actor, playing a role. I fixated on it being a part in a film, it wasn't me, but a fictitious unreal character.

Well that's what I told myself, in order to go through with it.

'All the world's a stage, and all the men and women merely players; they have their exits and their entrances.'

I was about to make my first entrance.

The house was huge, people were running around, setting up lights and cameras. Ross, and I viewed each other's negative HIV test to make sure we were safe before engaging.

The whole thing was utterly surreal. It didn't seem real. Well it wasn't. It was just acting, so go with the flow my brain ordered, and I did.

I was quite alarmed to see how many people were at this porn set. Why so many I asked myself?

I was soon to find out.

Making this film was also being filmed for a TV documentary. So not only was I about to make my very first porno, I was also being filmed for a documentary about a porn film being made in the UK.

How strangely exciting that made me feel. I would be seen on international television, all over the world, and fixated on the fame that might bring me.

However, typical of my naivety, I hadn't thought through the consequences of this kind of exposure. I never considered the backlash I'd face and how damaging it would be to my future.

It would, I'm afraid, seriously mess with my head, and create overwhelming issues for the rest of my life.

I wish I could rewind that dreadful day. I'd never have appeared in that film, and got the hell out of that place and gone home.

But you can't rewind life and start again, can you? As they say, life is a sliding door. You chose one way or another.

That day I chose the wrong door.

Debbie, had control over me now, having got me to sign papers that gave them consent to use me as they wished. Sign this, Debbie had ordered, and I did.

Stupid I had no idea what the heck I was signing up for, and signed away my rights. I just did as I was told, complied with what was asked of me, and got on with it.

As already noted, I was a puppet on a string, to be manipulated and moulded into whoever she wanted me to be. Debbie knew I was the new girl on the block with natural big boobs. She saw pound signs in my figure, a potential money spinner that would line her pockets with gold and silver.

Debbie took me through to the room where we would be performing.

Around the room, spotlights lit the scene, and cameras strategically placed, would capture the best of the action. Debbie briefed me on what to expect and what I was going to do. Ross had already outlined the story scene and I knew my part.

It was all very cheesy, most porn movies are.

If I'm totally honest with you, I've now opened a 'Pandora's Box,' that I really didn't want to open. I've chosen to close the lid on this part of my life, but the consequences of what I did, still ripple across time, causing me anguish.

It's been a long painful road, if the truth be told.

My past would be used against me on many occasions. The establishment would question my suitability to be Mum and would try to take my daughter from me. They failed. I have the perfect daughter and relationship with her, any Mum would be proud of.

So people will judge you because they cannot get their heads round why you would want to do porn.

I've known all my life, I was a bit of an exhibitionist. A show off. An attention seeker. So here was an opportunity to show off some of that talent in front of cameras. I was about to become a porn star, and to be truthful, I was very embarrassed about it, but no way would I show it. I blanked it from my mind, switched off and went with the flow.

They had to do a cut, while I sorted myself out. Many more cuts and restarts were to follow before the scene ended. Ross was a professional actor having appeared in many productions. He was well spoken and acted out his role with professionalism. I, on the other hand, was an amateur, and it showed. I put on a false accent and acted my role the best I could.

It was all a little bit cheesy, but after all, it was a porn movie.

Ross got into porn because he'd met Debbie, like me.

I guess everybody has got their own personal reasons for doing porn. You're reading about mine.

Halfway through the shoot, we stopped for a small break which I found a bit bizarre. A make-up artist came through and started to touch up my face.

I was beginning to feel very uncomfortable.

A lady, from the TV Company filming us, came over during the break to ask me what it was like, doing porn for a living. I admitted I didn't really know, as this was my first time. She politely said she'd never have guessed. I was a natural, and looked as if I'd been doing it all my life.

Praise indeed, for my acting.

It was all an act. It wasn't real. I certainly wasn't enjoying myself, I can tell you that. It wasn't like making love to someone you really loved.

No way.

It was just cold hard acting. Loveless, unfeeling, 'No emotion. Nothing!

This wasn't rape but it left me totally emotionless.

So we eventually came to the final scene which we all know is the money shot. Most porn films have the same structure and our amateur efforts would be no different to those professional porn movies. Our final scene and that would be that...

And that's what happened.

Immediately after, Ross literally got off me, ready to head off home.

Bang thank you mam and he was gone.

I laid there, for what seemed forever. Then it hit me, what the fuck have I just done? My skin felt uncomfortable. I cleaned myself up, desperately wanting to be out of this crazy nightmare I had got myself into.

Immediately Debbie told me to hurry up and we had to get back to London straight away.

I got dressed, and was handed an envelope with what I'd earned for being in the film. I said goodbye and left with Debbie. Ross was nowhere to be seen.

All rather weird.

So I'm heading back with Debbie to London.

We returned to the flat and bought a takeaway. One of the cameramen joined us and we shared it together.

Debbie and the cameraman carried on a private conversation about Ross, leaving me out of the conversation.

Rude, but that was Debbie.

Ross wasn't with Debbie which I thought was very strange. Maybe the boyfriend, girlfriend thing was but a ruse, for him to find girls for Debbie's business.

That's how they recruited me. I actually found Ross to be a pompous narcissistic Pratt.

I felt somewhat ostracised, and began to relive the events of the day. It was beginning to feel like I'd been used. Once they'd had their use of me, I'd been paid off and dismissed, without any praise or any thought on how I was feeling.

Debbie used people to get what she wanted.

On reflection she wasn't a nice person and here I was beholden to a woman who verbally abused and criticised me.

I'd only gone down for the weekend, Friday to Sunday, with the intention of going back to work on Monday.

But Debbie had other ideas.

She told me on Sunday she'd got me,' Escort clients,' to see. Again I was compliant to what Debbie told me to do.

Didn't question it. Didn't quibble. I just did as she asked.

I know what you must be thinking but that was me. I craved attention for my undiagnosed ADHD fixating on becoming someone important.

London supplied that fix and I couldn't resist its lure.

I went home to Manchester Sunday evening with more money, earned in three days than I would have working for a month at FX Labs.

Those three hectically insane days in London, took its toll. I travelled back to Manchester feeling drained and much stressed.

Debbie wanted me back in London as soon as possible. Her clients were asking for me...

Come Monday, I went back to work at FX Labs as normal. But I knew my life had changed with that weekend in London.

London was calling.

But did I want to go back? Go through more of what I'd experienced? Or stay safe and bored, and carry on with my normal life here in Manchester?

London life lured me back, so I rang and told Debbie I would come for possibly a week and decide after that what I would do.

She told me that was fine and she'd book me work for the week I stayed.

She told me I needed to change my wardrobe and to buy clothing that made me look sexy. She said she would arrange for me to do glamour modelling with a photographer and put me in another porn scene.

On reflection, I know it sounds too naive, but I had no idea I was being groomed. I guess my dopamine fix with the money, I could earn easier than working a 9-5 job, was the lure. I was hyper fixating on going back to London even though that first weekend was quite traumatic.

I was going back for more...

I didn't tell anybody about my trip to London. Not even Abby who by now had made new friends and was seeing a new boyfriend.

I didn't tell my family and I certainly didn't tell my work colleagues

I did however get in touch with Wayne. I wasn't angry with him anymore so whatever happened in London kind of reset my mind. I said I'd had an opportunity to make some money in London, but didn't tell him how.

So that was that. I gave myself the green light to go ahead with my visit to London and experience that new lease of life.

London would give me the opportunity, I reasoned, to make some extra cash, and maybe, that vital stepping stone, to what I so desperately craved. Fame, fortune and the Madonna lifestyle.

Madonna, had success with her X rated books, and stage shows sexual imagery. She wasn't afraid to use her sexuality to get what she wanted.

I thought if she can use sex to get where she did, so can I. It'll be no different to what Madonna did, or Pamela Anderson with her a sex tape. It made them Global Superstars, so why not me...

The truth, as I saw it, was people got famous for dealing in sex. I wanted the fame that came with it. My musical angle hadn't worked and was going nowhere. So why not fixate on sex, hoping that would bring me fame...

So I carefully planned my next trip to London. I purchase sexy clothes, lingerie, and makeup. I was going to go down to London to show Debbie I was the best!

CHAPTER TWENTY-ONE

SEX DWARF

I packed my suitcase, put it into the car and headed for London. I was riding high on dopamine with no idea what the next week would entail. I hoped it would be a life changing experience, and bring me closer to the goals I so desperately needed to achieve.

I arrived in London and waited for Debbie. On her arrival we entered the flat.

Once inside Debbie handed me an itinerary for the week.

As her worker, which now I was, I'd need to have a full screening for STDs and undertake another HIV check.

I was new to the industry, so the demand for my services would be great. According to Debbie, I had a great body and should use that asset to the best of my ability.

I assumed all her new recruits went through this kind of grilling. It was bizarre and totally confusing.

For me to do this work, I'd somehow have to erect a barrier in my brain to block out the reality of what I was doing. I'd done that before, with my past traumas so I hoped it would work again.

It was the only way I could go through with it. To the normal brain, it probably seems irrational, but with my ADHD dysfunctional one, it was a normal procedure.

Debbie had arranged a photographer to take pictures for my portfolio but first I had to appear on an X rated TV channel and do a live striptease.

Wow! Live TV, stripping I thought, excitingly, I am really going to become famous. I arrived at the studios, a makeup artist did my hair and I performed...

My dopamine level was high and I felt like a real professional.

I was even paid for the privilege.

I was riding so high on dopamine, now fixating on my stripping performance to the point I felt out of control with my brain.

I recall the presenter telling the viewers to look out for me in my latest film and realised Debbie had scripted him to say that to promote Ross's porno film.

Stripping in front of the cameras was fun. I felt free and confident. I was the true extrovert, completely in my element. Experiencing that madness only ADHD can create, with no consideration for anybody else other than what was pleasing me. I wasn't hurting anybody?

Well, I didn't think I was?

Clearly I'd got that wrong.

I'd no idea how many viewers this X rated TV had, or who watched it, but my performance on that TV show was to have a detrimental effect on my current career at FX Labs.

The next morning the manager of FX Labs phoned me. She was very angry, screaming at me down the phone.

I was fired for stripping on TV, and needed to return the car immediately.

In her anger she slammed the phone down, not giving me the opportunity to speak or explain.

I was in absolute shock...

I had worked there for three years...

It had provided me with the funds to pay for my mortgage. Now what the hell was I going to do.

This is what ADHD does. You get caught up in the moment and do things without thinking. You get caught in that dopamine rush and do erratic things without thinking about the consequences.

No concept on how it might affect others.

I called Dave, my work colleague at FX Labs.

I asked what the hell was going on. I'd just been sacked!

It appeared one of the lads had been watching the X rated TV channel, and recognised me, he then videoed it, and fetched it into work for all of my bosses to see! The bosses had seen my performance and I knew the rest...

I was the talk of the workplace. Fame at last, but not as I had visualised it. My bosses thought it'd embarrassed the company, and they had no other option but to terminate my employment. However, as it turned out, stripping was not a dismissal offence. Through Debbie and her highly influential friends and associates. I informed FX Labs that legally they couldn't sack me, so they had to reverse their decision and reinstate me.

However they were very disappointed in me for what I had done. Disappointed in me were they? A word I'm very familiar with...

I've disappointed many people many times in my life. Not often deliberately but inadvertently.

I'm ADHD dopamine driven, and needs to control her own destiny...

So at times I'm that awkward non-conformist that uninformed individuals find hard to control. So, in their eyes a disappointment.

I'm the one in control, so I took back control, and politely told FX Labs to stick their job where the sun doesn't shine, and I'd return their car on Monday...

And as for that pervert, who videoed me and took it to work for them all to watch and laugh at my expense, well; actually he did me a favour, because leaving FX Labs changed my life forever!

Panic set in!

I informed Debbie and she set about reorganising my life. She opened up with a promise she'd make me a star in the porn industry.

She would make contact with a national tabloid, and they would send one of their photographers, and a journalist around to photograph me. The tabloid would then run my story on page three in their newspaper.

More work, she promised, would come from the X rated TV channel, and from porn-directors across the globe. I'd get the opportunity to travel the world and become a famous porn star.

It was all a bit above my head. The whole thing sounded absolutely insane.

I was very nervous. My stomach cartwheeling over and over.

Had I made a huge mistake?

Who knew?

I know I was excited. The thought of appearing in a national newspaper, was sensational, it could possibly catapult my career in the porn industry to great heights, not only in the U.K. but worldwide. So I thought what the fuck, I've come this far, let's go with it, I'm hurting no one.

Technology, back in 1998, wasn't as developed as it is today, so the world was a great place to hide. My parents would never read or possibly see my life as a porn star so I felt safe in going ahead with my plans. I hoped my career in the porn industry would propel my desire to be a famous singer, the ultimate aim of what I wanted to be in life.

My planning was completely surreal. I wasn't really in control but conned myself into believing I was. I felt vulnerable with bills to pay.

It had to work. So I went along with Debbie's plans and allowed her to dictate progress. I didn't have a car, and needed one. I also had a mortgage to pay, so needed money. Debbie's advice was taken on board. She suggested I buy a car on finance, and take on extra work with her, to pay for the repayments.

So the tabloid photographer came round and took the photos. I told my story to its journalist, explaining how I'd be the victim of an unjust sacking. Stars spun around in my eyes, my fixation on the interview, enhancing my thoughts of becoming a porn star.

With the interview and photographic session at an end I waited apprehensively for their publication.

I wasn't sure if I'd done the right thing and thought of stopping it right there and then. History repeats itself, and here I was, yet again facing one of those decision-making moments.

Fuck it. Let's go with it, and that's what I did...

My life reminded me of the lyrics of 'Sex Dwarf' by 80's synth pop duo 'Soft Cell' from the legendary album 'Non Stop Erotic Cabaret'.

"I can make a film, and make you my star, making the headlines sounds like a dream"...soft cell.

I returned to Manchester...with the lyrics of Soft Cell whirling round my head...

I went to talk to Wayne. Because I needed to be clear about what had happened to us. He was actually pleased to see me, and we were actually amicable with each other. Laura had left him, unable to cope with the situation, and he told me he was doing well at college. I was truthful with him also, and told him all that had happened to me and what I planned to do.

Laid-back Wayne was very positive about my plans. Whatever makes me happy, he said, then do it...

'Whatever makes me happy,' became my motto...

I asked him if he thought I was doing the right thing? "Well if you don't try, you will never know," he replied...

So go for it was his message...

I always knew Wayne felt guilty about his affair with Laura, and we parted as friends. Wayne was to support me and judged me not. I was so grateful for his understanding and I left happy.

Go for it, was his message and I did...

In Manchester I went to the car dealerships to find a car...

I eventually found a suitable car dealership. I chose a silver 'Vauxhall Tigra' with modifications. It had a double twin pipe exhaust and a spoiler, and very sporty it looked too. I couldn't wait to deliberately show it off, like Debbie did, in her sports car. I'd be the owner of the latest, and best car on the block, and boy did I get fixated on that...

I handed the company car back to FX Labs. The manager wasn't there so I handed the keys to the nearest staff member. The atmosphere was understandably uneasy, and embarrassing for all concerned. I did get a few genuine smiles from some of my colleagues, which pleased me. I collected my belongings and left without any confrontations. On reflection, that was to be my last employed position, for nearly twenty years.

With the help and advice from Debbie, I then went officially self-employed, I even had my own accountant...so all was above board...

Refusing to take my job back at FX Labs had inspired me. I was now independent and able to seek my own employment, which I reasoned was an exciting opportunity to explore alternative job opportunities.

I was young and single, the world my oyster... with Debbie guiding me.

My decision to have a career in the 'Adult Entertainment Industry' was bold and unpredictable however, I wasn't hurting anybody, so I thought!

If anything, the only victim here would be me. But, as usual, I didn't consider the consequences of how this new chosen career would have on my future.

However, I would face my future, day by day and fixated on it being the means to become famous.

So my new career was to begin. It was to be a rollercoaster ride, of highs and lows. If I'd known, what I know about this business, now, I probably would have done things very differently. However, destiny was to lead the way so I can't really have any regrets.

When my new car arrived it was stunning and I couldn't wait to get to drive it on the motorway. London was calling. I had bills to pay so needed to get to London and start earning.

I plucked up the courage to speak to my Mum. I had to tell my parents something... It was beginning to bother me...I didn't want to disappoint them.

At this point, they had no idea whatsoever that I had even left FX Labs.

I didn't want to worry them. I had managed to turn my life around. I was in a stable good job, I had a house with a mortgage and of course a company car. As my parents used to say, I had landed on my feet. Even if I fell in shit, I would come up smelling of roses. They were very proud of me...

I couldn't actually tell them the full extent of what kind of work I was to be doing in the Adult Entertainment Industry now could I? They'd have been mortified... I needed to create a plausible reason for why I was leaving FX Labs, and why I was working away in London...

So I called my Mum on the landline, and told her that I had left FX Labs. She was a little shocked...

"I've found an agent in London, Mum"...I continued, "Who can find me work in the Glamour Model industry?" My Mum voiced that was not too happy with my decision...

I continued to tell her I was to become a Glamour Model, and do Page 3, just like Sam Fox. Which I hoped would get me into the music business... Mum knew how much I wanted to be a singer, so I guess she accepted this as the truth.

She voiced her concern about my finances. Would modelling provide enough funds to live on and pay the mortgage?

She didn't think it would...My Mum thought it was a bad and foolish decision to leave FX Labs. I had the security of a stable job with a stable income. Why would I want to mess it all up?

Indeed, why would I want to mess it all up? Well I will tell you why... I act purely on impulse... I had a dream, I had a dream of being the next Madonna. Farfetched and probably insane. But it was my dream. I had learned that to be successful you have to make a jump. Working at FX Labs was not going to fulfil my dreams of becoming a popstar...

I convinced Mum I was following my dream.. I was young and you only live once.... I reminded her of a story about Dad. He too had a dream of owning his own business, he made that decision to jump, which at the time, everyone thought he was crazy. It was a huge decision that he quit his shift work to fulfil his dream, and now was successfully self employed. Dad now had his own little business with the help and support of Mum... Dad taught me to always follow dreams... Mum still wasn't convinced, and we ended our conversation. Obviously I never told her the whole extent of what I was really going to do...

I was concerned, it would break my parent's hearts if they knew the full truth. I would have been an embarrassment, an outcast. I had got in far too deep now, there was no way of turning back...

My parents didn't need to know my real intentions, if they had, well I can imagine the upset and uproar that it would have caused. My crazy impulsive behaviour is now dominated over any logic...

So I headed to London, to start my new career in the industry, with a suitcase packed with all my sexy outfits, shoes, underwear, make-up and jewellery. You name it, I had it all.

When I arrived at the flat, Debbie informed me that another girl would be staying for the week. Her name was Sam. I instantly recognised Sam as the actress from that porn film, being filmed in Manchester.

Sam was a Mum, with a small child. Her boyfriend had no idea she was working in the industry. We were to become good friends, and eventually make lots of porn scenes together.

If it wasn't for Sam being there, I think I would've probably gone off the rails, who knows. Sam, thankfully, made everything fun. She never took anything seriously. A philosophy, I took on board, that helped me cope with what I was to endure. Health wise I looked after myself. Underwent the necessary tests in order to go about my activities safely. Such stringent health checks need addressing if you're going to make a career in the porn industry. Obviously you've got to look after yourself for your own safety and others.

So I was asked to make a lesbian scene with Sam. This I did..

We were two actresses, playing our part, in a movie.
We followed the director's directions and did what he asked us to do.

However on a personal level we were not lesbians, we were actors, acting out our character parts. We never thought of ourselves as lesbians. Everything we did was on a professional level, we were working actresses, being paid.

I would travel back and forth between London and Manchester regularly, in order to fulfil my client's needs in London and go about my normal life back in Manchester. Sam would visit me when I was in Manchester, and I would pick her up from Manchester's Piccadilly train station. Another girl called Chloe would sometimes join us. She was married and her husband knew nothing about her sexual encounters. So the flat was always busy with the girls. We were all girls in the same boat. All living double lives but wanting to earn money... My life fluctuates on two very different levels...

CHAPTER TWENTY-TWO

LIGHT

When I wasn't working in London, I was back in Manchester living a normal life.

In Manchester I was a member of a gym. I'd go there once or maybe twice a day to work out and train like a trojan.

I loved the freedom. It was like my escapism.

I was in control, unlike the regimental life I led in London. Here in Manchester, no one knew of my life in London, apart from Wayne. So I didn't have to explain to anyone.

I enjoyed the gym. I could switch off and just concentrate on me. I got to meet an assortment of its clients, including some famous ones. I recall Beverley Callard, one of the stars from Coronation Street taking aerobics classes.

Going to the gym, and spending quality time in Manchester, was an escape from the reality of what my other life demanded from me.

At the gym, my friend Becky, was the receptionist. She introduced me to her new boyfriend Sy. Now, Sy, was destined to be famous, with a boy band and have massive chart-topping hits. But that would be in the future, for now he was Becky's new boyfriend, and we had only just met...

Sy and I would become very good friends. In fact we became best friends.

It's the small things that neurodiverse people fixate on. I was upstairs, on the cross trainer, I would usually spend half an hour on the machine, that's when Sy and I began chatting...

He had come to the gym to see Becky, he impressed me immediately.

I recall he was wearing Becky's white tracksuit, and looked fabulous...

I can recall just blurting out, "With a face like that, he should be a model" my ADHD is now taking over... No filtering of words, just said what I thought, out loud...

His reply was somewhat surprising, announcing he'd just won, 'Face of 1998,' in, 'Pride Magazine'. A magazine targeting, 'Black British,' mixed-race, African and African-Caribbean people.

I was of course very impressed and could see why he won.

Instantly we had a strong bond and we hit it off as best friends...
He had just moved to Manchester.

Sy had an aura about him that radiates... He was someone that was slightly different from the norm, and my strong intuition told me he was destined for greatness.

My deep-rooted spiritual side, a sixth sense, if you like, a supernatural insight, I just instantly knew he was destined for stardom.

So we connected spiritually...

He didn't have a lot of money back then, and was struggling to buy nice things for his modelling auditions. I had a huge impulsive desire to just help him out. I was working, earning money and I wanted nothing in return, other than to help my new friend out.

I recall the day I bought him his first Adidas Shell Toe trainers. They were for his birthday, the look on his face when he received them was priceless... he was so appreciative. There is something wonderful about genuinely wanting to help someone, and not wanting anything in return...

However, Becky, Sy's girlfriend, was highly insecure with him...
My relationship with Sy was completely platonic. It was a brother and sister kind of love, just like the platonic friendship I had with Mike back in Grimsby years prior.

We were the best of friends and always would be. He wanted to become a male model and was planning to go to London and look for an agent. I knew in my heart Sy was destined for the big time. I just knew he was different. I had not met anyone quite like him. He was a tonic of fresh air to my madness.

I offered to take him to London...
On our first journey to London we strengthened our bond. Music creates memories and vice versa. I remember, on that first trip, we listened to Madonna's 'Ray of Light,' on the car's CD player. Creating genuine happy memories that will always stay with me forever. I told Sy, about my fixation on Madonna, and how I wanted to meet her in person one day. I opened up about my dream of becoming famous and how I love to sing just like Madonna.

He really hoped I'd achieve my dream someday...

I had some R & B, CDs which I played and encouraged Sy to sing along too.

He started to sing, and my God he could sing.

I told him how good he really was, and to consider making a career in music.

Modelling had been his objective but I could see by his face, I'd hit on something he'd consider. I suggested he should record a demo. and see if the music business thought the same way I did. He certainly had the voice, and the looks to do it, so should give it a try...

Our journeys back and forth from London to Manchester proved enlightening and our platonic relationship strengthened with every trip.
I eventually confessed to Sy, the truth as to why I was in London. I just felt safe enough to tell him...
He didn't judge me at all.
I would continue to drop Sy off, and I would continue on to the flat where I stayed.

Sy said the next time I picked him up , I should call in and meet his friend Ellie. I still hadn't met Ellie... Obviously I'd heard all about her through Sy, he told me she was a wonderful kind person. He said they were just good platonic friends.

Ellie had a boyfriend, whom she originally had met in Manchester, Ellie had since moved to London to study. She lived with a few student friends and Sy had an arrangement that he slept on her sofa when in London.
It was a perfect platonic arrangement, and Becky, Sy's girlfriend, had no reason to be concerned about Ellie and Sy.
I recall pulling up outside Ellie's flat and knocking on the door. She answered. Sy had described her perfectly...Her persona was warm and loving, with that affectionate personality one instantly liked and fell in love with.

We instantly hit it off. We had a good chat and laughed, I knew that I could easily fixate on her becoming my new friend.

On travelling back to Manchester I told Sy, what an incredible person Ellie was. It was only while we were driving back to Manchester, that the penny dropped and I realised who Ellie actually was...

Back in 1995 when I first started dating Wayne, he worked as security for a fashion shop in Manchester. At the time he told me a story, of a girl named Ellie, who worked in the shop and had spread unfounded rumours that I was cheating on him... it gets complicated;

Now, I never met this girl Ellie, but apparently back when I was dating Alex. Remember the guy with the Mercedes, back in Manchester. Well his brother Nick had dated Ellie. She'd found my name in Nick's phone diary, and assumed he was dating me on the side... Ludicrous accusations at the time...

So Ellie retaliated, and told Wayne I was a cheat! A misunderstanding that was now explained... All water under the bridge, as life has moved on.

So when I next met up next with Ellie, and explained this complex misunderstanding to her, she realised who I was, we both burst out laughing. What were the chances of us ever meeting up like this?

Well that's destiny, a meeting meant to happen. We accepted our fate and formed a long lasting friendship that is still strong to this very day...

I was now living a complex existence. My head is battling with complicating scenarios. Narrating this story isn't easy. Reliving, mentally, all I encountered during this period of my life, is proving difficult. I keep going off at tangents, my brain racing along at a hundred miles an hour.

What to include in my book, and what to miss out on, now becoming difficult decisions to make. So many stories it's impossible to put them all in...

Becky was now getting concerned about Sy going to London. She was convinced that there was more to Ellie and Sy than he was letting on.

I really didn't care.

I was only interested in helping Sy, I believed in him, he was a young lad striving for big things and success. He had so much potential, and my intuition kept telling me he would one day become famous one way or another...

Wayne, when we were together, had introduced me to a friend of a friend called Janet, she was a music teacher. If I could introduce Sy to her, I'm sure she'd see his potential, and he'd find success in the music industry.

I took Sy to see Janet.

He was nervous, a little shy, embarrassed and reluctant to sing. I just wanted Janet to hear him sing and listen to how professional his voice was. I literally pushed him through the door and told him to sing.

I was a bit bossy, but I just wanted people to hear his voice. I knew there was something about him that was exceptional.

When Sy did sing, Janet agreed he did have an exceptional singing voice, so gave him a few singing lessons. It was enough to give Sy confidence.

We never did see Janet again but her input gave Sy the boost to go ahead with a music career. Sy and I would continue our journeys back and forth from Manchester and London. Sy would eventually move on, and stay with a lad, whose brother would eventually play for Manchester United.

Sy always said, it was through my persistence and assurance about his voice that he persevered with his music. Although he would pursue his modelling career a little longer, it would be his singing ability that would make him a household name star...

He would go to singing auditions in and around London. Finally destiny met him up with a group of lads, to form the most successful Boyband of the Noughties.

Well done Sy, I'm beyond proud, to have been with you on your momentous journey. Our special platonic friendship will remain one of my fondest memories.

It gives my heart a proud and pulsating beat of pride, knowing that I helped encourage him to achieve his goal.

Now unlike Sy, who had the confidence in himself and the encouragement of close friends, I, on the other hand, lacked that confidence. I'd made so many wrong decisions, and upset so many people, I questioned whether I fitted in with normal society.

From 1998 through to the early 2000s, I lived a double life. I would spend maybe a week or two in London each month, travelling around the capital. Then the rest of the time I was back in Manchester being very normal.

Mum would eventually come over from Grimsby to Manchester, on the train, to visit and help me out domestically. She helped me decorate and select suitable IKEA furniture, along with bits and bobs for the house...

I would continue to see Wayne on and off, he would often stay at my house when I was back home from London. I'm not really into cooking, my ADHD is not suited for such a complex activity. Cooking's an ordeal, a chore I'm not very good at. I can cook, but wouldn't want to do it week in week out.

However, on one particular Sunday, I pushed my reluctance aside, and cooked Wayne his dinner. He refused to eat it.

How dare him!

That instigated a huge bust up. I remember him storming out of the house, and me following him in the car, with the Sunday dinner he refused to eat, on the passenger seat. I curb crawled and followed him down the street, screaming at him like a banshee. Probably, on reflection, it was a bit over the top, but I was angry, mortified, how dare he reject my food. I worked so hard to cook it.

What an insult...I took it personally.

So I stopped the car, alongside him, got out with his dinner still on a plate, ran up to him, and tipped it all over him. I got back in my car and drove off home. A few hours later, Wayne returned, with his Mum, and her boyfriend. They'd come to get Wayne's belongings from the house.

A huge argument ensued, at the front door. Liz, in a strong Jamaican accent, accused me of treating her son like shit. Went on to say I was a 'Blasted fool' and a 'fart faced lesbian.'

A fart faced lesbian was I? That brought a smile to my face...

Wayne collected his belongings and left...

However we did get back in touch a few weeks later, but our relationship wasn't going anywhere...

I worked with Debbie for about one year before she eventually told me that work was becoming sparse. She was a one woman operation, having only a few girls on her books. She was having a baby, so I think under the circumstances, she wanted to step away from it all. She suggested I go to work for an agent in Central London, however, I also did join a London based model agency as well.

The new model agency concentrated on glamour modelling, photo shoot sets for magazines, and extras for TV productions.

My ADHD brain at this time, was like an unabsorbent sponge, and not all events I attended can be remembered. I literally did everything on impulsive overdrive and recollections have become somewhat of a blur.

However, I remember working at the TV studios in Twickenham for mainstream comedian Chris Morris.

He was creator, and co-writer of 'Brass Eye,'

Brass Eye was a British television comedy series that parodied current affairs news programming on Channel 4 in 1997 and into 2001. He would produce a TV programme called 'Jam,' a British experimental black comedy mainstream sketch show. I played an extra in a scene titled 'Gushing'.

I even got to meet Bruce Forsyth on the set of the 'The Price Is Right,' I've still got the original name tag, as a momentum of having met the legend that was Bruce Forsyth.

I even appeared on a popular daytime TV show twice, which, as it turned out, was probably not a great move. Such shows were undergoing investigation for planting actors in the audience to create conflict and wind up the audience.

Such conflicts make good television. This show was notable for its guest's aggression and audience participation. Unfortunately, my Nanna saw me on this mainstream TV show. She was mortified that I've gone on national television and said I was a porn star. I told her it was to shock the audience into some sort of reaction.

Madonna would have done the same...

I told Nanna, I was a glamour model, working for an agency in London that provided actresses for TV work, and that I was paid to say that, which in fact was true. I was a glamour model, and had done some Page 3 work in a national tabloid. So in my eyes I wasn't really lying to my family...

As far as I was concerned, I was a glamour model, working in London... So here I was living this bizarre double life.

I was this self-employed glamour model, travelling the country, working in the adult entertainment industry and playing happy families back home in Manchester.

I paid my taxes and National Insurance like everyone else, so I felt legitimately employed...

However, living contrasting lifestyles, one in Manchester, and the other in London, would create anxiety. It would also aggravate my ADHD and bring on my Obsessive Compulsive Disorder. OCD...

CHAPTER TWENTY-THREE

SURVIVAL

In the spring of 1998, Debbie called to inform me, that I needed to bring my passport with me to London...
She had arranged an assignment for Chloe, and myself to go to Bahrain.
I was so naive,   I   really   had   no idea what was in store, and what danger's Chloe and I would be putting ourselves into...
Chloe was one of Debbie's girls. However, she was a lot older than me and was most definitely a lot more mature than I was. Where, I on the other hand, was impulsive, naive and starry-eyed.
Bahrain! Wow! I was excited, and fixated on seeing more of the world.
I had no fear and was looking forward to going to Bahrain while, to the contrary, Chloe voiced concern and caution.
I hadn't given it a second thought...
I never considered the dangers we would be putting ourselves in too by going to Bahrain. Women were treated very differently in the Middle East. Strict laws were imposed and harsh punishments followed if rules were broken.
On reflection, I should have researched more accurately what we were letting ourselves into, by venturing alone into the Middle East.
I had no idea what was expected of me. No idea where I was staying, and no idea what my purpose was. All I fixated on, was it sounded exotic and glamorous...

So I travelled to London and met Chloe at Debbie's flat.
Debbie met us with our tickets. However there was a catch.

Debbie informed us that in Bahrain, we'd be met by a guy called Mo. He'd paid for the tickets and we'd be expected to work for him. We were to stay in a hotel of Mo's choosing. His clients paid him directly, and not to us. Mo would take his cut first, then share the rest between me and Chloe. The cost of the tickets would also be taken out of what we earned.

Debbie had been sending girls out to the Middle East for some time. We were now her latest. The financial protocol had already been established between Debbie, Mo and his clients.

Debbie had full control over me, and everything she said I believed. My ADHD supports that conception. I was vulnerable and very naive.

Chloe on the other hand, already had her suspicions about going to Bahrain. I will be forever grateful that she had a suspicious nature, because her suspicious behaviour actually did save our lives...

We flew out to Bahrain, glamorous air hostesses saw to our needs and we had a thoroughly pleasant and very relaxing flight.

The complete opposite to what we were about to experience...

I've tried to block out this disastrous episode from my memory. So retelling it will be a little sketchy and very upsetting, but I'll try...

So a moment or two please, while I try to remember the details. My ADHD can be emotionally painful, especially having to recall such horrific events.

Our ordeal started on a high.

We arrived in Bahrain and were greeted by Mo.

We were greeted like princesses, and Mo seemed very pleased to make himself our acquaintance. However, by the time we got to his car we'd been downgraded to hired whores.

There would be worse to come...

He drove us both to an unknown hotel somewhere on the outskirts of Bahrain. He informed us both that this is where we would be staying.

Clients would make their private arrangements directly with Mo. Either they would come visit us directly at the hotel, or they'd arrange to take us somewhere of their choosing.

We arrived at this dodgy unknown hotel, and I could see Chloe wasn't pleased. She was acting edgy and very nervous...

I too felt a sensation of uneasiness. My sixth sense, kicking in something definitely wasn't right about this place.

The Hotel was not as we had expected. It was located in what can only be described as an unsavoury neighbourhood. Definitely a dodgy hotel, in an even dodgier area. Mulling around in this low rate hotel, were local males wearing traditional costumes. They stared menacingly at us, expressing displeasure of our arrival. They were sitting at tables, playing cards, sipping tea and smoking.
A frightening reception to be sure...

Chloe and I sensed their animosity. It was obvious the locals didn't want us there. Reflecting back, I realised we were in a Catch 22 situation, a dilemma from which there was no escape because of conflicting conditions.
Let me explain...
If we didn't earn the money to pay back Mo for the tickets, then we were trapped here until we did, and at the mercy of Mo. So we had to work to pay off our debt. Again how honest would Mo be. We'd no idea how much we owed him, or how honest he'd be when it came to handing us our money.
To me, Mo looked like a dishonest Arabian shark.
It was a no win situation, we were in a perilous position with no control over what we did, where we went, or our own lives.
The locals continued to stare at us. We were white alien females in a country where women hadn't the freedoms, like women have back home.
If looks could kill?
Chloe probably attracted more attention than me. She was dressed more desirably.
She was the typical Barbie. She had long blonde hair extensions, and polished
long nails. A slim waist, fake tan, and fake boobs.
A stunning figure worthy of any man's attention.

I had no idea what I was getting myself into, or how bad this trip would become. I wished my neurodiversity didn't make me so vulnerable, but it does.
I can't help being the way I am. I'm too trusting and people take advantage of that and use it against me...
It was obvious the local men knew why we were there..
Inside the hotel, we were shown to our room. Not perfect but acceptable. It had en-suite facilities and an extra room with a spare bed.
Chloe immediately voiced her objection, she didn't want to stay here and said I shouldn't either. She demanded another hotel in a more populated area. She honestly believed we'd end up dead if we stayed in this local unknown hotel. Looking back, Chloe was actually very accurate.

I didn't know what to believe, as my head was in a spin, unable to concentrate. My sixth sense knew it was wrong, but I couldn't think logically.

I kept trying to convince myself that Debbie wouldn't have sent us here to Bahrain if she believed we were in danger.

Debbie didn't give a shit about us, came Chloe's very honest and accurate response. Debbie was only bothered only about the money we would be earning her, she added. We had to get the hell out of here, Chloe warned.

Mo returned back later to our hotel, this time with two local men. We were ordered to strip down to our underwear and parade ourselves in front of them. We felt like pieces of meat, on display for the highest bidder. No respect had been shown for our femininity at all, but then you forget, we were in the middle east, and such attitudes in countries like this, towards women, were probably the norm.

So there we were, being displayed like meat, in a butcher's shop.
I felt very uncomfortable standing there, being ogled at. Being told to turn this way, that way. It was as if they were in a cattle market and we were animals for sale.

I wasn't surprised when they both selected Chloe. She'd told me, earlier, that they would. She'd warned me, the locals would choose her because she looked like the stereotyped barbie doll that men fantasise about...

I could see Chloe was panicking...
Mo informed her that she would be picked up by a driver and be taken to a location to meet a guy. After the encounter, she would be paid for her services. She was then to return to the hotel and give Mo all the money that the client had given her.

She was instructed to do as the client ordered, and to question nothing...

I recall being instructed later by Mo, that I too had a booking with a local client... I really had no idea the possibility of the danger I was putting myself in.
I was to be collected by a foreign stranger, who would then take me somewhere to perform an unknown sex act, on some unknown man...
What in the actual hell was I about to do?... Chloe was right. But it's too late now. We were in the hands of sex traffickers and we were their commodity.

I was met by a local, who told me to lay down in the back of his car so no one would see me. Once out of sight I was allowed to sit up. I snuck into the car and hid and once the coast was clear I sat up as instructed...

The drive seemed to take forever. I couldn't even tell you where this man was taking me. For all I knew he could be taking me to be gang raped or murdered, beheaded, my body sliced up and fed to the camels. My disappearance would never be investigated. I was a white sex worker, with a pimp named Mo, in a dangerous foreign country, about to meet an unknown client.

How precarious was that?

The car stopped and the driver told me to get out. He instructed me to quickly run to a building that he pointed out. This I do, and find myself in an unpleasant rundown flat with some strange foreign man I could barely look at...

My heart was pounding.

All I kept thinking, was to comply with whatever this man wanted, I wouldn't want him to turn nasty on me.

As it happened, the man turned out to be quite pleasant and my initial fears faded a little. However I still felt a little uneasy, so decided to comply with whatever I was asked to do.

He spoke in broken English, he talked about his family, and whether I enjoyed doing what I did for a living?

His question made me stop and think... Did I enjoy being a sex worker? No, I hated it, but I unintentionally stumbled into this life of vice. Having met Debbie, and doing whatever she compelled me to do. I then unfortunately had lost my job at FX Labs, and needed urgent money to pay the mortgage. I had now gotten myself too far deep into this mess, that I couldn't see a way of getting out of it...

...I complied with the man's request, and afterwards the driver took me back to the hotel. Again I went through the hiding routine in the car.

On entering the hotel, I was verbally accosted by a local man making kiss, kiss sounds. I felt like an animal. He stared at me, making this horrid kissing noise. Clearly he was making fun of me but I dare not retaliate.

I left the insulting local downstairs, and I was ordered by Mo to go to my room. No questions asked. There I had to stay until told otherwise...

Allsorts of unthinkable things rushed to mind. My concerns for Chloe grew. I was very frightened indeed. I was alone feeling vulnerable waiting for Chloe to return...

I walked up and down the room, pacing away my fears for Chloe. My heart was racing and I felt very uneasy. I also had the feeling I was being spied upon by some unseen pervert, through the keyhole of the hotel door...

Our hotel room door didn't quite close properly. An ideal spot for a peeping Tom, to lurk and get his rocks off.

What in the actual hell was we doing here? My brain logically for once thought!

How vulnerable and naive was I to listen to Debbie...

We were in the hands of real sex traffickers and it sent a cold shiver down my spine; it still does, even today and how lucky we were to have escaped their clutches.

Finally Chloe returned. She wasn't at all happy. On the contrary she was extremely angry. She insisted we left, right there and then. She explained, her client had been extremely rude, aggressive and rough. He had treated her inhumanly. She was having no more of this.

Chloe told me that we had to check out immediately from this hell hole of a hotel. It's too dangerous to stay here. She told me that we were to check into a respectable hotel in the centre of Bahrain. There we could then arrange to fly back home.

Chloe ordered a taxi from the reception, and told me to hurry up packing all of my

belongings, we were leaving immediately...

On our way to the new hotel, Chloe rang Debbie and told her what we were doing...

Chloe had a very heated telephone conversation with Debbie...

Debbie informed Chloe that Mo needed to be informed immediately where we were. Debbie said we owed him money for our tickets, and also owed him money, from the clients who had paid us for our services...

Debbie and Mo were the pimps, there is no two ways about that! How in the hell had I even got myself in this predicament...

Debbie was actually more bothered about us paying Mo back the money, than she was about our actual welfare...unbelievable...Chloe had been right about Debbie so it appeared.

We arrived at the hotel, and we both took a hugh sigh of relief.

What an utter transformation. This new hotel being luxury against that dodgy flea pit of an unknown hotel on the outskirts of Bahrain that we'd been imprisoned in.

Chloe informed Debbie that we had arrived at the new hotel. We were to learn from Debbie that Mo was not a happy Arab.

Far from it...

He was somewhat angry. In fact he was fuming that we'd changed hotels, as that had not been on the agenda. Debbie had given Mo the details of our new room number. She informed us that he would be contacting us. Mo relied on Debbie to send him girls and unfortunately we were his latest investment.

Victims are more likely...

Mo phoned our hotel and Chloe dealt with him. Apparently, he wanted us to attend a party that was going on in one of the rooms in the hotel that we were staying in.
They were Saudi citizens looking for female guests...
The laws in Saudi Arabia are much stricter than they were in Bahrain. It seems these guys had come over the border for the weekend to legally have a drink.

We were still beholden to Mo, so we attended the party and realised how
dangerous a situation we'd put ourselves into. Two western white girls, in a room full of Saudi males wanting a good time. Who were most probably worse for wear due to drinking excessively.

It was dangerous and barbaric when looking back...
Chloe attracted the most attention. Her Barbie doll appearance was a huge turn on. She was so different from the local women they were used to seeing, and they homed in on her. Like flies around shit, is the best way to describe this ordeal...

In a separate room, Chloe privately entertained one of them. Then later she would entertain another. However, she feared things were getting out of hand, and when the opportunity arose, we discreetly gave an excuse to leave, promising to return.

We left but never returned...

Back at our room Chloe urgently told me to pack. Chloe told me we were definitely getting out of the hotel and we were going home. Chloe could no longer cope with the abusive demands being asked of her and she feared for both our safety.
I'm not quite sure what happened in that room with those two guys but clearly it
was enough for her to say enough was enough.
We packed our suitcases. Luckily we still had our return tickets. But were they still valid?

When back home, Chloe promised to have strong words with Debbie. We should never have been put in this impossible situation in the first place. Chloe was adamant Debbie should answer to her, and why did she send us out there knowing it wasn't safe...

The situation in Bahrain was deteriorating, fast. Chloe was beginning to worry about Mo. Once Mo knew we had checked out the hotel, he'd be after us...
We were in a desperate situation. We owed this Mo pimp money and no way was he going to let us leave. Chloe knew we had to move fast, get to the airport as soon as possible and board a flight home.

When we first arrived in Bahrain, Mo said he'd be taking our passports, for safekeeping. More to stop us leaving more like... So how fortunate for us, he hadn't.

I dread to think what would have happened to us if he had taken our passports. Forever stuck in this dreadful place for certain and in the hands of Mo the pimp. Scary thought...

Chloe took control. Highlighting the fact that if we stayed we'd probably be raped or murdered. She was determined, we weren't going home in a coffin...

When we finally got to the airport, Chloe was magnificent. She managed to get us seats on a flight back to England that same day.

How? I never will know, but thank God she did.

Forever, we would be looking over our shoulders for Mo. If he should find us God knows what would happen..

We got our flight tickets, then we went through all the security checks at the gate and entered the inner lounge to wait for the announcement to board our plane.

We knew once we were through those gates we'd be safe...
A long glass panel separated the main airport lounge from the inner lounge that we'd just entered. We relaxed somewhat, knowing only people with flight tickets could enter this inner sanctum.

We at last were safe. Or we're we?
It was then we saw him. Standing on the other side of the glass panel was Mo.

He could see us and we could see him.
He glared menacingly at us, slicing a finger across his throat, gesturing he would cut our throats, if he could only get to us.

He couldn't, could he?
A shiver of coldness ran through my body, I realised the real danger we were in.
If it wasn't for Chloe's quick intuition, and awareness of danger I might not be here to tell the tale...
The announcement came to board the plane, and finally we left angry Mo on the runway and flew out of danger never to return again!

The airline were fantastic...On the plane home we got chatting to a Welsh sprint athlete and television presenter of the time. Who ironically had been in Bahrain training, a world faraway from what we had experienced. Fate would have us meeting up again in the future when I lived in Wales, but for now it was an enjoyable chance encounter.

I dread to think what would have happened to us if the airways hadn't let us travel back home for free.

We'd probably be dead, or in some Arabian despot's harem.

Once back on English soil we switched on our mobile phones, and almost immediately Debbie rang.

Chloe was reluctant to speak to her.

Debbie had excuses for everything, and would no doubt have one for what had happened to us. She should have helped us get out of Bahrain, when we asked her too, but she didn't. She was more bothered about her and Mo's money than making sure we were safe. Pure selfish greed.

That image of Mo, gesturing cutting our throats, remained a threat and for quite some time I felt a little insecure. I'd forever be looking over my shoulder to see if Mo was about to carry out his threat.

He never did, but the thought always terrified me.

However, Mo did ring Debbie, demanding his ticket money back. He also wanted money for the hotels we had stayed in as well. The incident was never discussed with me, so I assumed Debbie and Mo came to some arrangement.

After the Bahrain incident my trust in Debbie waned. I was very disappointed with the way she had handled it, and especially her attitude towards me and Chloe.

All she ever cared about was the money. She didn't care about what happened to Chloe and me. That I'll never forget...

I should have gone then, but getting away from Debbie is not that easy.

From the very beginning of our relationship Debbie had misled, manipulated and lied. She set me up for her own greedy needs on many occasions, manipulating my naivety to satisfy her own agendas.

Am I to blame, partly, but that's me I'm afraid. Debbie took advantage of my trust and vulnerability and used it to manipulate me into doing whatever she wanted.

How degrading does that make one feel?

So why do it?

To understand that, you have to understand my condition. My head is batshit crazy most of the time, my ADHD a major contributing factor, I'm afraid. My brain is always erratic, fluttering all over the place, from one thing to another. Never stable. At the time of this Bahrain affair, I was taking three Prozac a day, to help numb my emotions, and anxiety.

So put them all together and what have we got?

An emotionless individual high on dopamine cruising through life without a care in the world. A, bring it on, I can cope and deal with anything, kind of attitude.

Well that's how I saw life at the time. My ADHD is sometimes a godsend, but can also be a hindrance. So I exist in a Topsy-Turvy kind of emotional merry go round.

I guess there's nothing wrong with being the kind and trusting sort, but it caused me a lot of hardship, because people took advantage of my kind nature.

Debbie did and she continued to do so...

It's true, Debbie did use me. I was the new girl on the block so I would be in great demand. The novelty would eventually wear off, so she could get the best cash in while she could. So she had me doing anything and everything while she could and the money came pouring in to her.

I went back home to Manchester. Chloe said she'd never work for Debbie again, but eventually she did... That's what Debbie does, she cleverly manipulates you around her way of thinking, and you agree to go back and work for her...

Debbie called me often, offering me more work, but I needed time to consider my options. I told her I needed time to recover from the Bahrain fiasco, and I'd get back in touch with her when I was ready.

I tried to blank out the nightmare that was Bahrain and what Mo might have done to us. I thought about other girls that would be sent to him and wondered if they'd be treated similar to Chloe and I. Knowing Mo for the shark he was, I'm sure they too will be swimming in dangerous waters.

So back in Manchester I went about my normal routine. Bahrain becoming a fading memory. So it was back to the gym, seeing Wayne and going about a normal life. However the lure of London overturned normality, and the following week my suitcase was packed and off I'd go back to the capital and back into the hands of Debbie... it's all about survival...

CHAPTER TWENTY-FOUR

HOLLYWOOD

So again the weeks went by. Back and forth to London from Manchester.

I'd travel to London, I'd perform in scenes for various porn directors and pose for many glamour photoshoots. In Manchester, the opposite, it was back to reality, back to some kind of normality...

I didn't really trust Debbie. But she could manipulate and control a situation to her own advantage.

Take Bahrain for instance.

She said I was one of her best girls, but I'm sure she said that to all her girls.

It was her style. Boosting egos got results. You felt important and therefore more likely to conform and follow her orders.

I've been there and done that...

My ADHD fixates on such praise, especially if you're low on self-esteem. I wasn't at my best, far from it, but when Debbie informed me, she'd arrange for me to work in the USA, in Hollywood. A rush of dopamine sent me on an addictive high, and I fixated on becoming that famous singing star, I'd craved all my life to become. Like Madonna I'd find fame in America. Maybe not as a singer at first, hopefully that would come later, but as an international porn star.

Thankfully, memories of Bahrain had faded into unpleasant memories. On my return to London, I put aside that disaster, and concentrated on my work here in England. It's been months since then, so best left forgotten.

With ADHD we forget and remember things haphazardly. It's a random process that causes confusion. We also struggle to express what's in our heads. What we think, and what we say, might not always match up, hence our frustration. Oh, look, here I go again, away off on a tangent.

Back to my USA trip.

I have to say I was very excited about going to America. Debbie reassured me, everything would be okay and promised me it wouldn't be like the disaster of Bahrain. "Just porn" she reassured me, "No being a call girl."

You only had to look at the successful USA Porn stars that were around in the 90s to know I was about to embark on a life-changing mission.

I went to the USA on my own...

Chloe had stopped working for Debbie. An amicable arrangement by all concerned. Debbie couldn't manipulate Chloe as she could me. However, I do think the failure of Bahrain was her main reasoning for not going to the USA.

I, on the other hand, didn't really give a shit...

Whatever the USA threw at me, was okay. The fact I was going to Los Angeles, and Hollywood was a dream come true.

I mean, make it in Hollywood, and you've made it. That was my vision. I was going to become a Hollywood Porn Star, and bathe in all the fame that came with it.

I flew from London to Los Angeles by myself. I was so excited, I kept smiling
to myself, unable to believe I was actually fulfilling a lifelong dream.
I was actually going to Hollywood. I kept metaphorically pinching myself, to reassure myself I wasn't dreaming. Nothing would spoil this moment, not even my horrendous experiences in Bahrain. I was fixating on a high dopamine rush.

America, here I come...

I arrived in L.A and I remember how hot it was when I first stepped off the plane. I'd never imagined how hot LA could get, it was scorching.

I went to L.A in the summer of 1998, and while there, I would be celebrating my twenty third birthday. In my minds-eye, I was getting old, time was ticking by fast, and as I saw it, I needed to become a celebrity really soon.

I was briefed by Debbie before I left...

I was staying with an agent, a friend of hers called Brad.

I had no idea what this Brad agent looked like, or what kind of a guy he was, other than he was Debbie's friend, and could get me work. Another Debbie then, I told myself...

Brad, met me at the airport. I immediately took a dislike to him.
My God, he was gross. With the clothes he wore, he looked like he'd stepped back out of the 1970s. He was a short guy, with comb over black hair and a comical squeaky American accent.

Stereotypical of the 1970s porn star agent.

His dominating manner and dictatorial introduction was enough for me to dislike him enormously. I didn't like him, not even one little bit. I found him highly annoying. I wanted to like him, but clearly that wasn't going to happen.

I know Debbie controlled and manipulated me, but this guy was obnoxiously unbearable. His demands on me were quite unacceptable.

Brad would allow girls to stay with him, free of charge, provided they slept in the same bed with him. Initially he insisted I slept with him in his bed. I refused. We argued and clearly my insubordination wasn't going to be tolerated.

Submit to his will, I wouldn't.
He called Debbie and informed her, I wasn't conforming, I was difficult, and so he was sending me back to the UK...

Again, that phrase was difficult. Uncanny that, how so many people have used those words to describe me. True I was difficult, but I'm nobody's sex slave, especially not his. We would argue constantly...
I was being difficult, he kept telling me. No porn worker had ever treated him like this, and he'd expect me to conform to his demands.

No way...
He told me that if I wouldn't agree to sleep with him, and do as he asks then he wouldn't find me work... Blackmail to the highest order.

I called Debbie on the phone, she insisted I did as he asked, and against my better judgement I gave in to his demands and under protest gave in...

My forceful abuser had what we girls, in the business, call a micro cock. What the hell is a micro cock, I hear you asking...

It was a comical excuse for a penis. A physical abnormality or the result of some unknown medical condition. Whatever, it was a freak of nature, and I presumed this was the only way he could get sexual partners was to be a porn agent. I aggressively humiliated him about his abnormality, so much so that he just let me sleep in the other room on my own...He told Debbie I was a nightmare, but somehow reluctantly decided I could stay.

While in L.A, I performed in numerous porn scenes, working with various porn production companies... I was taken to 'Silicon Valley' to the studios of a few well-known production companies who sell porn movies worldwide.

Very slick and professional studios they are too.

This was the real thing, true professional actors earning big time money. I felt somewhat of a fraudster against such world class connoisseurs. I didn't have the Barbie image everybody seemed to want at that very time.

I performed in many screen tests and was told regularly I needed to alter my appearance. I needed to lose weight and dye my hair, possibly blonde. Probably not the best thing to say to someone who spent years battling anorexia and bulimia.

Being slim opens doors, gives you status and success, that's what I was constantly being told. I believed this utter bullshit, and as a result I became yet again seriously ill with an eating disorder trying to achieve it.

I wasn't fat or overweight...

However, such comments, in my past, have triggered uncontrollable compulsive behaviours. But now that I'm older, I can resist those compulsive urges. However, such comments can hurt, especially when you've spent most of your adult life battling with it.

My first assignment in the USA was actually in Beverly Hills. Can you imagine how insane that felt? A girl from Grimsby, in L.A making a porn film in Beverly Hills. The location was a Hollywood mansion, once owned by Jean-Claude Van Damme.

It was the classic multi million pound Hollywood mansion that overlooked Hollywood.

Inside was unbelievable.

It had an infinity pool that overlooked the Hollywood Hills. The house was breath-taking and the backdrop to my USA movie debut.

Brad, the creepy agent, would drop me off and pick me up like he was my pimp. Embarrassingly, I would have to conform to this as he was my agent and negotiator for my fee.

Before starting any porn work in America, like in the UK, I had to have an HIV test. This would be a regular check-up. What I did was a risky business. It's a dangerous occupation and you don't take risks. Health check-ups are essential and I attended them all.

So with the Beverly Hills filming done, Brad took me to another place. I was taken to Venice Beach. Venice Beach is famous for its muscle men, skating on roller boots, cyclists and the backdrop for endless movies.

The shoot had a cheesy storyline and had me being followed by a pervert with a camera. Who followed me around, taking photographs, and videos and we'd end up in this pervert's apartment...

That was the plot.

It must have looked realistic because at one point an ordinary bloke, not involved with the filming, became very concerned that I was being followed by a pervert taking pictures and videos of me.

That amused me...

There's no nudity on Venice Beach, and you certainly can't do porn scenes. So it was all done in this cheeky amateur way. After the shoot, I went with the producer on a coastal road trip to Malibu. We stopped at a roadside food shack, and had the most incredible milk shake.

I was really impressed.

I have to say my time in L.A was spent having lots of fun. It was a very exciting place to make porn. It was in Hollywood for God's sake, what could be better?

However, I became ill, originally with an upset stomach. Then with chronic cramps and diarrhoea. I felt very poorly for a few days. I thought it might have been something I'd eaten, or even heatstroke and dehydration.

I did lose quite a lot of weight, while I was in L.A. I became quite skinny, so why I kept being told to lose weight still remains a mystery...

When on days not working, I wandered around L.A exploring the locations. It got me out of Brad's dingy place.

Life was so different out here. Oversized and crowded.

Large cars, large buildings, food outlets around every corner selling large portions of food and drink. A walk around the block revealed more of the same, but even larger.

Everything here was colossal, and I was loving all of it...

I'd fantasise about Madonna, and imagine her walking along sunset Boulevard. Then my mind started to wonder... What about all those famous Hollywood film stars? Their handprints were found along Hollywood's Walk of Fame, for all to see and admire.

Maybe one day my handprint might join them...

I'd venture further and take in sightseeing tours. I visited the Hollywood Hills and saw the famous Hollywood sign. Not as big as I thought it would be, but I saw it. I visited Sunset Boulevard, and the Mall keeping a watchful eye on all the expensive shops and boutiques hoping to get a glimpse of a celebrity or two.

I loved Hollywood...

I wished I could have stayed longer. Obviously there was a time limit on my stay. My return to the UK was imminent...

However I did spend my birthday here, and much to my annoyance Brad bought me a birthday cake and he even treated me to a birthday meal at a restaurant. I still didn't like Brad but we tolerated each other.

My time in Hollywood was different...

It was a shame I had to stay with the dodgy agent Brad. Brad had already informed Debbie he never wanted me to stay with him ever again.

The feeling was mutual. No love lost there then...

I've experienced being a porn star in Hollywood, and that was a dopamine rush.

I wasn't to be a famous Hollywood actress, or the next Madonna. But I got the opportunity to be somebody in L.A. even if it was short lived...

That memory will always be with me, along with all my experiences.

It wasn't like Bahrain, it was a once-in-a-lifetime opportunity that not many people get. I did it and have no regrets for that.

So my time in L.A was over, time to fly back to London and continue my double life existence. So what did my next adventure have in store for me?   As my mentor, Madonna quotes; "How could it hurt you when it looks so good...

CHAPTER TWENTY-FIVE

SPANISH LESSONS

So I'm back in London at Debbie's flat. Fresh after my USA trip.
I'd experienced the porn industry on so many levels. However, Debbie had been right when she said I was the new girl on the block. Initially I would find lots of work. However, my popularity would fade, but not just yet...
My next adventure awaited me in Spain, with a European production company...

I would be working alongside, recognised porn experts, in Europe. However it was far from the professional set up I'd experienced in Hollywood.
On the USA circuit you always felt like a celebrity... But what the hell, it was another adventure abroad...

Debbie, for these porn assignments, would rotate me around with different girls. For my Spanish assignment she allocated Sam. Remember her, the actress I met in Manchester at Nik's studio.
So Sam and I travelled to Spain together. We arrived at the location in Spain, to a beautiful Spanish villa with a swimming pool. It almost felt like a holiday rather than work. We were also next to the beach. It was great fun.
We later went to the studio of the production company and filming began.
The film had a soundtrack, in which I was asked to record vocals. I went to a professional recording studio to record it. The film's script was based around the main characters being pop stars and musicians, hence the need to record a song.
You can imagine my excitement and delight. Recording an actual song in a recording studio. This time I'll make it, I told myself. Fame at last...

I'd spent a lifetime trying to achieve being a popstar. I will become that famous recording artist I told myself. Look here I am, recording a song, in a studio in Spain. I was thrilled at the opportunities this would bring.

But there was a drawback...

The leading actress, a very pretty girl, would frustrate my ambitions...She was contracted to sing, with me, on the record.

The problem being, she just couldn't sing a tune, she was tone deaf! She kept singing all the notes way out of tune. However, when challenged, she accused ME of singing out of tune.

To say I was pissed off with her, would be an understatement. She not only ruined the song, but my future ambitions...

But that's show business for you.

The shoot however was very relaxed, the film fun to make, with all us actors and crew members having lots of breaks and downtime.

It was Spain and the sun beckoned...

So off set, we went to explore and enjoyed ourselves. We went jet-skiing and did all the tourist bits, and chilled out round the swimming pool.

All the actors and actresses had built up a great relationship with each other and formed great friendships. We all felt relaxed in each other's company.

As you know my ADHD has no boundaries. I do things without thinking, without any thought of being rational.

I'd never in my life, up to this point, done a live sex show in front of an audience. Yes, I've made porn films, but never a live sex show on a stage.

So whilst here in Spain, the production company wanted to promote the film, this involved doing a live sex show in front of an audience, in a nightclub.

So do I do it, I questioned myself?

Well, I am an exhibitionist, but performing a live sex with onlookers was exhibitionism on a far higher level. Am I that much of an exhibitionist I asked myself? I'm impulsive. Yes, I am, with absolute no cares or thoughts in the world.

Please open your mind here; Forget the actual sexual act. When I say, "I loved it" what I actually mean is that I loved the attention it created.

I rushed on the fact that people clapped and cheered. They were worshipping me. My ADHD drives that dopamine rush to dizzy heights. I was riding high on their applause, I was fulfilling their fantasy and in doing so fulfilling my need to be loved and appreciated. I was feeling as high as a kite on my ADHD dopamine rush.

Reaching an euphoric out of the body experience high, like what someone on narcotics expects to feel, but with me, it wasn't, this was a natural ADHD high, the one my neurodivergent brain craved.

Dopamine in abundance, I was high, rushing on pure natural dopamine.

I imagined I was Madonna, attracting all the attention she does when she performs. I fantasized being like her on a stage, her audience adoring and worshipping her.

To some people, what I did was highly controversial. Throughout my life, many people have been offended by my inappropriate behaviours in one way or another. This however then, was my then profession, I performed and people watched. I was an actress simply acting out a role. So making the video, recording a song, and performing a live sex show on a stage in Spain were once-in-a-lifetime experiences.

Over the years, I've been repeatedly asked, what was it like making porn films? The answer is simple. It's a job, like any other, except in this job you're paid for sex. Like any occupation, health and safety are paramount, so you take care of yourself. You had regular screening for the usual sexual diseases and I found, most of the people in the porn industry, were probably the healthiest and cleanest of any worker in any occupation. It was as simple as that. When all was said and done, I was trying to earn a living, like everybody else.

During my days doing porn, there was no internet or social media. So obtaining the material I was making, could only be obtained from sex shops, mail order companies, or even from the top shelves of certain newsagents. Obtaining porn, back then, was an under the counter kind of secret most people kept to themselves.

I honestly thought I was not hurting anyone. No one would see these films because I didn't think anybody knew I was doing them. It was my secret, shared only with a trusted few.

However, I had no idea how this would affect my future or that my past escapades would be used against me.

With my work done in Spain, as always I'd return back home to Manchester.

Back to my secretive double life and my adventures were set to continue on in Sleazy City...

CHAPTER TWENTY-SIX

SLEAZY CITY

So onto my next adventure making porn films in Europe, this time it would be in Paris... However, before I continue on with my story, I need to address a few things about my ADHD; At this particular point in my life, understanding now, how my undiagnosed ADHD, had affected me.
I'm beginning to understand why I did what I did, and why I made some of those bad erratic decisions.
I was at the time taking up to three Prozac a day, for depression and anxiety...
I believed Prozac did help me cope with my porn and escorting escapades.
ADHD can also make you very depressed and anxious, so taking this into consideration, I was being bombarded from all sides with debilitating conditions. Whether Prozac was an appropriate drug to give me is also up for debate. I took it for approximately a whole decade, so whether this along with my ADHD contributed to my decision-making is conjecture.

However, I'm amazed how people can quickly judge you for taking antidepressants. Back in the late 90's, people rarely spoke openly about mental health, as we openly do today. Had it been in today's time, I'm sure, a better understanding of my condition would have been judged less, and with more compassion.
Let me demonstrate an example of this ignorance and judgement...

I was being my friendly bubbly self, and got chatting to a man I knew in the gym. We talked, he listened and I was quite open to him about me taking Prozac for depression. I thought no more about it...

However, returning to the gym the next day, on my arrival, I was taken to one side, by the manager. The man I'd been talking to yesterday, had said, after our conversation, he'd discovered four hundred pounds had gone missing, and because I was taking Prozac, thinking me to be a mental case, accused me of stealing it.

I was mortified to think how innocently discussing my mental health problems with this man had made me a thief...

My ADHD brain had problems dealing with that.

To be accused of something I hadn't done would adversely affect me. I take things literally, not able at times, to discriminate fact from fiction like a normal brain would. So being accused of theft left me somewhat traumatised.

God knows why he should accuse me of stealing his money, but he had and that upset me. I've never stolen anything in my life. I work bloody hard to earn my own money. I always have done and always will. I did, however, confront the man over his accusation. He wasn't having any of it, and went on to accuse me of being a mental case on Prozac, and went away convinced I'd stolen his money.

So, attitudes such as this, as I've encountered on many occasions. It's as if being honest, and disclosing my mental health situation, which my ADHD inadvertently makes me do sometimes, is an excuse for society to unjustly hang the appropriate label on me. In this case, a thief. I'm no thief and will never ever be one.

This incident still upsets me. With ADHD you feel guilty for doing something you haven't done. Being accused falsely, messes with your head and you go overboard to prove our innocence. To clear the air, even though I was innocent of any wrong doing, I said I'll give him the money.

Again my ADHD is taking control...

I don't know why I said that, because it made me look guilty. I wasn't, but that's what suffering with ADHD causes you to do.

So let's roll on to my next adventure....back to Sleazy City...

I left Manchester with Sy, he was still travelling to London to do his many auditions.

I loved driving backwards and forwards to London in those days.

The motorways weren't as busy as they are now. I was a fearless traveller, an expert map reader, so I really didn't get lost.

I would play my CDs, in the car and sing and drive along to Madonna and other great artists of the day.

The music prompted memories, my favourite being, Madonna's' Ray of Light' album. It was legendary. Driving to London, I would play it full blast, and the memories would come flooding back.

Here I go again, going off at a tangent. I was living this crazy double life in Manchester and London, and enjoying every minute of it.... On reaching London, I dropped Sy off at his friend's flat...

Sam and I had been assigned to go to Paris, we were to work for another European production company. Before we travelled, we met Debbie who quickly briefed us, as to what was expected in Paris. We were to travel by Eurostar to Paris...

As mentioned in a previous chapter I used to enjoy working with Sam, purely because she made it all so much fun. We always had a laugh together. She made our assignments together, one big holiday. Sam was easy to get along with and like me got on with whatever she was asked to do.

So Sam and I are on the Eurostar, heading to make yet another porn film, but this time it's in Paris...

Sounds so glamorous doesn't it?

I guess, yet another once-in-a-life time opportunity.

On reaching Paris, we were picked up and driven to a large French chateau. It was absolutely stunningly beautiful. I wanted to share its incredible beauty with my loved ones, but unfortunately that might give rise to my reasons for being there, and I just couldn't let that slip out now, could I?

I knew, if they knew, it would upset and disappoint them. So I kept myself to myself and admired its beauty silently from within. I've experienced working in some amazing locations around the world, and now this chateau in France.

Yet another stunning location.

A full production crew manned the set, here in Paris. Such crews aren't cheap and these were obviously professionals. A lot of thought, money and expertise had gone into the making of this film.

Before filming, I would sign the required documents, giving permission for the company, making the film, all the legal rights to my performance. This allowed them to make commercial videos of me, and distribute them with my consent.

I didn't receive any royalties either. I was paid a one off fee for performing and that was all. Such videos were reproduced and sold all over the world. I never ever read the consent forms, I just signed them as instructed to do...signing my rights away.

So in Paris, Sam and I performed at the chateau. It was hectic, we performed a lot of girly stuff together. Very cheesy and typical 90s vintage porn. More than likely, we got dubbed over, with the appropriate European languages. Proper cheesy stuff it was too. I, as usual, was being swept along by my ADHD madness in control. The numbing effects of Prozac also added to my, 'devil may care,' euphoria.

But to tell the truth, my memory of those days is very sketchy and as curiosity killed the cat, maybe it's best to let certain sleeping dogs lie...

I was controlled, it's true by Debbie, who unwittingly, I agree, used my undiagnosed neurodiversity to get her way. Like the dysfunctional creature that I was back then, I followed her lead.

To enlighten my reader I need to retrace my steps.

Being a porn star seemed quite glamorous. You got your own make-up artist, a hairstylist and lots of attention. You were generally treated with respect and you felt important. Qualities that fed my dopamine rush...

I was a professional, acting out my scenes, as directed, with professionalism.

No different to any other profession.

So back to Paris...

The Parisian shoot had many scenes and we worked long hours. Sam kept me amused as she always did making these movies.

I can remember nearly slicing my finger off in one of the scenes.

I was asked to move a sofa, which had a protruding metal nail that cut my leg and sliced my finger. Carnage and blood was everywhere...

The director went ballistic, aiming his anger towards the makeup artist who'd innocently asked me to move the sofa. I still have the un-faded scars, on my hand and leg, from that Paris shoot. In my relative short period in the porn industry, I worked with quite a lot of European production companies. Many of them came over to the UK and usually Sam and I made ourselves available for filming, should we be required.

Other girls, under Debbie's protection, were also recruited and such companies found English girls successful porn actresses. Many of the girls under Debbie's care would make successful careers in the industry. There was Lucy to name but one, a major porn star in the making. However a girl called Jess, having succeeded in Europe, had a disastrous adventure when she went to Australia.

Jess wasn't the brightest button in the box and fucked up trying to get there. But more about her and Australia later in my story...

So this was my life. In London I was doing all things immoral, and in Manchester, I was seeking normality. In Manchester, there was Wayne to offer stability, and on the phone there was my Mum, to be reassured of my wellbeing. She knew nothing of the true adventures, nor did my Dad. I, of course, preferred it that way, as I didn't want to disappoint them.

I kept to myself. My private life was for my eyes only. That way I didn't have to explain my double life to anyone but myself.

However, I did meet up with an old school friend, whilst visiting Mum in Grimsby. Now I kind of thought she would have been open-minded about such things. So I told her about my Page 3 exposure. I would have possibly disclosed much more, had she not reacted so horrified, on hearing what I'd done.

I can't imagine how she'd have reacted, had I gone further and told her more what I really got up to.
In her eyes, I'd degraded myself, let myself down. She'd been very judgmental, her words unpleasantly scathing of what I'd done. At the time I took her comments to heart, and felt hurt and somewhat deflated. I just felt she was unjustly putting me down. However, on reflection, possibly there was some truth in what she said. After all, she lived a completely different life to me, so possibly in her world, I would probably be considered somewhat immoral. Possibly, if my old school friend had travelled the same roads I had, and undergone the same experiences I'd had, then she might have seen things differently. But of course, she hadn't. She led the normal life, a life I only encountered in Manchester, so I could honestly understand her concern for me.
We parted friends, but I knew I'd have to do a lot of explaining, if we were to re-establish our old school friendship...

I see things in pictures, I'm not at all confident in expressing things into words. My brain races along at a breakneck speed. I'm likened to the spinning wheels of a ticking watch, forever turning, never stopping. I have millions of flashbacks, stored up in my brain, a million images of my life, stored away in memory.
    Accessing them becomes a chore.
Having opened the box to access one memory, it closes, and is quickly replaced by another. So it unfolds, the pictures of my life.
    Capturing them before the lid closes is art. Hopefully, I'm successfully doing that now, through the pages of this book. Writing this diary has been a very satisfying therapy helping me overcome my life traumas and finding some inner peace. At times, it's been hard, truly emotionally tearful. It's been an emotive soul search for the truth....

A roller coaster of a ride that will continue to excite and enthral my reader.
But for now, let me finish this chapter, quoting the title of director,
Serio Leone's epic spaghetti western. Still to come... 'The Good, The Bad and The Ugly,' parts of my sensational diary...

CHAPTER TWENTY-SEVEN

JESSIE

So, Debbie informed me that myself and Jess, were booked to fly to Australia, to work with a porn production company based in Melbourne.

How exciting was that? Australia. Wow!

I have to say I was incredibly excited about this opportunity of going to Australia. My parents had spent a holiday over there visiting relatives, so I guess I felt I had some kind of emotional attachment with the country, through my family connections.

Our tickets had already been purchased for us by the production crew in OZ.

Whom Debbie was liaising with, and all we had to do was get ourselves there.

However, there was one small problem. We were informed, by Debbie, that we had to tell the Australian passport control, we were tourists on holiday.

The Australian authorities had strict rules on who could and couldn't enter the country. And if we were to tell them the real reason for our visit, we of course would be refused entry and be sent packing on the next plane home.

However, if we were to fool the customs officers into letting us in, we would have a Melbourne address. However, we had no other contact details, no telephone numbers, nothing. We'd have no idea who would meet us, or what we were expected to do.

I sensed another Debbie disaster waiting around the corner...

I can remember picking up Jess from her house in Yorkshire and driving down to London to the airport.

Jess was a simple girl, a sandwich short of a picnic, if the truth be told. Not the brightest button in the box.

If anyone was going to fuck up this trip to Australia, it would be her.

The flight to Australia was uncomfortably long, having to sit in the cheapest seats available. Rigid and unpleasant. I was just bored shitless. My attention span is going AWOL. We flew to Bangkok, refuelled and on to Sydney. From there we flew to Melbourne.

A twenty seven hour flight in total. It was horrendous. But we made it.

Now to face customs.

I told Jess what not to say at customs. Don't tell them we're here to make porn films, we're here on holiday, visiting friends. She said she understood, and would do just that.

But would she?

Queuing at customs was confusing. First in one line, then redirected to another.

My sixth sense kicked in and I knew this wasn't going to go at all well for us. I went through customs first. When asked the reason for my visit, I churned out my practised response.

I was on holiday, visiting friends.

They asked where I was staying and offered them the address Debbie had given us.

So far, so good, then they asked Jess. Disaster was about to erupt.

She blurts out, she thinks she's on holiday, and when asked where she was staying, mumbled, not sure.

So alarm bells started ringing in the minds of the customs officials. Because we were together the next thing I knew my suitcase was being searched. Unfortunately several of my items came under scrutiny along with my PVC porn outfits and accessories. Literally the customs guy was lifting them up and looking at me as if to say, well what kind of a holiday are you expecting.

Jesse's suitcase followed, and as I feared, she had bought receipts from being a call-girl!

I knew she was a bit scatty, but bringing evidence you were a call-girl, in your suitcase was asking for trouble.

Despite a barrage of excuses, the custom officers were having none of it.

Our nightmare got worse. The more we argued, the deeper we'd sink.

What a complete shit storm of a mess we were in. Thanks to dilly Jessy and her call-girl receipts.

In erratic desperation, I said I had a cousin who was a lawyer based in Sydney. They asked me to give more details about my cousin Peter. My cousin Peter was a successful lawyer. So I boasted to customs that he was a very successful lawyer. I impulsively asked customs to call him. This they did, and of course he hadn't a bloody clue what the hell was going on...

Why should he?

He had no idea that I was even in Australia. Looking back at what I did, what the hell was I thinking, bringing my innocent family into all this?

Peter, would tell me, the custom officers suspected we were coming into the country to be prostitutes. I of course denied it, but his voice told me how confused and shocked he was.

I was there to make a porn film but what the hell, I wasn't going to tell customs that, or cousin Peter. The phone hung up, I was feeling very embarrassed, why had I dragged Peter into all of this. I panicked and thought Peter might call my Mum, to ask her what was going on, which would have seriously gotten me into trouble at home.

Fortunately he didn't. Many years later, I would meet Peter, at a family wedding, here in England, and we would laugh off the incident. All in the past, we agreed, and nothing more was ever said about it again.

Again, this incident with Peter in Australia, was a classic example of my ADHD. I acted erratically, illogically. Not considering the consequences of what I was doing or how it would affect Peter. I acted on impulse, and as always hoped things wouldn't go tits up.

They did!

I do believe our interrogators at the airport had sympathy for us, and I'm sure deep down, they felt quite sorry for us. I think they realised we were quite harmless, however because of the incriminating objects found in our suitcase, especially Jesse's receipts, they had no alternative but to deport us, and to send us home on the next available plane.

We were to be put on the same plane we arrived on, after it had been refuelled and turned around ready to return to England.

I don't think we were in Australia for more than four or five hours.

I was truly pissed off with the whole incident and especially with Jess. If only she'd have done what I'd asked. But no! She had to bring those stupid receipts with her.

And Look where that got us.

Deported!

What would Debbie say? Was anybody's guess, she wasn't pleased, that's for sure.

In Jesse's defence, Jess said she was sorry, but why fetch those blasted receipts? Jess said she liked to keep everything together, so she had control of everything. My God, and I thought I was bad, with my controlling behaviour.

So back to my Australian fiasco...

I do remember the custom guy actually smiling and I do believe he saw the funny side of our dilemma.

We were very lucky that we didn't get our passports confiscated or be banned from entering Australia.

More embarrassment was to follow. We were told to collect our suitcases from the baggage carousel. The customs officers hadn't closed my suitcase properly, so dangling out of my case, in full view of everyone, going round and round the carousel, were my sexy, PVC outfits and a rather revealing object. On our journey back to England, the air crew felt sorry for me and Jess. They took a shine to me, and informed the pilot of what had happened, and he invited me to sit in the cockpit to experience take-off and landing.

This, of course, was before 911 when pilots could do this.

Jess wasn't in the cockpit with me, and slept most of the way home. When we landed in Bangkok, the pilots changed, and I wasn't allowed in the cockpit from there on. I sat back in my seat having experienced two memorable take-offs and landings...

We were absolutely beyond exhausted when we finally landed in London. We decided not to go to Debbie's flat, and on Jess's request, I drove from London, to Yorkshire to take her home. I should never have done this, considering how dangerously delirious I felt.

I was on autopilot.

I got Jess home and then set off for Manchester, and hopefully for a very long sleep. I must have been speeding because the next thing I remember was a blue light flashing in my rear mirror.

This is all I needed. One, more bloody disaster after another.

I pulled over, stopped, and a policeman got out of his patrol car and came over to me. He asked me if I knew what speed I was doing, and then I started to cry quite hysterically.

I was so overtired, so distressed.

In my hysterics, I blurted out, I'd just been deported from Australia which had been a horrific experience and I just wanted to get home and go to bed.

I turned on the charm, and said I was sorry. I showed him my passport and the recently dated Australian stamp, to prove my story.

Fortunately, the police officer believed my story and took pity on me. He gave me a warning, suggesting I slowed down and drove at a safer speed. It was a very dangerous road I was speeding along, and I should have taken more care of my speed.

Thankfully no speeding ticket was issued.

When I finally got home, my head was throbbing. My body was shaking, my nerves on edge. I even had a nosebleed.

I went to bed without unpacking my suitcase and slept for over twenty four hours. Physically my body was reacting to the trauma and pressures I'd been subjected to over the last two to three days. I was unwell, my body dangerously out of sync, and I needed time to recover.

When I recovered, I eventually spoke to Debbie. She was very unhappy with me. The production team in Australia, had questioned Debbie, over our absence, and were obviously unhappy. They'd paid for our tickets and we never turned up. Debbie had been quite sharp with me. Probably, she was still pissed off over Bahrain, and my attitude towards Brad when in the USA.

I wasn't in a good place with Debbie, not at all...

I had a friend, Louise, a journalist at a tabloid newspaper. She was always looking for stories. You got paid for stories, if published. So, I got Louise to do a short story about my experience with customs in Australia.

This she did and it was published. It was a win, win situation for me.

However, I never did go back to Australia. I've thought about it, on several occasions, but was so haunted by what happened to me out there, I couldn't do it...

CHAPTER TWENTY-EIGHT

EROTIC

I was fixated on Madonna, who'd appeared in a 80s soft porn film called '
A Certain Sacrifice' and that had inspired me...

Richard is an Italian pornstar, director and producer.

All everybody talked about, in the porn industry, was Richard. All the best pornstars had worked with him.

At this moment in time, my involvement with his work came through my association with Candy, a friend of Debbie's. Candy was famous for doing glamour modelling. She had met Richard, fell in love, and then got herself into the porn industry, and her world dramatically changed.

Richard was renowned for making violent porn films. People get slapped, spat upon and the sex is rather violent. If I'm honest, I wasn't really looking forward to working with Candy on a scene. Intuition, and that gut feeling, told me this wasn't going to be pleasant.

In fact I hated every minute of it...

I've done plenty of porn films, and most have been with respectful actors, considerate directors and understanding producers. With film crews who respected the art and dealt with the subject professionally. However, with Richard his productions are very unpredictable with an edgy climax.

This I assume is the reason why he was so popular.

What you see in Richard's porn films are real. You fear the worst and you get it!

I was going to be in a scene, filmed in London.

Candy was a complete nut, and did whatever Richard told her to do, without question. I realised now, they were obsessed with each other, a vile and dangerous relationship if ever there was one.

Candy was wild, there was no doubt about that, and rode the pornographic horse to the extreme. I feared the outcome, pushing the thoughts of what was to come, to the back of my mind.

The result was a painful memory, best forgotten.

Before we'd even begun, I'd had an alteration with Richard, who'd said if I didn't comply, he wasn't going to pay me.

I got quite shitty about it. I called Debbie and told her Richard was threatening me. She tried to smooth it over, but I was being difficult.

I should have walked out, it didn't feel right, my vibes were telling me to get the hell out of there. They were not the kind of people I wanted to be with, I wasn't their kind of porn star.

At the time, Richard said he could make me a very famous pornstar. Such was his command of the porn industry. He could crush you, or make you, such was his influence.

I wanted none of that. He was a narcissistic manipulative bully and I wanted none of his bullshit.

I compromised for Debbie's sake, and remained. Richard in the porn world, was a legend, and here I am, challenging his authority.

The scene began with Candy slapping my face. I remember it was a real slap and on impulse I wanted to slap her back. Obviously I didn't but I sure as hell wanted to. But that was Richard, forcing you into violence, you're his puppet and he pulled the strings.

To those who are reading this, I promised the truth. My involvement in the porn industry really happened and the various people I got involved with have had a very damaging effect on me. With lots of reservations, I regret nothing.

I made the film, it was the typical porno of its time, and featured Richard's
Candy as its star. I was set up to be humiliated in the film and that's what they did.

As you know by now, I don't like to be out of control, and I felt way out of control in this movie. I was way out of my depth.

I just went ahead with it because that's what I do. At the time I thought myself an actress. This wasn't for me at all.

If I'm totally honest, Debbie groomed and manipulated me into this business, luring me with lofty thoughts of becoming a star.
All I ever wanted was to be famous, so I went along with it.
Now, instead of being famous, I felt infamous.
I felt utterly depressed after working with Richard and Candy.
My mind wandered back to the time when Kim and Dean, had raped me and again that feeling of being taken advantage of, overwhelmed me.

I took a bit of a nose dive. I felt lost, my sparkle no longer sparkled and I felt despondent. Feeling sorry for one's self, is definitely not for me. I'm more resilient than that. I'd gone through hell on many occasions, and come out smiling, on the other side. So I wasn't going to let this porno thing get the better of me. On the contrary, it inspired me to do better.

So what next I thought? How about the music business? If I could only get a shot at becoming a singing star I'd become rich and famous, just like I've always wanted to be.

However, working with Richard was not for me and I'm sure he was pleased to see the back of me. I hold no grudges and wish him well...

My experiences over these years had hardened me and I was able to overcome most obstacles. Not all my porn productions were like Richard. There were some good guys.

I'd been asked by Debbie to travel to Reading and do a scene for a UK Porn Legend. He was a popular 90s porn star and producer and his productions were very amateur, but funny. Wayne randomly decided he was going to come with me to support me on this particular shoot.

He'd never asked before so it was a bit of a surprise. I insured Wayne to drive my Vauxhall Tigra, and he insisted on driving me to Reading. I was a little bit apprehensive considering he'd crashed my other car.

We set off on the motorway to Reading.... However, just before we arrived a police car pulled us over...

The police officer said Wayne had been driving over 100 mph. As an excuse for Wayne speeding, I started crying explaining I was pregnant and needed the toilet. It was a lie, the policeman quite rightly saw through, and Wayne was booked for speeding. Which led to a year driving ban...Wayne didn't have much luck when it came to my cars!

Porn fascinates people, and my porn past certainly does. It's apparent, when people find out you've done porn, they tend to perceive you somewhat differently. Regardless of the reasons why you ended up doing porn in the first place. I didn't go out of my way to be a pornstar, it was an unplanned destiny. That fateful day meeting Ross in that Manchester studio, and the rest is now history.

Do I have any regrets? I regret nothing! I can not erase my past...I can only learn from it.

Things in life happen for various reasons, and destiny found me along this dark debauchery path. However, having been actively involved in the porn industry, I have to admit, it did cause conflicts and complications for me later in life. Especially when I became a Mum, more on this in my second book.

I am driven by my dreams...

All I ever dreamed about was being a pop star. Being famous. Being adored.

So, I thought, being a pornstar at the time, was my way of becoming famous.

I was actively employed in the porn industry making films. The beauty of having a neurological brain like mine is, I can easily forget. The memory of an event, pushed to the back of my mind and forgotten, I then can successfully move on.

So, Dear Reader, this is me, authentically unmasking and exposing my life as I remembered it. It is the truth as I witnessed it. An honest account of my life as I lived it at the time. I've now opened up that dark abyss of Pandora's Box. That has sheltered me from all the pain it caused. Now open, for me as a therapy, to share with you with no judgement......Once you put your hand into the flame, it will never be the same...

CHAPTER TWENTY-NINE

JUSTIFY LOVE

Debbie put adverts in newspapers and magazines to advertise, discreetly, her agency...

I was very naive, and worked as one of her call-girls. Age and wisdom makes you wiser, but back then I was neither. Wisdom wasn't a priority, doing what Debbie asked me to do, was!

News back then, warned a man was going around attacking call-girls.

To be honest, I'd never considered I was in any danger, I'd always believed I was safe. I was so naïve and so trusting....

Look how trusting I had been about going to Bahrain, but thanks to Chloe who sensed the life threatening danger, luckily we didn't come to any harm.

But now there was no Chloe around to protect me...

Debbie took the call for this one particular client, and a booking was made for him to visit the flat. I can't remember what name he gave, but Debbie said he was on his way, and I was to be there to meet him.

He arrived, and I felt uneasy, he was distracted, not himself. I didn't want to appear concerned or judgemental, so greeted him as I would any normal client.

I explained to him, I had to ring my associate, Debbie, informing her of his arrival. This unnerved him. Nervously, from a room in the back of the flat, he looked at me anxiously. He looked off his face, either through drink or drugs, which I couldn't say.

Then my sixth-sense alarm bells started ringing in my head...

All I remember, he suddenly forced himself on me. Despite me, telling him to get off, he ignored me. He literally wouldn't get off. History was repeating itself, I was being raped, yet again...

His eyes were wild, rolling around as if drugged up beyond reason. It was unbelievably scary. I felt I was being crushed and suffocated. However, I weirdly remained calm, thoughts of happy times filling my head. Flight or fight adrenaline filling my body.

After about what seemed like an hour of this bizarre behaviour, I managed to calmly persuade him to get off me, fortunately he complied...

Five minutes after he left, I just laid there in silence. I then started to get this overwhelming feeling of panic and distress... I'd been a victim of rape. Yet again.

It was at this point, I realised how dangerous my life was. I thought about the man who attacked those call-girls and wondered if he was the same man.

To this day, I'm still not sure. But he fitted the description. I get the chills, thinking about that fact. Thinking about him makes my skin crawl. So possibly, I'd had a lucky escape. One wrong move on my behalf, could have resulted in me being seriously injured or even murdered. I realised now what a vulnerable position I'd put myself in and how fortunate I was to still be alive!

Debbie didn't give a fuck for my wellbeing or my safety. All she was bothered about was booking in another client. My complaints to her, about my rape, in one ear and out the other...She didn't give a shit about my welfare, only about the money I could earn for her. Just like it was in Bahrain and America, I was merely a commodity that earned her money.

I told Debbie I didn't want to do another job in the flat, not after I'd been raped.

I no longer felt safe there. I never told anyone, other than Debbie about the rape. I never even reported it as a crime...

Why?

Because at the time, just like my previous rapes. I thought in my neurological mind it was always my fault...I know now this is so not true.

I thought if I reported it to the police, no one would believe me...I was a sex worker, so probably was asking for it...It was probably my own fault, I thought.

So like every other time, I did not allow myself to become a victim and I learned to mask it, be strong and move on....

Resulting in more future mental health issues, creating post-traumatic stress. Again, I did not seek out any professional support. I was a very naive vulnerable girl, who was very immature and far too trusting. Severely struggling with an undiagnosed neurological mind....I had however become hardened to the traumas, I was using my body as a weapon to overcome my pain. Nothing could or would hurt me no more...

Debbie eventually gave up renting that horror of a flat. She then set up another flat in a different area. But it didn't work out there either. So she moved to the outskirts of London. After the rape, I needed some respite time away from London...

So I went back to Manchester, to my other life. I set about trying to heal myself. I fixated on decorating my home, along with going to the gym twice a day. Anything to take my mind off my trauma...I was happy going about a normal life, and if I'm honest, that's all I ever wanted, a happy normal life.

But I couldn't see a way out of this nightmare, it was a mess, I was a mess. I had gotten so far deep into this mess, there was no way out. But that's the problem with my ADHD. My brain reacts erratically, and there's no such thing as a normal life... so I thought.....

My music ambitions were on hold, and going nowhere, I needed money to pay my mortgage and pay for my car. So I reluctantly called Debbie, pulled back to her by this invisible cord.

I asked her if she had any work for me around the Manchester area, rather than in London. She informed me she had a contact nearby in Yorkshire. She said she would arrange work for me, at this Yorkshire based Adult Entertainment Production Company. She reassured me it was owned by a nice pleasant man....

Why did I still keep allowing myself to keep trusting Debbie? She was a dangerous pathological liar? But I kept going back to her...why?

So I arrived in Yorkshire, about to do a shoot, at this Yorkshire based Adult Entertainment production company. Recommended highly by Debbie. However, I instantly felt very uneasy with him... The director of this production company...

He was obsessed with wanting me to dress up as a schoolgirl, sucking a lollipop, and acting like I was a young girl. I felt very uncomfortable and again I thought what the hell was I doing here? He reminded me of that creep, Brad in America, and made disagreeable demands of me...

He wanted me to dress up, like a young girl, on a bed-spread depicting flowers. I felt physically sick, it was wrong on so many levels, I just couldn't do it and I found the strength to actually stand up to him and screamed No! Fuck off!

My instincts proved me right, this freak of a pervert, was eventually sentenced to prison; he was actually a paedophile! The headlines in a local newspaper at the time highlighted the following:-

A porn king was jailed after hundreds of indecent pictures were found on his personal computers. He admitted making indecent photographs of a child.

I wish I could delete these horrible memories from my mind;
However, I cannot change what has happened to me in my past. It certainly doesn't define who I am, or what I am today. I challenge myself to overcome these uncomfortable chapters in my life. Challenging them face on....I did everything I could, to hide the truth about my past. Protecting my family all my life, feeling very unsure on how they might react to such stories ...

So why am I now trying to justify myself?
That's a great question. Because I've mentally been a prisoner of my past. With no support for nearly all my life. Throughout the pages of my book, they are my therapy. You are witnessing my life journey of discovery, helping me find my peace, releasing me from years of mental imprisonment and trauma. I feel liberated within these pages. So thank you, My Reader...I am healing.

Eventually in January 2000 I called it a day. My involvement in the industry at an end. After which I wanted the whole thing to stop and go away. How wrong I was...I stopped, but a few years later, the newly invented Internet and Social Media didn't. Faced with the pressures they would exert on me, the only way I could deal with them was to embrace them...

When I started my job in 2019 at the car garage here in Grimsby, I at first didn't tell anyone about my past. I didn't think it was necessary. I feared I'd be judged by my past, and not by my ability to do the job I'd been employed to do.

However, unintentionally, in a room full of managers and staff, I let slip that I once worked in the 'Adult Entertainment Industry' At first they wouldn't believe me, until, eventually they realised I wasn't lying but telling the truth.

The truth was out. So now what? I feared the worst...But, I shouldn't have worried. My employers and fellow colleagues weren't in the least bothered about my past. They supported me wholeheartedly.

I finally felt liberated and free, no more fear. It felt truly wonderful to speak the truth, without judgement... Thank you Team GY xx

CHAPTER THIRTY

HANKY

If you remember, I did a live striptease on an X rated TV channel, and my bosses at FX Labs saw it, and gave me the sack and then were forced to reinstate me. I refused to be reinstated and left them if you remember. Well that incident of the live TV striptease, initiated my porn career...

So I returned back to the X rated TV channel.

X rated TV was probably one of the first soft porn channels at the time. I guess now they are awash with these channels but this one was probably one of the first.

I enjoyed working for X rated TV, true, it wasn't the BBC or ITV, nevertheless, it was proper TV. I had a make-up artist, a hairstylist and a production team, so it really felt professional. I became a TV presenter for the channel. I had an Autocue and would introduce the viewers to the artists who were to appear in their soft porn productions. I actually thought, at the time, I could have made a mainstream career in television, and been a famous TV presenter.

I'm a larger-than-life personality, so becoming a TV presenter wasn't beyond me. Far from it. I'm loud with a bubbly personality. So becoming a television personality was well within my grasp.

Why I never pursued my TV career further, I will never know. Possibly my neurodiversity brain caused me to lack self-confidence, and have no belief in myself.

I know that's hard to believe, considering I'd performed in explicit porn films. But back then, I was very insecure, and didn't think I'd be good enough. A bizarre conundrum I know. Only my neurodivergent brain understands, it's weird.

Whilst working for X rated TV, I had the opportunity to appear in other shows.

These were great fun.

It was all done very professionally, and not in the least bit, seedy. It was my first experience of working on live TV shows and I loved every minute of it.

I didn't feel embarrassed or ashamed. Most of the time you just sat there, with your boobs out, having a laugh.

During 1998 and 1999 my ADHD had me running around, like a Duracell Bunny, constantly on the go. I wasn't aware of having ADHD back then, but now, knowing I had, explains the physical and emotional chaos I went through. I would crash and burn, become paralysed with fatigue, have meltdowns and burnouts.

Thankfully I had my near normal life in Manchester to give me the opportunity to recharge and recover. Without this I probably would have had more, serious mental and physical issues.

In the autumn of 1998, I flew out to Spain, with Debbie, Ross and a few of the girls. My suitcase was packed with loads of sexy outfits, dresses, shoes and make-up. I'd become more conscious about my appearance now that I was in the porn business.

I'd lost weight, dyed my hair blonde and now looked a lot more polished.

We were flying to Spain to go to the Porn Awards. The Porn Awards in Spain are held every year to celebrate producers, actors and actresses in the porn industry. It basically is like the Oscars or the BAFTAs of the porn industry. They have a similar one in America.

It's important, insisted Debbie, to go and be seen by visiting producers and directors. It was an opportunity not to be missed, as it could easily result in being offered work. It all sounded so glamorous. It put all the drama of the last six months into perspective.

There could even be the possibility of winning an award, who knows.

However, I doubted that.

Porn actresses and actors from all over Europe gathered, and I felt somewhat humbled, a bit of an, 'impostor,' if I'm honest. I felt a little drab and frumpy when compared to these established porn beauties.

But that's me I'm afraid.

It always amazes me how my ADHD self-esteem issue overrides my confidence and I feel I'm not good enough.

However, I did get noticed and secured a little work, and performed a few scenes with a couple of directors.

On campus, in one of the buildings, ongoing sex exhibitions were staged. I was asked to perform on stage in one of their shows.

I felt very uncomfortable at the time, despite having done something similar before. But, the music started, and I performed. But my mind was elsewhere. I was with Madonna, in her infamous MTV awards performance, as she sang 'Like a Virgin,' rolling around, showing off her lacy knickers...

People clapped, cheered, my solo sexy dance, a surreal and exciting masterpiece. They shouted my name and I felt like a celebrity.
I enjoyed it immensely. Wow did I get a real dopamine buzz from my performance.

The award night was a grand affair. It took place in a large hotel, and everyone, including ourselves, dressed themselves in their finest attires. Dare I say it, boobs dangled everywhere, but you would expect that, it was the porn awards.

I didn't expect to win anything. I hadn't been in the industry long enough to even be considered for an award.

Candy, a girl I worked with, when filming with Richard won the 'Best New Porn Actress'. Making that film with Richard you may recall, was unpleasant. I vowed I would never again work with such a horrid man. I was annoyed, to think, an award went to the girl, who violently slapped me across the face.

At the time, I thought it was a bit of a fix. Richard was the king in the porn industry and I'm sure working for him influenced those who selected the winners.
Candy only worked for Richard. But fair dos, she won and I guess she deserved it.

It was during these porn awards that I realised this wasn't the life for me. In an attempt to pursue my dream of becoming a real celebrity, being a porn actress wasn't going to achieve that ambition.
I knew I was better performing on stage singing than doing porn to gain fame.

I wanted to focus more on my music, pursue a music career, and be the next Madonna. So from this moment in time, I was to focus more on the music business rather than the porn industry.

I had the conviction to do this. I didn't take drugs or drink and knew I could control and project myself towards my musical dreams.
I'm grateful in a way that my ADHD brain is the way it is. Not being wired normally does have its advantages sometimes.
I was in control, but out of control, if that makes any sense. My life is a colourful montage of extraordinary experiences.

I am unique and believe I was put on this earth for a reason.

My life has had a learning curve of encounters.

Everything I did, I believed, was driven by destiny. Life lessons to endure and learn from. True, at the time, I may not have fully understood what those lessons were teaching me. I would eventually, when given all the facts. However, it was all an important ongoing process to enlightenment.

I reflect on, those life-changing incidents that have influenced my behaviour, my dad's illness, my rapes, all the sexual abuse, my life style and actions. I refuse to be a victim and learnt to let go. My ADHD went undiagnosed for so long I was left to my own devices and made some bad choices.

But at the time I thought I was always doing the right thing, but clearly I wasn't...

Madonna's encouraging words guided me...No Matter who you are, no matter what you did, no matter where you've come from, you can always change, become a better version of yourself....

CHAPTER THIRTY-ONE

SINNER

So on my return to Manchester from Spain it was time for a lot of soul-searching.

Do I stay in the porn industry or move on?

Did I like what I was doing or not?

Well if I'm totally honest I don't recall enjoying it, it was a job throughout this era. I was on Prozac the whole time. I was numb, no feelings. I was acting out a fantasy. It wasn't real, but what I did love was earning the money. To me it was an addiction to earning money. Typical ADHD creating an addiction fixation, and that's the truth, that's what I craved, money.

I think I've gone over this before in a previous chapter. I apologise for repeating myself but that's ADHD. We tend to forget what we said, seconds after we've said it, I'm afraid.

So when I got back to Manchester I wanted a complete break from all my porn activities. Returning to the real world was not going to be easy. Finding employment might prove difficult.

I was used to the freedom of being self-employed and making my own decisions. I was in control.

An employer would inevitably impose their own restrictions, and there was my past to consider. If I were to disclose my past to employers, what would be their reactions?

That was going to be my problem. Was I to disclose my past, or mask it?

As narrated earlier, I went to the gym, to relax, have fun and take time out to rethink my options.

I fixated again on my trainers. My Velcro Asda zooms were replaced by Nike air TNs, and I bought them, in every colour available. I loved wearing them at the gym. I enjoyed my gym classes. I met and interacted with many people from all walks of life, but I never disclosed, to any of them, what I did for a career.

With no technology developments yet in social media, and the like, I was able to protect my secrets, and live anonymously. Facebook, Instagram and social media would eventually catch up with me, but for now I was safe, masking and hiding my past.

However, when I reflect upon my obsession to become famous, I regret the internet, not being there for me in the 90s. If it had been, as have so many others, I could have launched my singing career on the net and become famous. I guess nowadays people are famous for the hell of being famous.

At least I did have talent. I could sing, I could dance. I could take great photos and had the personality to accompany my skills.

But, sadly, I went unrecognised and never quite made it.

Now had the internet been there? Who knows, I might have become as famous as Madonna.

I soul-search and question, on a regular basis, life and the meaning of life.

My own life included. Why are we here? Why do we do what we do?

What my parents would think, if they knew the truth about my life. What would they say?

Such a question has been my Achilles' heel, and one of the reasons, I'm writing this book.

So I took a few months off and stopped my porn and escorting activities. However, I knew the decision to stop would have to be temporary. I wish it could be permanent, but knew the money would draw me back into it.

However, for now, I'd stopped. My mental health needed to recover as I was worn out. I was mentally and physically exhausted.

Burnt out!

ADHD can paralyse you like this. Unable to sleep for days, sitting procrastinating. My brain metaphorically fried while trying to come to terms with everything.

My mind is an absorbing sponge, evaluating everything I'd done in the last six months since I left FX Labs.

Debbie had worked me to the bone. I was absolutely knackered.

Having ADHD can create eating disorders. This I've discussed, earlier in my narrative, in great detail when writing about my teenage years.

I again, was controlled by what food I ate. I didn't eat properly and couldn't be bothered to cook.

Again my ADHD takes control of my wellbeing.

During the time away from my activities in London, I got a job in the tanning salon at the gym. I only did it for a couple of months till Christmas was over.

The wages were poor, and I realised I could earn triple this amount doing porn.

However this was what life would be like living normally. I was interacting with normal people, wiping down sun beds, listening to music and generally going about life in a conventional way.

The owner of the salon was a very pretty lady. I'd not mentioned my previous occupation, so she knew nothing about my past. She owned and drove a beautiful blue brand-new Mercedes SLK.

I fixated on that car. It was a brand new model, the same model Mercedes had given to each of the Spice Girls.

It was gorgeous. I wanted one but I wasn't going to get a Mercedes SLK, by working in the tanning salon now, was I?

My time working in the tanning salon was short lived. I worked with another girl. She'd worked in the glamour business, been a photographic model, in several top shelf magazines, so we kind of shared a common interest.

I, for some unknown reason, would open up to her, and talk about my experiences in the same industry.

She would keep my secret, as I would hers.

We never really became friends, and we parted company when I handed in my notice.

The job, never satisfied me, so I left, but continued to go to the gym.

I enjoyed myself immensely in the gym.

At this time, life confused me. I didn't know what to do with it. I'd built up a few relationships in London, and I was holding on to Wayne. I knew he represented normality to me.

He accepted my life in London, whether he liked it or not.

I rekindled my friendships with Abby and Ellie, and we'd go out clubbing through Manchester's club land.

I'd try to make my life as normal as possible, but there was always that fixation, the urge for more. Always on edge, anxious waiting for the next big thing, the next big fix. Like a drug addict, needing the next high, I was addicted to earning money, lots of it, in order to achieve my dreams. No matter what, I was going to achieve those goals.

So I reluctantly contacted Debbie again.

Debbie said she didn't have any work for me anymore. She'd turned her life around. Life had drastically changed for her. With her baby on the way, she'd moved out of London and was now living on the outskirts.

However, all was not lost, she did invite me to stay with her, and she'd see what she could do...

The flat was long gone. Debbie now lived in a small place outside London ready to become a mum to her first child.

Debbie, knew of a Madam, with lots of girls on her books. I was to see her and if accepted, she'd find me work.

Debbie took me into central London to meet the Madam of this escort agency.

Trust me, it was a large operation too.

I was to meet Isobel, with noticeable cosmetic work done on her face. She had fake boobs, with a thin figure and dressed very elegantly and was very wealthy.

She informed me, I had a beautiful face but needed to lose some weight. Words I had heard so many times before, I mean what a thing to say to a young girl. Especially a girl like myself who had battled eating disorders and I lived for the gym.

I wasn't fat, I was in great shape and very athletic.

So what the hell was she on about?

Any rate, I was accepted to work for her and could start any time. I told her I'd be available the following week. She said she had a house in London and girls could stay there for a rent fee.

However it was also used as a brothel, where girls could entertain their clients.

Isobel had contacted Debbie asking for photographs of me. A portfolio she had demanded. I didn't have one. I would arrange to have professional photographs taken and present her with a portfolio.

So I took it upon myself to go back to Manchester, to get some classy photos taken, to put them into Isobel's photo albums, to then get as much work as I possibly could...."I'm a sinner, I like it that way"...

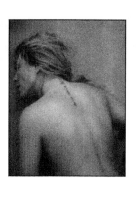

CHAPTER THIRTY-TWO

CANDY

Returning back to Manchester, I set about getting a portfolio of pictures for Isobel. I fixated on my dream of becoming a pop star like Madonna and my portfolio could be the means of achieving that aim. So I was determined to have them done professionally.

As you know I collected and kept in a chest, at my parent's house in Grimsby, a collection of all things Madonna. I'd done this throughout my childhood, and that Madonna collection was like a child's comfort blanket, to me. This attachment, obsession, can be traced to neurodiversity, as we tend to store things that remind us of our childhood, and happy days.

Madonna was my mentor as a child and I aimed to be like her one day. Whilst working for FX Labs, I came into contact with many professional photographers and their studios.

There was, of course, Nik's studio, where I was introduced into the pornographic world, but there were more legitimate photographic studios I delivered film to.

I finally ended up going to a commercial and fashion photographer called Scott. He was a nice guy, good looking, chatty and full of life. He owned a cute Dalmatian dog. He remembered me from FX Labs and agreed to make a portfolio of my photographs. He hired a make-up artist, and took some amazing photographs.

I absolutely loved them. They would be perfect for the portfolio Isobel demanded from me. In recent times, I discovered Scott sadly passed away RIP Scott xX

So again, it was back to London and a return to my old life of vice.

I'd replace Debbie with Isobel, London's top Madam, and I was back on the same merry-go-round once again.

I handed my portfolio to one of Isobel's girls, who was quite impressed with them. They were perfect, and would certainly attract clients.

Looking back, the set-up was probably no different to that in Bahrain. I recall feeling uneasy, somewhat concerned, and even a little bit scared.

As it happened, I was in far saver hands than I'd ever been with Debbie.

I was given a key to a very basic flat, in London. It had a living room, a bedroom, a kitchen and a back bedroom. I chose to sleep in the back bedroom.

It had its own key, so I could lock it safely, store my belongings, and had the bonus of having its own private en-suite.

It was a professional high class escorting agency. It had receptionists in Central London who booked girls for clients, after they'd selected them, from, looking at their photographs in their albums.
The clients would then come along to the flat, to view in person, their selected escorts. Most of the agency's clientele were the richest in London and would hire their escort, for the perfect night out. Either to satisfy some personal fantasies, or be seen on the town, with the perfect female accessory.
Their ego was enhanced, their acquaintances jealous, envious, and their status greatly improved.

At the time, it was the best escort agency in London...

However, at the start of this new relationship, nothing really had changed. Like with Debbie, Isobel was using me as a 'cash cow'.

I was billed as a porn queen, the agency promoting my pornstar image. I guess, if truth be told, a fair description of me at the time. I had a petite figure, with large boobs, blonde hair and had worked in the porn industry.
After all, I was good looking, I was young, with that Madonna look and figure.
However Isobel had fixated on me losing more weight. She and some of her clients thought I was too athletic, her customers wanting me to be less curvy.

I was young, energetic and had inside me the drive to be the best at what I did, and work that little bit harder to be noticed.
I hoped to make Isobel proud of me. So I considered her quest.
However, I was up against a lot of competition. The agency had, at the time, absolutely dropped dead gorgeous girls. They'd come from Estonia in Eastern Europe, and were stunning. They had the perfect body, they were slim and very desirable.

They looked like supermodels.

In fact, some were professional models, and would regularly walk the catwalks at London fashion week and the like. Being a call-girl would top up their fees.

I now realised, it was safer working for Isobel than it had been under Debbie's regime. All Isobel's clients were vetted.
I got into a routine working with Isobel. One week on, one week off, so I knew exactly where I was. It was a regular routine. One I could easily cope with.
No pressure.
I was in charge. I would control my returns to London, and Isobel would book my clients in advance according to my wishes. The system worked and I was under no pressure. A system diary, recorded the agency's clients, and business practices, and was done very professionally.
I was happy and relatively content for a while.

So I enthusiastically threw myself into my job. I bought and wore the latest clothing designs, changing my wardrobe whenever I wanted.
Working for Isobel, was a High Class. Expensive and exquisite.
I was living the high life as a first rate call-girl, and loving it. I felt important, classy and valued. My porn activities slowly disappeared in my past.

Thankfully, Debbie was becoming a distant memory...
She would try to entice me to do porn again or ask me to return to glamour modelling. I wasn't really that interested. I was happy working for Isobel. I believed Debbie was quite curious about how I was getting on working for Isobel.
Doing Ok I'd replay.
I liked working for Isobel, but pondered the fact that my clients would want to see me less curvy.
Maybe they did. I would try...
But how standards have changed. Curvy is seen as the norm today. Big ass and boobs, with a bit of weight, a sexy lure.
But back in the late 90s, it was the era of the supermodel.
Maybe I was ahead of my time, but what the hell.

When I think about this period of my life, I'm reminded of a controversial quote by Kate Moss, who once caused an uproar announcing,
'There is nothing sexier than feeling Skinny.'

So Isobel, the Madam of The Agency, in Central London fixated on being skinny.
She would constantly be fixated on me being skinny.

I would say naturally, I'm not a skinny girl. I'm naturally curvy. I have a bust, a backside and do carry a little weight around my tummy.

Isobel wanted me to become slimmer. My ADHD alarm bells rang. Triggering again, my past eating disorders, and my obsessive behaviour with food. That you've already read about, so you can imagine my reaction to Isobel's request to get a little slimmer.

At the time, I never classed myself as a big girl. I felt slim, I was normal with a normal body frame. To this very day, I don't eat properly. I either binge or starve, or do the opposite. I'll eat one type of food for weeks until the hyper-fixation of that food goes away. And so on to the next fixation...

Such is a classic example of ADHD eating habits. Crazy behaviour I know, but it's the norm to us people with neurological brains.

And here I was, being asked, by my very pretty, but skinny, new boss, Isobel, to slim down.

What is an acceptable weight?

Today, I'm probably the heaviest I've ever been in my life. I'm quite big, not obese, but it's probably the first time in my life I've actually accepted who I am.

However, back then, in 1999, I was a young girl embarking on a life as a high class call-girl and being told constantly I had to be slimmer.

So here we go again...

One of the receptionists at the agency had told me that she once worked in a pharmacy. And how she knew the pharmacist, who could supply me with slimming pills, and did I want her to get me some?

I agreed, and the next day I went with her to the pharmacy. According to the pharmacist, the slimming pills she offered me were revolutionary. If taken after food, it would stop the fat absorbing into the body and be expelled in your excrement.

Revolutionary indeed. I was going to shit myself slim.

I was offered an alternative, an amphetamine based one, that, again, according to the pharmacist, would suppress my appetite and I would, literally, just not want to eat. So that was my choice. I either starved or shit myself thin...

I decided to starve myself slim rather than spend extra time on the toilet.

After being diagnosed by my psychiatrist for ADHD in 2022, one of the medications prescribed to me is ironically amphetamine based.

Very similar to the amphetamine I took as a slimming pill all those years ago. Amphetamine based drugs are given as medication treatment to help treat ADHD, with proven evidence they raise dopamine in the brain and keep you more focused.

I did lose a lot of weight by taking the slimming pills, and became very skinny. Isobel had suggested that when in the gym, I concentrated more on cardio activities. This would raise my heart rate to a level that would burn off fat and calories...

No shit Sherlock! Extreme!

Not only was Isobel an Escort Agency Madam, but now my bloody personal trainer...

So I hardly ate any food, and was living on slimming pills and smoking tons of cigarettes. I don't drink or take hard drugs, and am in full control of my life. However, the moment I lose self-control, then that's when life turns to shit...

Isobel was delighted, I'd lost lots of weight and because of that factor, she said, I'd get more work.

However, in Manchester, I made my own decisions...

Balancing my diet was becoming troublesome. In Manchester I would let my hair down and eat takeaway food, and put on a pound or two. Then when back in London, I would starve myself.

Not a sensible way to eat, but this I did to please Isobel.

My work for Isobel took me to the top London hotels, in black cabs, to spend an hour with very rich clients.

On Isobel's advice, I bought the best makeup products from Harrods and was to seek make-up tuition from there as well.

So everything I used to wear was of high quality. Nothing was cheap.

Isobel didn't do it cheap.

I remember a client booking me and Sam to party with him for the whole night. He was staying in a big expensive hotel in London and liked to go clubbing. So we became his escorts for the night, visiting VIP nightclubs and other venues.

I recall, Brown's a famous nightclub at the time, for celebrity clientele. I remember this particular scene of Whitney Houston and Bobby Brown partying.

They both looked like a train wreck. Whitney was struggling, at the time, with a drug problem. So here I was, hanging out with this client, and Sam at this celebrity nightclub.

That night, I met Whitney, in the toilets. Quite a surreal moment. A pinch yourself, is this really happening to me, moment.

So there I was with Whitney Houston and getting paid for the privilege...

During my call-girl days, I would think I'd love to write a book about my adventures in London. Such stories I had to tell...

However, if I'm honest, what a Pandora's Box that would open.

I recall, only a few years later, a book and TV series had been written by a call-girl and I recall saying I could have written the same with my stories...

So I continued to live my double life existence. In Manchester I was now more relaxed and life was full of fun. In London my agency work was profitable.

I was riding high and loving life. Every other week, I enjoyed going back home, to my house in Manchester.

I renewed my friendship with Abby. She was living in a flat, she had painted in vibrant opal fruit colours, in Manchester. Like me, Abby was never frightened to embrace her passion for bright colours.

I was still taking three Prozacs a day, during my time working as a high class escort in London. My overactive brain, mostly, calm, and pretty mellow now.

Prozac, I believed, gave me the dopamine levels my ADHD craved, or was it the amphetamine slimming pills?

So my life in Manchester would introduce me to people outside the sex industry.

I was determined to get my music career off the ground and started.

I became a good platonic friend, to a lad called Tim, we used to work together at FX Labs. Tim introduced me to the absolutely delicious foods of the Greek, Iranian and Persian restaurants.

Living in the same block of flats as Tim, was a member of 'Take That's' fame.

I had the absolute pleasure of meeting him, face to face, one night whilst visiting Tim's flat. A great number of 'Take That' fans were hanging around in the car park, wanting to get a glimpse of their 'That That,' hero.

He came upstairs with a girl who also lived in the flats. I realised those living in the block had built up a unique relationship with each other. I remember getting super-hyper-excited when I met him. My ADHD brain went totally off its trolley with excitement.

I'm sure onlookers, seeing me, thought I must be some sort of mad woman, totally crazed or off my head on drugs.

Which of course I wasn't.

I was loud, yes, over the top loud, I admit. I tend to do this, when nervous and excited. My ADHD is ruling my head trying to create dopamine.

Quite off-putting for others, I agree. But what do you expect, it's me...

Tim was now aware of my London escapades. I told him everything, and he was never judgmental. We would share many a chat, exchange many ideas and have a laugh together. I will be forever grateful for his friendship and companionship.

My relationship with Wayne was virtually non-existent by 1999. We still met up but I couldn't completely cut him out of my life. I don't know why, I just couldn't.

I think possibly, I was frightened of his reprisal, him knowing all about my other life in London or was it because he was some kind of comfort blanket if the truth be known. I just didn't know.

This would drag on like this with Wayne, until I would eventually meet my future daughter's dad, John in 2000......."You can have it all your way....

CHAPTER THIRTY-THREE

ANGEL

So for one week, I was a high class call-girl for the agency in London and the following week, I was back home in Manchester living a near normal life...

When in Manchester, I'd go to the gym, then meet up with Abby and Tim and on an odd occasion, visit and chat with Wayne. I also liaised with my friend Sy. He was pursuing his musical career, down in London, and whenever possible we'd meet and discuss the music scene. We'd meet both in Manchester and in London.

In Manchester, I led as near a normal life as was possible. In London, the opposite. I don't think being a high class call-girl would be deemed as normal.

So, the need for my double life.

Fortunately my parents didn't know the extent of my escapades. I masked it by saying I was a glamour model, which was partly the truth. I did appear in top shelf glamour magazines to name a few.

I was a glamour model that part was true, but the thought of them knowing the full truth totally embarrassed me. I felt ashamed and it was best they didn't know that part. I was in fear of totally disappointing and destroying them.

My parents are wonderful people and I love them dearly.

I didn't really get to see my family as much as I wanted, however, when my busy schedule allowed it, I'd make the effort. True to form, my ADHD out of sight of mind.

Having already outlined my ADHD behaviours, in earlier chapters, you'll appreciate how easily it is for me to give up on tasks and friendships. I get bored easily and adopt an ad hoc approach to both. Such an attitude has resonated throughout my life, and still does, even as far as my present circle of friends.

Now being aware of my condition, enables me to understand the nature of ADHD and gradually learn and come to terms with its nature.

Writing this book has enlightened me, on how my ADHD, in my past had influenced and actively been responsible for some of my behaviours and the relationships I formed.

For example, Wayne.

If we analyse, in more detail, the relationship I had with Wayne, I can now see my fixation on me, '*needing him,*' and not the other way round. I knew he didn't need me, he cheated on me, but that was deliberately erased from my thoughts, because, all I fixated on was, '*I needed him.*' A strange concept, but that I know now was partly due to my ADHD conditioning.

Penning this book has not been easy, however it's given me a deeper insight, and greater understanding of the decision making behaviours that influenced my life.

I knew my life was different. Very different. Possibly a lot more sensational than most. Unbelievably, fascinating and very colourful, to say the least...

I believed my extraordinary life story would be very different, so I felt I had to write it, warts and all. Your journey through this book is my journey too. It's a learning curve for me, an empathetic read for you...

ADHD has always been present in my life, and always will be. Now, having been diagnosed with its presence, I'm now aware of the influence it has had on my life. A life I'm now sharing with you...

Having to dissect my life, as I'm doing writing this book, has opened my eyes to many things. It's broken me at times, made me sad, made me cry, and even made me smile. However, I'm beginning to understand how complex my life has really been. At times out of my control, despite me thinking how in control I thought I'd been. That being the result of my undiagnosed neurodiversity and post-traumatic stress.

As you will be speculating, how can anybody have done what I did, without it affecting their mental stability?

Well you'd be right. I've had many years of trauma that's affected my mental health resulting in PTSD and Panic Attacks. Obviously I did and still have a lot of mental health issues relating to my once undiagnosed and now diagnosed ADHD.

However, whatever destiny threw at me, I was mentally strong enough to overcome adversity, pick myself up, and move on. Exerting this inner strength enabled me to be a survivor, not a victim...

Should my reader have similar issues to me, I hope my narrative gives you hope and inspiration, and the strength to be the real you.

Other readers, I hope, for an empathetic understanding of the, 'The Secret Diary of an ADHD Martyr.'

And in true ADHD fashion I've gone off on a tangent yet again. Haven't I?

The narrative of this book is going to take forever to finish. I never get to the point. Trying to remember and get into the appropriate zone of where I am, that's the problem.

So where am I?

Yes, back in 1999. London with Isobel and the agency and Manchester, living my double life.

I'm back on track, back in the right zone.

I celebrated my twenty-fourth birthday in 1999.

Mum and my godmother came over from Grimsby, and brought with them a birthday cake in the shape of two boobs.

However, I'm getting ahead of myself. Rewind!

During the early 1999 I did more Page 3 work in a national tabloid, along with a professional photo shoot of stripteases called, 'Fantastic in plastic. I wore a black PVC catsuit, and daily, throughout the week, stripped down to me, 'Monika's,' showing off my magnificent boobs.

So you could say, I had my fifteen minutes of fame, as Andy Warhol so famously quoted. Not the kind of fame I desperately sorted, but nevertheless, Page 3 notability. I did have opportunities in this weird world of Page 3 fame, but not the kind of Madonna, superstar fame, I craved.

However, I was a Page 3, regular knockout babe, thanks to this newspaper.

Being in the adult entertainment industry has seriously influenced my views on sex. I consciously made the effort, not to have, or contemplate physical sex with male companions. When you worked in this business, you hardened up your attitude towards sex.

So dealing with men on a platonic basis was the norm.

I never saw men as either a boyfriend or a casual partner. A philosophy that worked for me in my past.

In 1999 I worked solely in the sex industry, and didn't have a personal sexual relationship with any of my porn colleagues. It was work, not love, so it never crossed my mind to have a loving relationship with any of my work colleagues.

I met up with Wayne, but that too, more of a friendship.

Being in the business I was in, you had to be resolute. I'd been through a lot, had many hard knocks, but I was determined to get through the ordeals I encountered. Yes, at times I was aggressive, and had to be too forceful to survive. You had to be strong to have gone through what I went through.

However, friends and friendships on my journey, would help me cope, and Sy was one of them. Sy also introduced me to Ellie, a friend of his, and together, Ellie and I, would become very good friends, and share wonderful times together.

It was a period of behaviour extremes. Calm one moment, and bat shit crazy the next.

I do however recall a few such violent occasions...

I owned a Mercedes SLK, more about my fixation on owning such a car, later. Anyway, I pulled up at the service station. Ellie was with me. A car pulled up in front of me and took my place at the petrol pump.

I went absolutely bat shit, lost my temper, raved and ranted. An unwarrantedly aggressive, over-the-top reaction if ever there was one. I was banned from that petrol station for being too aggressive and very erratic.

So that was me, around this time. I didn't give a shit. I was fearless and could quite happily tell people to, fuck off, or else.

Maybe, displaying this kind of aggressive hardness, was a defensive ploy, a protective barrier, against what I did to earn money and all the sexual traumas I'd suffered.

My ADHD head reasons like that along with Post Traumatic Stress. There were many such unwarranted occasions where I reacted aggressively.

Again I was in my car, with Ellie, going to Moss Side carnival. I had the roof of my car down. It was while driving past a gang of girls walking on the pavement, I lost my cool. They shouted abuse at me and my car. So, while still driving, I tried to get out of the car and take them on.

How dangerous was that?

Yet again, over the most trivial, insignificant thing, I became aggressive, fearless, that hard case, not to be trifled with. Ellie was horrified and tried to calm me down.

Whether I was driven by my ADHD fixations, or just defending my self-esteem, I just couldn't say. I'd been through hell, taken on board a lot of abuse for one so young, so maybe I felt, at the time, it was justifiable to react to these detrimental insults.

Such was the Topsy-Turvy status of mind at that time.

It was the year 1999. I had my own mortgage, and was driving a Vauxhall Tigra but fixating on owning a Mercedes SLK, like the one the owner of the tanning salon had. I had my heart set on a brand-new Mercedes SLK and no barrier would stop me getting one. I called in at the Mercedes garage, to make enquiries about the SLK, and as coincidence, would have it, the same guy who sold me my Vauxhall, had changed dealerships and had moved to Mercedes. What were the chances of that?

So I told the car salesman what I wanted. I had a goal...

Something to hyper fixate myself on. I was getting rid of my Vauxhall Tigra, replacing it with a brand-new, shiny Mercedes SLK. I was obsessed about owning it for months. I had to wait a while to get my brand new Mercedes SLK.

My parents aren't materialistic. So I haven't inherited my need for materialistic objects from them. Now, my Auntie, sadly no longer with us, just the opposite. When alive, she was obsessed with sports cars and owned one. So possibly I've inherited it from her gene pool.

When my Mercedes SLK arrived it was gorgeous...

In the summer of 1999, Isobel had booked me to attend a client's twenty first birthday celebrations. I and a couple of other agency girls were to be picked up, by a Limo, outside the offices in central London.

The Limo arrived, and we all got into the car. We were greeted by Sebastian, the birthday boy, and his brother and a friend. Sebastian was a lovely young lad and was training to be a pilot.

We cruised around in the Limo.

We had a great laugh that night and it was more like friends celebrating a birthday. I'd just celebrated my twenty-fourth birthday so to me it was like a double celebration. I did keep in touch with Sebastian after his birthday, and I hung out with him and his friends.

Once while back in Manchester, Sebastian and his friends hired a plane to come and see me...I'll never forget that day.

I invited Abby to come along, and we all went inside the cockpit of the plane and messed around with the controls. We didn't fly anywhere, but it was just exciting going to the airport and messing about in a plane.

I took them on a tour of Manchester and showed them the sights.

Sebastian was well spoken, and I recall Abby commenting, 'What would Wayne say, if he knew you were with someone who spoke with such a posh voice?'...

...'Why would I be bothered by what Wayne thought? I replied...

Sebastian went to live in San Diego, in the USA to finish his training as a pilot.

Before he left for the USA, I drove to where he lived with his parents, to say goodbye and wish him well in becoming a pilot. We agreed, on his return from the USA, that we'd meet up again.

As a going away gift, he gave me a bottle of very expensive vintage champagne, a bizarre gift considering I am a complete teetotal. But I kept it for many years, then was to pass the gift on to someone who would appreciate it.

I never saw Sebastian again. Tragedy struck and he was killed instantly in an accident whilst training. I of course was absolutely devastated, on hearing about his death. He was only twenty one years and had the rest of his life ahead of him, and destiny, sadly, had him dying, in a plane crash.

Although he died doing what he loved, it just didn't seem fair. Sadly, life isn't fair and the older you get, the more certain that becomes.

I met up with his brother who was absolutely heartbroken. Talking to him, about his brother, moved me to tears. I was deeply touched, because obviously, Sebastian had spoken about me to his family.

Sebastian's death hurt...

It would affect me badly. You know how spiritual I am. I believe in the supernatural and the paranormal. After Sebastian's death, I honestly believe I can still feel he is still around me.

I could feel his spirit, my psychic power sensing his presence. When detecting his presence, the room would go cold, my breath visible icy. I even saw a huge white orb moving slowly around my landing light. I know this was a spiritual sign from him.

I sometimes see a black silhouette shadow, from the corner of my eye. All spiritual signs that I still believe Sebastian is still around me.

The other month at the car dealership, where I work, I met an incredible gentleman. He was a clairvoyant, and he said to me, *'Who is the young man that is always by your side?'* I felt goosebumps on my arms, and the hairs went up, on the back of my neck. I knew exactly who the clairvoyant was talking about.

I said, 'Yes it's Seb.'

The clairvoyant continued and said, *'He's there always, with you, guiding you. He seems very protective.'*

I already knew this, but the clairvoyant had now validated that. It gave me great happiness, knowing Seb, is one of my spiritual guides, a guardian Angel,

Protecting me throughout my life...

Rest in peace Sebastian x

  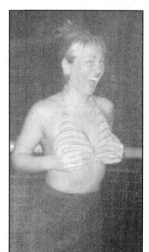

CHAPTER THIRTY-FOUR

VENI VIDA VICI

I want to talk about my platonic good friend Tim. We used to work together at FX Labs. Tim thought it was funny I'd stripped live on the X rated TV channel. It was fantastic he thought, and called me a legend. Tim was a really nice guy. He was from a really good family. He had no money worries and lived in a most desirable apartment, not far from Barça, the bar that was owned by Mick Hucknall. The same place where I celebrated my twenty-first birthday party.

Tim had a recording studio in his spare room, and liked to play around with making music, and being a DJ.

I was introduced to Tim's friend, Nick H. They were very good friends and enjoyed their music. Nick H, had already had some success in the music industry. Especially in the Manchester club scene.

I asked Tim about me doing some music demo work with his friend Nick H. Tim said he'd be more than happy to do demos with me. Wow, I was excited...

At last, I'd met somebody who wanted to record music with me. We'd make professional musical demos that could be sent to record companies.

I was so sure I was going to be the next big pop star.
I mean come on, all these years following Madonna's career, my mentor and guide, and it had to be my turn. Hadn't it?

It was back in 1999, that I first was introduced to Tony. Now Tony was a big time A & R man for one of the largest,' Record Labels,' of the time. An A&R (Artists and Repertoire) representative is responsible for finding promising new artists for a record label, or for a music publisher to sign them up for a career in the recording industry.

Now Tony was known to regularly hire girls from my escort agency. Never the same girl twice and would ask for a different girl every time.

Sometimes he would go to the agency apartment, where we girls stayed, or he'd pick the girl up directly from the agency in his sports car.

Speaking from experience, he would take you to a hotel of his choice.

Tony will need a chapter, all of his own, so I'll leave him there, while I continue with my story...

I started hanging back with Abby loads more, which was always great fun. We both used to love the Manchester club scene. Especially a few years prior in the 'Holy City' days and here we in 1999 enjoyed the Manchester club scene yet again.

Nick H was one of the local DJs, and we'd tour the nightclubs where he was DJing and became his devoted groupies.

Looking back, I felt sorry for Nick H's girlfriend, we would continue to dominate, his time and attention. I can understand her concern. On her birthday she asked us to back off Nick H. He was her boyfriend and she felt we were getting far too close to him.

But as you know, it couldn't be on a boyfriend and girlfriend level. That wasn't me, if you recall I just wanted to be close to him because you know, how I fixate on people. He was feeding my dopamine rush. He was a music producer, and we'd record demos together. I was musically drawn to him, and it excited me.

All I ever dreamed about was to be the next Madonna, be an international singer superstar and Nick H, was my chance to do it.

Nick H had a TV producer friend called Colin. Colin was well known for being in the first reality TV show called 'The Living Soap'.

Colin was at the time working for a channel called Rapture TV, where he did the producing and presenting of a TV programme called, 'Trainspotters.' Each week they would go to various nightclubs and interview clubbers and top DJs.

It reminded me of a slick version of the late 80's and early 90s TV show 'The Hit Man and Her'

Now, Nick H, was going to Rimini in Italy, to DJ. It was being filmed for Rapture TV. He asked, would I be interested in going with him to Italy. I'd meet his friend Colin, and maybe get the opportunity to do some TV work.

An absolute fantastic opportunity, to meet Colin and hopefully, get the chance to appear on TV. The opportunity, possibly to become famous, and an opportunity not to be missed. I returned home, packed my suitcase, eager to go to Italy and meet Colin.

Nick H and I flew to Italy and on our arrival in Rimini, met up with Colin and his film crew. I have a tendency, as some might know, when meeting people, to be loud, over the top and act rather stupid. I dont realise I do it. Might be nervous energy, creating dopamine for my ADHD brain.

Not sure.

I just don't know how to behave accordingly, in certain situations, so I act like an idiot in the hope of getting everything out the way quickly, and then I just chill. I guess that's why certain people find me difficult to handle. I have a tendency to go over the top with my personality when confronted with new and different situations.

By myself or with people I know I'm normal, but sometimes, when introduced to other people, I become this 'show person' and an extroverted exhibitionist.

That's another side of me!

We all went out to a restaurant in Rimini for a meal. There we chatted and exchanged stories.

Colin took a great interest in me. I revealed it all. I told him about my porn, and escort work and how I wanted to be the next Madonna, and become a famous singer. He listened intently, I'd told him I had worked in television, appearing on X rated TV and would welcome the opportunity to again work on TV, possibly as a presenter.

Colin said he'd keep me in mind when planning his next TV schedules, and I felt I'd made a good impression on him.

We were both filmed and interviewed by Colin for Rapture TV. Nick talked about his music and about how the both of us were making music together.

That excited me. It seemed like a dream come true, at last!

After filming, we all had fun on Rimini Beach. We sunbathed, laughed, and had loads of fun on the pedal boats.

The opportunity to fulfil my dreams was at last within my grasp. That's what I do in life. I found opportunities, without even searching for them, and this was a golden opportunity not to be missed.

It wasn't as if I'd manifested this opportunity, it had to be my belief in the law of attraction. In other words, positive thoughts bring positive results into one's life, while negative thoughts bring negative outcomes. Life's a journey along a road. Sometimes you take the wrong path, sometimes the right one.

Positive thoughts had led me along the right path, because before we left Rimini, Colin took me to one side and said, he'd a few presenting assignments, he'd like me to do.

He'd be in touch, to arrange when back in the UK.

I'd cheekily asked if my friend Abby, my clubbing buddy, could do it with me, and to my delight he agreed.

We only stayed in Rimini for a couple of days, and then me and Nick H got on a train to Venice. It was an amazing experience. It was a steam train, like the one in Harry Potter films.

Very old-fashioned.

It travelled along the coast of Italy from Rimini to Venice. I recall, the journey being absolutely boiling hot. The train had no air-conditioning and the weather outside matched the heat in the train.

I'm not quite sure why we went to Venice, but I think Nick H wanted to show me some of Italy's famous tourist sites. Venice of course, being the most famous. He knew Italy very well indeed. He worked here, his music well known, as he worked with many Italian producers on his dance tracks.

In Venice, we met up with several music producers he'd worked with making dance tracks. I didn't realise, at the time, what a golden opportunity I had with Nick. However, as you well know, I get a hyper fixation on somebody and then I lose interest. Move on and do something more erratic.

Typical of someone with ADHD, like me, I never follow tasks through.

So Nick H showed me the sights around Venice. I kept pinching myself thinking, Wow! Here I am in Venice, with probably one of the top music producers, meeting other music producers, and I hadn't yet I still haven't recorded a professional song.

So when back in the UK, Colin as promised, contacted me and we arranged an assignment. It was presenting various slots on the TV show, 'Trainspotters,' for Rapture TV. I told Abby I had arranged for us both to work together presenting for Trainspotters, this would include interviewing top club DJs and clubbers at various venues up and down the UK, as and when they needed us.

She was ecstatic.

I was to work on TV with my best friend, Abby, presenting a TV show. A dream come true. Fame was just around the corner.

I hoped...

I've had many friends throughout my life. Some influential, others simply acquaintances. By connecting with the right people in your life, which I felt I had, would enhance my chances of becoming famous. Closer to those dreams I so craved to achieve. So, 1999 was the year where things started to change. The dreams I had all my life were slowly becoming a reality...

Through Tim I met Nick H. A famous name in the Manchester dance music scene.

I had the opportunity with Nick H, to finally make it. But would I take it...

Colin, who is now a very well-known TV producer and director, has produced many, factual documentaries on Netflix and mainstream TV. He's also been involved in, 'Celebrity get me out of here,' and has even worked with Jane McDonald.

An impressive biography of work.

In 1999 Colin was involved with producing and presenting the TV show called, 'Trainspotters, for Rapture TV', where Abby and I were to be presenters.

Colin and I would become friends, and we still keep in touch in recent times, via our social media platforms. Colin's always got some adventure going on, and I thoroughly enjoy watching the antics of his street cat from Dubai called Achmed. Achmed, who is known to some as a hooligan cat, on the internet, who causes nightmares for the locals in Hackney.

Working for Rapture TV would see Abby and I travelling the country interviewing club DJs. This was a great opportunity for us to appear on proper TV as presenters, and hopefully be the platform, a portfolio maybe, for even more television presenting.

I would fear, with justification, my porn and escorting days would hinder me in some way. Back then when I was younger, everything bothered me. Not so much now, but back then, I was very wary of how my career would be hampered, because of my past.

So, our first TV presenting gig myself and Abby did, was at a club in Derby called 'Progress.' It was known for its club nights, playing Progressive House. I recall meeting our TV crew there at the club.

I had blonde hair, and was dressed in a red satin tie bodice that had metal rods in it, with a long black skirt. I wore black gloves, and red lipstick. I had that million dollar look and was eager to start interviewing.

Abby wore a white PVC dress, and had dark hair extensions. She looked quite exotic. We were a good pairing of me and Abby and we bounced off each other really well.

I was very nervous, and stage fright struck me. Here was my golden opportunity to be a TV presenter, and I was bottling it. I was going to be on TV and I was smitten with a wave of stage fright.

I didn't think I could do it. Now, I do know my ADHD, unfortunately can flare up bad anxiety and panic attacks. At the time my condition wasn't known to me, so I'd no idea why I felt like this or what had come over me. My brain had gone completely blank.

Classic ADHD.

I, just, all of a sudden, went into some weird meltdown, I couldn't understand. I froze with fear. I'm normally good fun, but somehow I felt I wasn't good enough to do this.

I was mentally paralysed.

The crew noticed I was nervous, and helped me compose myself. I was to interview the club owners, Russell and Pete. Luckily, for me, when I interviewed them, they were quite chatty and obliging. I remember just standing there hardly asking any questions, just smiling.

They did most of the talking. The camera would roll, and they'd carry on talking about the nightclub and its venues and its connections to Boy George.

I have watched this video on YouTube, and looking back at it now, considering how scared I was, I hid it quite well. When all was said and done, only I knew how paralysed I was, no one else...

Abby and I interviewed many of the club goers. One guy was asked what he'd do if all nightclubs were closed by law? Such an ironic question, don't you think, considering over twenty years later, our COVID-19 pandemic did just that.

Coincidence, or was it my paranormal abilities reading the future?

Who knows?

Another, silly thing me and Abby filmed, was asking some of the male club-goers, if they fancied us?

Abby got all the yes's and I got all the no's.

Well, you win some and lose some. I tend to lose a lot...

I often watch back, with amusement, the videos of our interviews. I, on some of them, look off-me-trolley. As you know I don't drink, or take drugs. I'm as sober as a judge doing these interviews.

But you wouldn't believe it, if you saw my antics.

Clearly it shows how my ADHD presents itself. I go into a kind of possessed, hyperactivity.

It's a kind of a defence mechanism.

As you know, I like to feel, I'm in control, which I am most of the time. But there is a side to me, in certain environmental situations, where I become overpowering and hyperactive.

Maybe a fellow Neurodivergent will understand that. But sometimes it can really let me down.

If I go out to nightclubs or bars, due to my ADHD, I act like I'm absolutely pissed. I go over the top, drawing a lot of attention to myself. I've been known to do inappropriate things. I'd do anything to attract attention to myself, but then I don't really want to draw that attention.

But I do despite not wanting to.

I have meltdowns, get poorly and desperately need to escape the situation.

So you can clearly see this behaviour on the Progress episode of 'Trainspotters.' You see how deranged, my ADHD makes me look. I also interviewed Alistair Whitehead, a top legendary DJ that night as well.

I feel Abby and myself were good interviewers. The programme was aired on Rapture TV and we were absolutely delighted with our performances.

We were very proud of ourselves.

Colin too thought we were good, and gave us two more assignments. We went to a London nightclub to fim, I can't remember what it was called. While we were there, Abby and I got into a huge argument. It turned nasty. Probably, it was me that triggered it. Maybe I said something inappropriate, I honestly can't remember, however it escalated into a huge row. Insults were thrown and Abby left. It didn't go down well, with the TV Company who had to abort the session.

My final assignment for Rapture TV 'Trainspotters' was at, 'Gatecrasher's,' a nightclub in Sheffield. I remember I had a PVC clear dress, you could see through, with a PVC silver bra and thong. 'Gatecrasher's' nightclub was a well-known nightclub, famous for its rave scene. Everybody would wear neon type, crazy outfits. Such dress was the norm for the club. I interviewed the resident DJ, Tall Paul, who was big at the time on the club scene.

After that night at Gatecrashers, I was never asked to present for 'Trainspotters' again. I asked Colin why, and he replied that there wasn't the demand, so there'd be no more interviews. At least I got the golden opportunity to present on a TV show. An opportunity that not many people would ever have...so I very grateful to have been given the opportunity thank you Colin xX

So I continued making my music demos with Nick H in the hope I could send them to a top Music Mogul, who I will explain more about in the next chapter...'I came...I saw...I conquered"

CHAPTER THIRTY-FIVE

ME AGAINST THE MUSIC

So, I return to London, to continue my work for the agency, where I'd be introduced to Tony, a V.I.P. in the music industry, responsible for finding new recording artists.

I remember the night we first met.

I was waiting in the agency reception area, waiting for a booking. Some nights you could wait hours for a client to call.

On this particular night, our receptionist received a call, and I heard her telling the client, over the telephone, she had a girl, who was available, was a bubbly, fun loving, curvy blonde porn star, who was very discreet.

I loved the way our receptionist would describe you, to our clients. It was like she was describing a takeaway menu to potential customers...

Popstar, Robbie Williams formerly of Take That. Was popular in the charts at this time with his hit 'She's the one.' It's crazy how I remember the popstars and groups that were around at the time... Music transported me back to that very moment. Sorry going off on an ADHD tangent again...

I remember before meeting Tony, the receptionist had commented, how big a Music Mogul he was in the music industry. He represented a top London based record label, he had signed up loads of artists as an A & R scout.

The receptionist said I had to go to a top London hotel. Now this hotel was made famous because of Lady Diana. In the 90s, before she so tragically died, she used to use the hotel regularly. She was photographed regularly in and around at the hotel, as it was rumoured she used to use its gym.

As I've mentioned before, my work took me to many famous London hotels, which were popular venues for call-girls like me. However, I'd never been to this particular hotel before so this was a new experience.

I must admit, I was quite excited.

However, this hotel wasn't an easy access, unlike the other London hotels I visited.

Normally, I'd just walk in a hotel, take a lift and find the room. No one batted an eyelid. The staff knew who you were, and why you were there, and they didn't want to upset their rich clients, so they would never challenge me.

This however was different...

In this particular hotel, you needed key passes to get everywhere. It was a new security system, something I hadn't come across before, so I sought the help of the hotel porter.

Fortunately, he was the nudge, nudge, wink, wink, sort. Who knew exactly who I was and why I was there.

No question asked kind of guy.

We exchanged the obvious banter, I smiled politely, he smiled knowingly and I headed off to the room, I was to meet Tony in...

Now, Tony, would use a different name in hotels and when booking us girls. Our receptionist, of course, knew that. She'd give us the man's background history, and we all knew he liked to, discreetly, entertain a different girl each time. Never the same girl twice.

So I knew it was a once only encounter.

I recall thinking he must be a very wealthy man and feeling excited about meeting this Music Mogul. If only I'd made some music demos to play to him, I pondered. I was yet to arrange that with Nick H, so even if I'd wanted to, I had no demos to play him...

But I wasn't there for that, was I?

But, hang on, I do have a demo...far better than any recording could be...Me! I can be my own demo.

What a golden opportunity, this was for me to shine and present myself, personally, to a V.I.P. in the music industry. Hopefully I could use this intimate get together, to show him how good a singer I was, and hopefully for him to sign me up to a record contract. Well, that's what was going through my mind before I knocked on the hotel room.

I was dressed, to kill, as they say. I had a leather jacket, a Karen Millen outfit and high heeled shoes. I looked like that sexy dream girl, my clients fantasised over. I'd swallowed down, slimming pills, worked out in the gym, and it was no longer that plumy girl, clients complained about, but a thin, slim, desirable young girl.

Butterflies fluttered in my stomach, pure, uncontrolled excitement, thrilled my senses. I was actually going to entertain the main entrepreneur in the record industry. So, I'm knocking on the door of the Penthouse Suite, in the Hotel, waiting to be told to enter.

I knocked again.

'Enter,' said a voice from inside the room. I walked in...

I entered the Penthouse Suite, and walked along a hallway of mirrors to a large, magnificently decorated, living room area. It had a panoramic window overlooking a London landscape. A magnificent room with a magnificent view. Just the location, to warrant the status of the man who stood before me.

He was quite short, well-dressed and very well spoken.

My God, I thought, he looked like Mel Gibson.

Typical ADHD behaviour, not thinking before I spoke, I just blurted out what I thought. 'You look like Mel Gibson,' I uttered, 'also Robbie Williams,' no idea why I said that. I think he quite liked that and was flattered.

'Do you think so? Never been called that before but I'll take that.'

I continue to talk utter crap. Uncontrollably I started to show off, as I do, my ADHD driving my fixation. I went off on tangents, rambled on about wanting to be a pop star, needing to be famous and becoming the next Madonna. I just couldn't control myself, spewing out verbal diarrhoea, in every direction and all over the place.

I started singing Madonna songs, feeling all nervous, and making a tit of myself, so desperately trying to impress, my head unable to think straight like I was drunk. But the excitement of meeting a Music Mogul with the potential of making me a star sent my dopamine through the roof!

Back then Tony was well known in the music industry. If in hindsight, I'd have known how influential he was, would I have been a little more reserved, and not spouted out all that shit about myself, or told him he looked like Mel Gibson and Robbie Williams...

He'd just signed up a girl band, hoping they'd take over from the 'Spice Girls,' but I don't think they ever succeeded in doing that. He said to me, if only I'd have met him a few months earlier, he would have probably auditioned me as part of that girl band...

At the end of the evening, said, he'd enjoyed himself and I'd been fantastic. However, I can't help but think, had fate been kinder, I'd have met him earlier, and possibly have had that audition, for his girl band.

I was gutted that another opportunity to be famous had been lost. During our time together, we'd talk openly about the music business, and he told me if I wanted to break into it, I'd need to get connected to the right people.

He suggested I should consider session singing, and of course I asked how I should go about becoming a session singer. He suggested, I consult adverts in music magazines, go to auditions. There were always recognised singing artists, wanting to employ backing vocalists. You then would get a chance to go on tour with them, and possibly get noticed. It's who you know that gets you recognised, he reinforced.

Reflecting back, I wish now I'd have listened more enthusiastically. Again, typical ADHD trait, of not listening. I should have probably looked deeper into becoming a session singer.

But I didn't.

I'd have probably made a bit of a career out of doing that. I had the voice and would have been a good backing singer. Possibly even had got spotted, and been destined for stardom.

But no! I had to do it my way.

He also suggested I come to some of his house parties and meet up with famous influential people. Meet up with TV presenters, producers, pop stars. They all came to his parties, and I was invited. I'd get myself known, and I imagined myself being introduced to the 'Who's Who,' of the record world. How exciting would that be, me amongst all record producers and pop stars?

Tony suggested, if I record some demos, he'd listen to them and give me his honest opinion on whether or not I was good enough, to make a record and possibly become the next Madonna. You can imagine how fixated I became knowing this Music Mogul was going to listen to me sing.

However, all this potentiality would never materialise. I never did go to any of Tony's parties and would be left wondering, what actually went on at these social V.I.P gatherings.

Why?

I think, at the time, I expected him to listen to me sing, sign me up, then and there, without all the hullabaloo, he suggested I go through. I thought he would pay for all my demos, knowing I was destined to become a superstar. But it doesn't work like that does it? But that, I'm afraid, is me. Impatient, I wanted it all, and I wanted it now. That's what It's like having ADHD...

When reflecting back on my encounter with this Music Mogul, I can honestly say, he was a very pleasant and worldly man. I at the time had a lot of respect for him.

He was honest, considerate and very polite with me.

A true gentleman. A very nice man indeed.

However my opinions on him would soon change, more to come of that later...

Had I been more experienced, and possibly not suffering from ADHD, I might have listened more carefully and followed his advice. I was impatient, at the time, and wanted everything immediately. An ADHD trait that has caused me many mishaps.

Maybe, when I left Tony's room that night I should have set my heart on becoming a session singer. God knows I was talented enough. Maybe I should have gone to his house parties and hooked up with all those celebrities and music producers? Maybe? Life's full of maybes!

However, Tony and I exchanged contact details. He told me to give him a call once I'd got the demos done. He'd then arrange for me to come to his offices so he could listen to them. This I did and we kept in touch via text and phone. On numerous occasions we'd chat about my music. I was unsure how genuine he was about helping me with my music. Or whether he was paying me lip service, knowing how we met, and me being a call-girl he'd hired.
Maybe he wanted to keep it a secret, and was safe guarding that promise. Any rate we kept in touch. It was a connection I wanted to keep.

In Manchester, I continued to work with Nick H and told him I'd met this Music mogul who wanted my demos.

Nick H was working with a girl band, and had recorded a backing track with their songs. He suggested that, for my demo, I sang, 'Heat of the night,' and 'Supernatural,' two songs from the girl band's recording. However, despite them not being the type of songs I sang, I did record them in his recording studio.

I then contacted Tony, who said he'd look forward to hearing the demos.
So this was my first encounter with Tony, which doesn't end there. It was me against the music...

CHAPTER THIRTY-SIX

ATTRACTION

I spent the Christmas of 1999 with my parents in Grimsby.

There's something special about going back home for Christmas and regardless of whatever I was doing, I would always try and spend Christmas at my parent's home. Christmases at home were always special. My parents would have a real Christmas tree, which we all helped to decorate, with sentimental, old toy decorations from the 80s. My parents had a lovely dining room, due to an extension they had built in the mid-90s. It made the room very homely and Dad, every Christmas, would decorate the dresser, with Holly and Ivy. The dresser displayed my parents' collections of Minton and Willow patterned pottery.

Very festive and very cosy.

It was a great couple of days, meeting up with all the family again, and of course, enjoying the turkey, or goose, Mum would cook, with the help of Dad, for our Christmas lunch. Mum's Christmas dinners were unbeatable, very delicious and traditionally sentimental. I would come over all nostalgic, my mind reliving the Christmases of old. It was always lovely to see my sister, who I believe was pregnant during this Christmas, get together. I recall her being quite tired, and not as sociable as she normally was. She didn't have a drink of wine, or go with us to the local Church, for our traditional, midnight Mass.

The family always went to Christmas, midnight Mass. We'd done this for years.

Ed's Mum, and family were also regular Christmas Mass attenders.

I remember Ed's Mum loved singing, and when she was younger, sang in a band. She also sang in a choir, and like me, who was in the school choir, loved to sing hymns. Traditionally, when meeting up with Ed's Mum at Christmas Mass, we tend to bounce off each other, and together, sing the descendants of Christmas carols. We got a laugh and a buzz, doing those descants, which drew attention to our singing, which we believed was better than the church choir were doing.

Like me, Ed's Mum was a boom box, very loud and I had a lot of fun singing with her.

I remembered this Christmas Mass of 1999, very well, because Ed was home from wherever he was, at that time. Both our families were all there, at the church together and I really couldn't keep my eyes off Ed.

He was absolutely gorgeous.

I remember trying to get Ed's attention at the church, but he would look away, and avoid eye contact. There has always been a kind of awkwardness, between us. An unexplained attraction, a connection that nobody would ever understand, but us.

Ed was shy around me, and I felt really embarrassed around Ed. So the tendency of my ADHD hyperactivity would always come out and make a fool of myself in some shape or form.

As families, we all walked back home from the church together. Ed dawdled at the back, and I kept turning around to look at him. On reaching our respective homes, which were very close, I recall telling Ed how absolutely gorgeous he was, and should seriously consider being a model.

I literally just blurted it out, and Ed went coy and awkward. I could see how embarrassed he was.

Ed made his way back to his house and I turned to get one last look at him. He too turned, and we stared lovingly at each other.

At that moment I thought, wow! He's absolutely gorgeous. The most beautiful man I'd ever seen.

And that's the truth.

However, self-doubt, and past history, told me I wasn't good enough for him.

Ed deserved better than me. Well that's what I thought at the time. You only had to look at where I was, and what I'd done, to know I was out of my depth and well out of Ed's league. Again my low self-esteem telling me I wasn't good enough. I always underestimated myself. And still do...

If you recall, both Ed and myself, left Grimsby at the same time, in the early 90s. He went away to London and then to Nottingham, while I went first to the West Midlands, then to Manchester and London.

After which I'd go to South Wales. More about that later...

I would then prepare myself to go abroad for the millennium with Rick and his family. Rick was about ten years older than me. I was twenty four, he was thirty four. He always had a melancholy sadness that made him look a little pissed off with life. If I'm honest with you, I think he was just lonely and wanted some companionship. I got the impression that he'd just separated from a girl, who he clearly hadn't got over.

I also got the impression that the ex-girlfriend was a bit of a socialite. He mentioned that she appeared regularly in 'Hello,' magazine. A girl around town type, a bit of an IT girl.

He said he was friends with an 80s pop star. Didn't really understand that, but he always talked about his pop star friend. I discovered he owned horses. However, a little unhinged, when I first met him, if I remember rightly.

Jealous as well...

Rick asked me if I wanted to go out for lunch with him as a friend. I agreed. So we went to a bar near Harrods. We then walked around Knightsbridge together and we started to form a friendship.

This confused me. I didn't really understand why, most probably, my psyche was telling me I desperately needed to get out of the business and get back into the real world. I had a mortgage and a car to pay for and needed the money. I liked nice things. I liked nice clothes. Getting out of the industry wasn't going to be easy.

I got the impression Rick had lost a lot of money. I don't know how, but he gave that impression. He would, intuitively, give me snippets into his life. He didn't fully trust me, at this time, but I knew he wanted to be with me.

Very confusing.

One Sunday Rick invited me to the stables where his horses were kept and we went for a hack out together...

I can remember feeling free. It took me back to my childhood when me and my sister used to ride, 'Muffin,' and, 'Firecracker.' It took me back to those very innocent times of my life. Happy memories came flooding back, and I felt all warm and cosy.

Rick asked me what I was doing for celebrations for the up-and-coming New Year's Eve 2000, Millennium. I really had no plans, so he invited me to go abroad to meet his family.

So we flew abroad together and we stayed with his family. It all seemed so romantic and everybody was so lovely, and they treated me normally.

Rick kept telling everybody that I was going to be a singer, and was recording records. He was exaggerating the truth, a little I know, but it was lovely to see how passionate he was, telling people about my ambitions. One of his aunties took me aside, and quietly, told me, I was much nicer than the money grabbing girl he had before.

It's funny, isn't it, because I didn't think this relationship was going to last forever, or an exit out of the call-girl business? I didn't know where to go with my life, so I carried on being a call-girl even though I continued to see Rick.

I never officially thought we were boyfriend and girlfriend. Rick, I believed, was trying to get over the break up and I just wanted a little bit of the, 'norm,' away from this world.

We continued to see each other up to the end of February, when things started to go a bit pear-shaped between us...Trying hard to get away...as all we do is fight...

CHAPTER THIRTY-SEVEN

ORDINARY WORLD

Ray is my guardian angel, a knight in shining armour.
He basically is the reason why I got out of doing what I was doing.
I will forever be eternally grateful to him. I met Ray in 1999 at the agency.

Ray lived on the outskirts of London, with business connections abroad.

It was obvious Ray had money.

He was a pleasant, down-to-earth, Northerner who made you feel like you were human, instead of the call-girl that you really were.

In our very few times together, we would discuss my dream of becoming the next Madonna, and hopefully a career in the music industry. I voiced a fear, I'd never be able to achieve this, as I felt trapped, and unable to escape from the industry I was in.

Ray would listen, with genuine empathy, and highlight the fact that there was more to life than being a call-girl, and if I so desired, I could change my lifestyle. How ironic was that, coming from a married man with children, who had a desire to see call-girls.

But who am I to judge? But he was right. My destiny was in my own hands.

I'd just come back from being abroad, with Rick, where we celebrated the year 2000, Millennium. I was also working with Nick H, recording my demos, for Tony, the A & R man to listen to.

Ultimately, I wanted to make it in the music industry, but felt trapped working as a call-girl, because I had a mortgage to pay and an expensive car to run.

Together, an expensive, financial expenditure. My work for the agency was paying for it.

So leaving the industry would be a financial disaster and I just couldn't afford to give it up. It paid well, and was a financial lifeline. I also doubted whether or not I'd be employable in a normal job.

Would I be good enough, and have confidence in myself?

I'd been in the Adult Entertainment Industry for over a year, and didn't know if I could adapt to normal life. Would potential employers want to employ an ex porn star and an ex call-girl, and what were the possible repercussions that it might cause?

Such questions flooded my mind with confusion.

I really didn't know what I wanted to do with my life, other than be a singer and become a celebrity. I could become a photographer, I reasoned, I was good at that, but that old enemy ADHD said I lacked confidence and possibly not as good as I thought I was.

Bloody ADHD!

I was clutching at straws as the only thing I was confident at was being a high class call-girl.

I so wanted out, but how? I had too many commitments to escape its lure.

Getting out of the industry isn't easy. It's bloody hard if you ask me.

You know, you're going to be judged and people will, or don't want to, understand the reasons why you went into it in the first place. You're a vulnerable target, to potentially bigoted, prejudices, and I knew, I just couldn't cope with having to explain myself, to these misinformed dogmatists.

I reasoned myself, into believing I'd got a cushy number. Working part-time, alternative weeks, but being paid. Full-time wages.

So should I stay, or should I go?

So one cold afternoon, whilst sitting in the London flat, I was to have a heart-to-heart chat with Ray about my future. I'll never forget that discussion, it would be the foundation stone that would change my life forever. Ray looked me straight in the eye and said, why, in God's name, was I working as a call-girl? Such a nice girl like you, deserved so much more, and I shouldn't be wasting my life doing this type of work.

He went on to tell me, he'd been with many call-girls and I wasn't like any of them. I was special, and shouldn't be wasting my talent, entertaining men. I had a purpose in life, other than doing this, and I should pursue those dreams of mine.

Get the hell out of this business he'd insisted, and be yourself.

I felt a lump in my throat. What inspiring, wonderful kind words he was saying.

He'd meant every word, and God, did I take notice.

Ray saw something in me that others probably didn't. You see when you have been struggling mentally all your life, being criticised for your behaviour and how you look, you begin to doubt your worth.

I've had a lot of self-doubt in my life. I had dreams but didn't believe I could ever make them come true.

So much self-doubt.

What he offered me next was the lifeline to change my life. He offered to pay my monthly outgoings, and living expenses, if I was serious about wanting to stop work as a call-girl and pursue those dreams we'd talked about.

I just couldn't believe what he was offering. I'd fallen for similar promises before, and sadly, then used by my so-called benefactors, for their own gains. So was Ray, just another one, out to use me, or was this a genuine offer, to help me get out of this industry.

He asked me to give him a monthly figure that would cover all my expenses, and he'd put that amount into my bank account, every month, until I was financially back on my feet and secure.

Was this for real? You bet your life, it was for real!

But what did he want in return?

I sat there, on the bed, open mouthed.

Why? I enquired, what do you want from me, if I agree?

He wanted nothing, there wasn't a catch, no conditions attached, he genuinely just wanted to help me get out of the business, to get back into the normal world and live a normal life.

He wanted me to follow my dreams, focus on my music, and find the love of my life and settle down with him. When I'd achieve that, he'd stop the monetary assistance and from then onwards I was to make my own way in life.

There was no one, at the time I would say, was my permanent boyfriend or a prospective partner for life. I'd just come back from being abroad with Rick but that was more of a passing time fling, that really wasn't going anywhere.

There was, of course, Wayne, my ex-boyfriend, but that relationship had broken down. We saw each other only as friends now, but we still confided in each other.

So there were no potential husbands waiting in the wings...

However, it was agreed, I just couldn't just walk away immediately, so I'd stop at the beginning of the next month, after fulfilling the bookings Isobel had made for me. That would be the end of January.

I had arranged with Tony to meet him face to face at his record label headquarters in London in February. I had finally finished recording my demo tracks for him, with Nick H. Tony had invited me directly to his record label offices so he could personally listen to them. I arrived at the record label, signed myself in. I even got to meet his PA who was absolutely lovely.

I remember feeling very overwhelmed inside the record label offices.
Walls were adorned with platinum albums of award winning artists that Tony had successfully signed. Imposter syndrome overcame me, and I started to feel, not good enough. My low dopamine ADHD brain telling me I was not good enough, I was not worthy of being there.

Tony was friendly and sat in his huge leather A & R chair overlooking all of London. He oozed importance and here I was about to play for him my two demos. He listened to them both and quite bluntly told me that they were not good enough. He said my voice had a similar tone to Lisa Stansfield. That was a huge compliment as I adore Lisa Stansfield.

Tony just instantly confused me, I was completely disheartened, and here I was yet again being rejected. I had my huge golden opportunity ripped away from me in seconds, my confidence shattered into pieces.
I asked Tony what I should do next, he told me not to give up, and told me to send the demos to other record labels...

My ADHD brain by now was totally overwhelmed at that very moment in time. I had been working so hard with Nick H on those demos, to then be told they were not good enough.

Totally confused, that's how I honestly felt, my body and mind deflated.

My only chance with Tony was completely blown.

I just wasn't good enough. That's what I truly thought. Looking back I should have fought for my music. I had one of the top A & R men in the country in front of me and I crumbled...I just wanted to give up, not taking too well to the rejection.

It totally felt a right fuck up. Especially in my neurodiversity mind, I just couldn't handle his rejection.

It's important to mention; I only was paid by Tony once to be his call-girl and that was the very first time we met at the posh London hotel back in the autumn of 1999. I took his advice on board. I literally did what he asked me to do, and that was to record him some demos. Which I worked hard on preparing with Nick H.

I did exactly as he asked, and now, to be told, I wasn't good enough...

I was totally confused. Not actually accepting what he was saying...

He said I had a great voice, just like Lisa Stansfield! I mean WTF, Lisa Stanfield's voice is incredible, I would imply that as a huge compliment, It was all too confusing, far too much for my neurodiversity head to process and take in.

I could feel myself going into a meltdown, my face was burning up, churning sensations in my tummy, a lump in my throat, I could feel my voice quivering, and my emotions were just starting to take over... I felt out of control.

In a complete state of desperation and panic, I just kept asking and repeating over and over to him, what did I need to do next... my hands were clammy, and he just simply replied "Just keep recording more demos" I mean what the actual... he then said, adding more to my mental confusion...

That I should send them on to other record labels! I mean what in the hell... he then added that I should let the other record labels know he said that!

Looking back now, why would I inform the other record labels about Tony's rejection, surely that would sound so wrong! Oh Tony rejected me, saying I wasn't good enough, but he thinks your label will be interested in me....I mean come on!

Honestly it was too much confusion... a complete mental head fuck... I felt I'd been taken for a complete ride. I had! I felt he really didn't want to help me, it was all lip service, pass the book kind of bullshit....and I took it literally to heart.

I felt used....I just couldn't accept his rejection... I was broken.

Tony clearly knew I was upset, so to pacify me he invited me as his guest for dinner with him at his home...

So my second encounter with Tony was now, not as a call-girl, but as his personal guest, I would even go as far as saying a date... a one night stand!

He never paid me to stay the night at his house...

Looking back now, I don't know why I went, well I know why I went. I was desperate. Still hoping I would get something out of it, get my well-deserved break in the music industry, that I so had wanted. My ultimate dream was in the palm of his hands, hoping he would be the golden ticket...

I do recall him asking me if I had any of my porn films for him to watch. Somehow I managed to get one, don't know how but I did. That's all I was to him, an ex porn star and a pop star wannabe! He literally could do what he wanted with me, and he knew he had the power to do so.

I was totally used by Tony and I never got anything out of it. Other than broken dreams...

I will always remember Tony telling me that night at his home, I had the most beautiful soft hair, but if I wanted to be a pop star I would need to lose weight! What in the actual hell! Really not a clever thing to have said, when I take things literal, along with my then history of eating disorders. I was Tiny, probably didn't weigh 8 stone wets.

Talk about having a hard detrimental knock back...

Why would my weight defy me from being a popstar! Utter bullshit! That was the problem, I really was being conditioned and programmed by so many judgemental people. Everybody was constantly telling me `If you lose weight you will get more work!' 'If you lose weight you will be successful, you will be desirable.'

I was developing severe complexes that would haunt and dominate me for most of my adult life. I really believed that being skinny made you successful... which I know now is complete bollocks! But unfortunately at this time in my life, this is what I was up against daily. It created so many detrimental effects, by the time I turned forty years old, my body suffered from so many complications with years of eating disorders, my overall health has not been great over the last few years...These will all be addressed in my second book. I would describe myself now as in full recovery from an eating disorder, but it's taken having serious bad health to get there...

I stayed the night with Tony at his London home and that would be the last time. In the morning my Mercedes SLK had been clamped outside his house. I also got a parking fine which Tony obliged to pay. I did however laugh as the men who unclamped my car did ask me if Tony was my dad...

I know now, my underlying motives to sleep with Tony were based on the fact I wanted to promote my music career... There is no doubt about that.

The idea of the 'casting couch' Syndrome thinking if I slept with Tony he would sign me up as his popstar!

Does that make sense?

Being a call-girl, at that time in my life had been my job. It would mean nothing to me at that time, other than possibly pleasing Tony into getting my career in the music business. I know now it's totally immoral, but I was desperate. I was vulnerable, trusting and literally believed everything...

Now, I want to repeat and put the record straight. I've stayed silent for far too long for fear of reprisal. I slept with Tony, the A & R man on two occasions. But only, once as a call-girl.

Just once.

A fact that would be disputed later in my life, but more about that, later in my story. But for now, it's important, to know Tony would eventually accuse me of being paid, to sleep with him on three occasions...Total lies!

Now, that was a huge lie, and it's my right to expose that lie, and speak openly about a secret I've kept to myself, for many years.

Writing this book has given me strength. It's been a liberating exercise that has freed me from censorship. I'm no longer fearful of speaking the truth....

I left the industry, and felt so proud about it. There would be no more, porn films, no more escorting men and no more prostituting myself. I was finally free to be me and live a more normal life.

Ray was true to his word, and financially supported me, through my conversion to normality. This he did until I met John, my future daughter's dad, and who at the time, I really thought, was the love of my life.

It was in November of that same year, when I informed Ray, I'd found the man of my dreams and our financial arrangement came to an end.

I was never to hear from Ray again.

Ray never wanted anything from me, other than to help me get out of the industry.

I was very lucky, I had Ray. Others like me, were not as lucky. The industry is notorious for drawing you in. Getting out is very difficult...

So I'm eternally grateful for Ray. He was my Richard Gere, in Pretty Woman, me of course, his Julia Roberts, the call-girl he saved. Thank you Ray, for getting me out of a life of vice...

It's now time to rewind to the day I realised I was pregnant...

I started to feel very poorly. I felt sickly, was very sick, I was gaining weight, my breasts swelled. I knew this wasn't normal for me, I felt different. I've polycystic ovaries, so I didn't think I was pregnant. However, I took the test, and there it was clear as day.

I was pregnant.

My hormones raged. I was confused. I cried and cried.

What was I to do?

I'd always said, if I fell pregnant, I would keep the baby. But my situation at this point in my life was not good.

Well, fucked up, actually.

I worked it out that I must have fallen pregnant in February. I'd been intimate with two people in February. That being Tony and Rick. So the baby's real dad was unknown.

I wanted to keep the baby.

I felt confused. My head was a shed. My life was inside out and upside down. I'd just come out of a life of vice, with Ray financially supporting me.

It was a mess. A bloody mess. I'd got myself pregnant and was in one hell of a mess. I felt scared, frightened it was a horrible challenging situation to be in at that time in my life. The timing was all wrong! I spoke to Abby and she told me it was ultimately my decision. She said it would be a life commitment, and was I really ready, especially with my mental health problems, to have, take care and raise a baby? So I confided in a family member who told me, in my circumstances, a termination was for the best.

I was really confused. However, I eventually opted for an early termination.

Trust me it still haunts me to this day. I have many moments of guilt. I sometimes wonder what my baby would have looked like. I think about people who so desperately want a baby and can't, and I feel selfish for my actions.

However, at that moment in my life, it was not the right time for me to have a baby.

I don't know why, but I told Rick I was pregnant, and was thinking of getting an abortion. I wasn't sure who the baby's dad was, it could have been, either of them. So a termination, I thought, would be for the best, all round.

However, Rick was a bit of a nightmare with it, to say the least. He would beg me to keep the baby and threaten violence against Abby and me, if I did go ahead with the abortion.

He was very unhinged, about the whole affair, and thank God, I would, survive his threats, and eventually get him out of my life.

After which I never heard from him again.

Maybe I should have told Tony I was pregnant.

I will always question whether my aborted child was Rick's or Tony's, but that will remain a mystery, never to be solved.

I had at the time, my whole life ahead of me and despite the moral issues involved with abortion.

I know, it's a debatable argument, and understand both sides of the abortion lobby, however, despite my reservations, I went ahead with the abortion.

Wayne, believe it or not, supported me, and was there for me during my abortion. He came to the hospital, stayed with me, and looked after me.

I've always wondered whether he did this through guilt, trying to appease me for deserting me for another woman, or was he genuinely, being caring.

Not important now, I'm sure.

So I had my termination in Manchester under general anaesthetic. I felt grief afterwards. I felt I'd made a huge mistake, but back then, I'd never have given my baby a decent start in life.

After my termination, I struggled with emotional grief, I felt traumatised and hormones were raging. It was horrific, I was full of guilt. However, I was determined to get my life sorted.

I called my first baby Lucy.

I'm adamant I was carrying a little girl. I think about her often and I hope she forgives me for not letting her have a life that she deserved. I know it's so controversial and a contradiction of right and wrong... I'm so sorry Lucy Xx

Life in London was no longer an issue. Ray had released me from all that and I was free to find a new life.

Duran Duran came to mind, and their song, 'Ordinary World,' would inspire my new lease of life. The lyrics of that song were so true of me at this moment in time.

However, finding my way back into the ordinary world was not going to be easy. I'd left the trauma of London behind me, but my mental instabilities still remained. I should have considered counselling, seeking psychiatric help, but that wasn't me, as well you know. So instead of getting help, I picked myself up, dusted myself down and got on with it.

I was determined never to be the victim again.

So, I got on with the normal Manchester life I knew. I did everything I could to find peace within myself.

It wasn't easy I can assure you.

I concentrated on starting a music career and sent my recorded demos to record producers along with letters introducing myself to them, desperate for one of them to recognise my talents, and sign me up.

Tony's comments, about becoming a session singer, resonated with my reasoning, so I concentrated on writing songs for other artists. I still had regular contact with Tony, via the phone and we'd chat about my prospects. It was friendly banter, nothing more and I never told him about me being pregnant.

We would discuss his record company and my attempts to break into the music business. I told him I'd recorded more demos and had distributed them to record producers.

All I ever wanted from Tony was for him to sign me up to his record company.

But that was never going to happen, was it?

It was a very frustrating time for me. I desperately wanted to be recognised for my musical abilities. I so wanted people to believe in me, help me achieve that dream of becoming a famous recording artist, but instead, it was rejection after rejection.

However, I grew stronger knowing Ray had believed in me. So I would be that normal person in a normal world, I owed Ray that.

But hell, was it proving difficult.

I'd gone full circle. From 9-to-5, employment, as a sales rep, in Manchester, to a debauched life in porn and prostitution, then back into the normal world again.

Full circle, but now without employment.

I was, at this time, still being financially supported by Ray. That of course would continue until I met my knight in shining armour. That would be John, but I'd yet to meet him. So during these turbulent times, I thought I'd never meet the love of my life.

After my abortion, I became much closer to my best friend Sy. Sy was concentrating on his music career, and recording songs in London. Destiny would make him a future musical star.

But, I'm so proud of him. His support and guidance during my troublesome journey into normality, inspired me.

I'll never forget that.

He was amazing. Thank you Sy, for being such an understanding counsellor.

Love you SY. xx

There was of course Ellie…. She was like my sister to me. She became my special friend. A kind-hearted girl with a heart of gold. Ellie lived in South London, but regularly came back to Manchester, to see her family.

I started to come and visit Ellie down in London.

Memories of my old call-girl life would haunt me on every visit, but that life was now well behind me. I put such thoughts to the back of my mind, and got on with my normal life.

Ellie was studying at the time, and was living in a house in South London, she shared with some girls.

She was struggling financially.

Ray's money was still financing my lifestyle, so I had the funds to help her. 'Pay it forward,' I thought. So responding to Ray's kindness to me, I helped Ellie. It would at least help pay her rent, I thought.

I would stay with her in London, while I went around looking for and attending singer auditions. I would also visit record companies with my recorded demo records, hoping to get signed up to a record label.

It all fell on stony ground.

What a pity, because I do believe I've recorded some very good record demos.

Worthy of being released.

God knows why record companies have rejected them. People who I've played them too, agree with me. They're good.

Bloody good if you ask me.

But that's the music business. As Tony once told me, it's who you know that gets you noticed.

I think he was talking shit.

Looking back he had the key to open doors for me, but he kept them firmly closed. Tony could have seriously helped me a lot more than he promised.

I felt very let down by him.

However, I still hoped he would give me that golden opportunity. Nothing happened, other than adding to my self-doubt. That I now believe to be true.

I did find a producer in Sheffield who wanted to record a garage track with me, I recorded a demo called 'Missing you'.' There was also a guy in Preston I collaborated with, but again nothing became of either.

Having ADHD fogs up your brain. Often, tasks undertaken, left unfinished, and forgotten. Throughout my life, I've needed support but the network for managing that help is not always available.

My ADHD, as you know, went undiagnosed for most of my life back then, so I became frustrated with being rejected by the musical world.

I knew I was good at it, but obviously not good enough to achieve the recording contract I think I deserved.....
Inspired and guided by the lyrics of Duran Duran... An ordinary world that I had to somehow find...

CHAPTER THIRTY-EIGHT

HUMAN NATURE

As you know, my ADHD leads me off on tangents, so instead let me take you off on one that I've instigated.

So let me set the scene.

It's Britney Spears' tour, in the UK, she had a few tour dates at 'Manchester Arena,' in the year 2000.

Now, at this time, I was undergoing 'Reiki'.'

Now, 'Reiki,' is a Japanese homoeopathic technique for reducing stress, and encourages relaxation.

It also promotes healing.

It's administered by 'The Laying of Hands,' and is based on the idea that unseen, 'Life Force Energies,' flow through our bodies, and heighten control of your own life-forces.

Reiki became a spiritual therapy. Its ideology, working wonders for my psyche and self-belief. Reiki was the saving grace of my life, and together, with a trainee Reiki student, I began to understand the power of such techniques, and what it could do to improve and enhance my outlook on life.

Self-help was only fifteen minutes away, and I would attend my Reiki sessions, with the hope of the renewal of a life I so wished to achieve.

During these periods of renewal I would carry a silver cassette Dictaphone, it was perfect to record my inspirational thoughts, mainly words for lyrics so I could write songs. Creating my own unique melodies and words that hopefully, I could use when creating my music demos. A perfect tool to keep with me at all times, as inspiration can be found all around us, especially when we least expect it.

I recall on this particular day, as I was walking to my Reiki appointment, I noticed this Black Tour Bus outside the very luxurious Hotel in Manchester's city centre.

As I walked by I noticed a group of people all wearing Britney T-shirts and holding a few Banners saying, 'We Love you Britney'.
I asked someone what was happening, to be told, they were waiting for Britney to leave the hotel. She was to take the Black Tour bus to the arena for her sound check as she was performing that night at the city's arena. I can remember feeling really excited, I was about to see, 'Britney Spears.'
It all seemed very surreal.
I can remember thinking why haven't I got my camera with me, the days before the smartphone. It was fun hanging with her enthusiastic supporting fans.
It reminded me of my devotion to Madonna.
We were not waiting long... and her fans were not left disappointed. I remember how, petite she was, exiting the hotel, through its revolving doors
She was extremely tanned and I used my diaphone to record the occasion.
I recall, shouting, 'Britney I love you, Britney I love you.'
She looked pleased, and waved at everybody. I switched on my Dictaphone and recorded all the people shouting for her as she came out of the hotel.
It was all very amusing.

I look back on this moment in time and smile, I remember thinking damn,
Why did I leave my camera at home, and how can I prove I had seen Britney Spears, no one will believe me. That's when I realised I had my Dictaphone, and in that quick split second moment I pulled it out of my handbag and just started to record. Bizarre I know and it still makes me chuckle at my quirky little story.
In the modern day world we take for granted the Smartphone, had it been modern day times it could have been recorded live and straight onto social media platforms for millions to see.

I have the utmost respect for Britney Spears. Our lives have been worlds apart, she's been the ultimate pop princess, with the world watching her every movement and then my life... well it's just been a world of chaotic fuck ups, with me wanting so hard to be the ultimate pop princess and failing my ultimate dream.

But I feel we both have some kind of very similar connection, and do have things in common. We both have been through a lot from a very young age. The word, I feel fitting here, is 'tortured souls' we have both been 'victims' of others taking advantage of our kind vulnerable natures, both been victims of control and silence.

I appreciate her, with what she's been through with her own family, in her own legal battles to repair and preserve her way of life, over the controversial conservatorship. The conservatorship meant she had no voice, no control for many years. It seemed her human rights were taken away from her. From being told what to wear. What to eat, the whole thing sounded horrendous. 'Free Britney' and she finally won her freedom!

Most of my life, I've been silenced to speak my truth. Because I was too afraid I would upset people or offend them. Worrying too much what others would think, petrified of being judged. I never reported my rapes, believing no one would believe me, or people would think it was all my fault. Leaving me with years of mental torture, imprisonment inside my mind.

I too have had similar legal battles, fighting in court, and silenced. So I wholeheartedly can understand the trauma of such an encounter.

I never challenged the legal document I was summoned with. Because it was all about inflicting power, money, and fear on me. My ADHD was undiagnosed at the time and crippled with my dyslexia. My emotions at the time we're high, that eventually would lead to a full meltdown of confusion and fear.

It left me with a form of mental paralysis, where I couldn't think straight. If I'm honest with you I didn't even read the documents, I couldn't even understand really what the documents meant.

I never had a fair legal representation, I wish I did back then. I also was bankrupt and had no money to fight it. Now thinking back about it, I was bullied. It was a one-sided affair that I could never win.

One thing I have a clear conscience about, is the truth, and the truth will always prevail. In life, honesty is always the best policy. We have to own up to our mistakes.

Don't get me wrong. I'm not perfect and as you know. I've made many mistakes. However, I know one thing, I now know myself. I'm strong and bearing the truth about myself. I now have the freedom to talk freely without any prejudice.

Take from me what you will, but I no longer can be harmed.

It took Britney a long time to find her freedom. It didn't come easy to her either. Even Britney, who is an international superstar, had to fight for her freedom and still is to this day, she is still fighting for her freedom from her years of mental abuse, that she's still overcoming I'm sure.

I've been left with years of emotional trauma, resulting in PTSD. I went decades without no professional help. I've masked out the psychological pain and built up my own coping strategies to enable me to survive. To appear normal.

Now, I'm finding my true inner peace.

When I was diagnosed with ADHD in the summer of 2022, I started to grieve, I grieved because I had known all my entire life I was born different, born unique.

All my struggles I had endeared in my life all now made sense.

I started to eventually understand myself and accept my brain works uniquely. I can't erase my past, and yes my story is uncomfortable to read in some of the dark abyss places.

But imagine what it feels like holding on to such secrets and traumas.

Having my diagnosis has given me the strength to speak my story and hopefully, inspire others to do so as well. Break down the stigma of mental health conditions.

My book is only the tip of the iceberg to my real story. But I hope it has given you an understanding of having a neurological brain and it's chaos it has caused.

I know my book will possibly break some of my friends and family's hearts, I'm sure I will be challenged to why I've exposed myself in this way, but it's deeper than my chaotic stories. Writing my book has been therapy, going back to facing the demons that haunt me.

A quick note; Madonna has always been with me, as I've said, she doesn't know me but her strength, and what she stands for, has always been there in my heart, for a lifetime. It made my heart feel good, knowing Madonna helped Britney fight for the truth. Britney has and still continues to gain her freedom.

I feel free in my mind. I feel free knowing my truth.

No one will ever take away our freedom again.
As famously quoted and inspired forever by my mentor Madonna...
"I'm not your bitch don't hang your shit on me and I'm not sorry"
Love you **Britney** and love you Madonna... keep fighting for your truth!

CHAPTER THIRTY-NINE

TAKE A BOW

John, the Diet Coke man as I called him, was handsome, all the girls had a crush on him.

Why call him the Diet Coke man? Well let me explain.

Can you remember a 90s advert for Diet Coke? It featured a workman, in a workman's outfit, showing off his chest. Women gushed around him as he sexily opened his can of coke.

Well that personified John.

I first noticed John when going to the gym. He had a business, in a unit on the same industrial estate where the gym was situated.

A blonde woman, who gave everyone a dirty look, was often seen going in and out of the unit. I assumed this to be his wife, and thought nothing more of it.

John would, when visiting his business unit, say hello and we'd exchange pleasantries.

With Ray's financial support, I was beginning to find myself again.

I felt free. However there was always this underlying voice, in my head, that said, what if Ray stopped the support. Where would I find the money to pay my mortgage and the Mercedes?

I hoped against hope not to face that scenario...

Gina, a friend from the gym, had invited me, and the Diet Coke man, to her birthday party in Manchester.

However Gina also fancied him, and was adamant she was going to get him. I was still, a little unsure, as to whether he had a girlfriend or not. I knew about the blonde woman who came to his unit where he worked, and wondered if she was his wife?

I remember, going back to London, telling all the girls in South London, about the Diet Coke man I fancied. They were all really excited for me, especially Ellie. She knew I'd been single for a long time, having confessed my past to her. She obviously knew everything about me, but I trusted her completely. I still do to this very day.

Ellie held no judgement on me. She was delighted, I had a crush on this Diet Coke man.

'Go for it,' the London girls chorused. So I did.

I bought a new outfit from Karen Millen, consisting of a tight denim part leather skirt, with matching jacket. The dress had an unusual dog-collar neck that was very sensual indeed. To finish off my sexy look, I bought mock snakeskin high heels. I had spent a fortune on this outfit, just to impress this Diet Coke man.

I turned my house upside down, getting ready for Gina's party. Literally upside down. It was a mess. I even had a chair on my bed.

It was just chaos.

I met with Gina and we made our way to the nightclub in Manchester's city centre. On the way, she would tell me how she wanted to date the Diet Coke man. Much to Gina's annoyance, on arrival, the Diet Coke man made a beeline for me. Blanked everyone else, and homed in on me.

We exchanged niceties, and he asked if I would like a drink. What really caught my attention was his voice. He had that Eton, public school, scholarly voice you wouldn't associate with a workman like he was.

He was originally from Wales, and I told him two of my girl-friends in London came from Wales. I told him their names. When I told him all about Lynda his mouth dropped to the floor.

It turned out he and Lynda went to school together in Wales. He knew Lynda, and I'd unknowingly, when in London, told her I fancied this Diet Coke man.

What were the chances of that, what a coincidence? In life you're confronted with numerous opportunities. This way or that way, forward backwards, sliding door connections.

So was this coincidence or an opportunity.

Small talk with the Diet Coke man continued, and I told him I didn't drink, and declined his offer of a bottle of champagne. I asked for sparkling water instead. He enquired what I did for a living and I told him I worked as a glamour model, but was now concentrating on my music career. He said that he'd seen me many times going to the gym and was very impressed with my Mercedes.

As in all developing relationships, the usual questioning followed.

Was I single, yes?

Was he, yes? Sort of. He'd just separated from his partner. I asked was it the blonde girl I saw going in and out of his unit? She was his business partner, he insisted. He convinced me he was now single, and that the girl I'd seen at his unit, was not his girlfriend.

To substantiate these claims, he went on to tell me, they buy properties together, refurbish them and sell them on for a profit. They were actually in the property market together buying and selling houses.

I then asked where he lived. He hesitated a little, then said he lived with this blonde woman, but they had separate bedrooms, and he would soon be looking to move out.

Again, he sounded so convincing, so charming and that voice was so posh, you had to believe him.

Why wouldn't I believe him?

I looked around and could see Gina giving me the eye. I could see in her facial expressions, she wasn't at all pleased. I was muscling in on her attempt to hook the Diet Coke man.

She wanted me, the hell away from him, so she could step in. No way! I wasn't moving, me and the Diet Coke man were engrossed in conversation. So why should I? I'd got him hooked and by the look of it, he was hooked on me.

I had heard in the gym rumours, that he had a history of dumping girls like hot potatoes, however that was far from my mind at the time.

Should have recognised the signs but didn't.

After the party, I had to drop Gina back at her flat.
John, his real name, had asked for my mobile number, which I willingly gave to him.
I told him that I'd come back to the nightclub, after I'd dropped Gina back home.

I really wanted to get to know him.

I took Gina home. She was absolutely gutted. Annoyed with me I could tell. John hardly spoke to her that night, and it was her birthday. She'd invited him, solely to get off with him.

She' hadn't I had.

It was me who'd hooked him. She obviously saw how strong a connection there was between me and him.

I remember that night, a voice inside my head, telling me it's now or never, go for it. My mind was as clear as daylight, on a cloudless sky.

Go for it, my emotions were telling me.

So that's what I did. I went for it. Full steam 100mph. He was mine for the taking. Not at all thinking logically, I acted as usual, on impulse.

On my return, I found him outside the nightclub. I could see he was drunk. Don't like dealing with drunk men. Drunk men are very unpredictable, the drink making liars out of all of them. Upon John seeing me, he said how amazingly beautiful I looked. Boosting my ego, that was so full of insecurities, he was a real charmer from the beginning.

Was this the drink talking or did he really mean it?

I took him at his word and invited him back to my house.

So I drove back to my little house and forgot what an absolute bombsite I'd left it in. It looked like somebody had ransacked the house. I felt embarrassed, very uncomfortable having to invite him in and be confronted with all this mess.

I actually went shy. That's weird isn't it?

I made him a coffee, and we sat on my yellow and blue check sofa, in my yellow and blue living room, and chatted.

We chatted, with me feeling embarrassed and awkward. I was sober, and my verbal diarrhoea went on and on, my ADHD on overdrive.

Sometime during the conversation, he lent forward, whispered for me to shush, he wanted a kiss.

In all fairness he was a gentleman and didn't push it any further.

It all felt surreal. This was a normal guy, who didn't want anything more from me.

I hadn't been with anyone since the abortion.

I drove him back home to his house in Manchester.

The next day he messaged me saying he wanted to see me again. However, I had planned to go back to South London to see Ellie and the girls, so texted him to say, I was going to London, but would on my return. He replied saying he'd take me out to dinner. I'd planned to stay a few days in London so it meant I'd be back at the weekend.

It was arranged that we'd go out for dinner on my return.

I couldn't concentrate, driving to London. My mind was on John. My stomach churning, my heart all dithering. I couldn't get John out of my mind. I really wanted to turn the car around and go back to him.

Quite impulsive, really magnetic.

When I got to London, I couldn't wait to tell the girls all about him, and the connection between John and the girls from Wales, especially Lynda, the girl he'd gone to school with.

When I got to South London and went inside the flat, I just blurted it all out. All about my night with John and that he went to school with Lynda. Lynda was shocked and went on to warn me about him. She'd said he might seem like a nice guy, but be careful, he's not what he appears to be.

I was totally confused. Why would she say that? It didn't make sense. I'd just met this incredible guy and here she is telling me, I've got to be careful of him and he's not what he seems to be.

Now at the start of any relationship, you're absolutely blown away with the amazingness of it all. You don't think there is anything wrong with the person you're with. Everything seems incredible.

I just didn't want to believe Lynda. I just thought she was being bitchy, nasty actually. As it turned out, Lynda had been with John, a few years back when they were both in Wales. They went to a music concert together. He was pissed, and kept telling her, he loved her, they'd snogged. She'd found him rather freaky. She again warned me to be careful, the man was a real freak, please be careful.

Do I ever listen to anybody?

No! I always have to find out for myself, the hard way.

I was determined when I got back to Manchester, I'd have that meal with John and we'd start dating. I ignored Lynda's advice, and refused to listen to her.

However, the craziest thing was, Lynda was right but I would find that out the hard way, many years later after the birth of my daughter.

The desire, to get back to Manchester, and satisfy my dopamine fix of wanting desperately to see John again, took over.

I drove back to Manchester, my mind fixated on seeing John. As soon as I got back, I told John I was home.

He picked me up dressed in black trousers, a black leather jacket, and polo necked top. We drove to a cash point and I got out of the car and withdrew money. When I got back to the car he said how gorgeous I looked. We went to a restaurant in Manchester City centre.

All night, he was the perfect gentleman, he was so charming, and I knew Lynda must be wrong about this attractive man. I thought, if I'm going to make this relationship work, I need to be honest with him.

I didn't want to be holding back secrets. There's no point in starting a relationship, and later finding out your partner has betrayed you and hasn't been honest with you. So I decided to be upfront and honest, and tell John about my past. If after that, he wants to walk away, then so be it.

As long as I've been true to myself, I owe it to myself and John to be truthful, the truth will always prevail.

So, there we were in this really posh, swanky restaurant. John was into 'Fine Dining,' and this restaurant was one of his favourites. We ordered our meals and John, appearing to be genuinely intrigued about me, started asking me questions. His questions were all about me, and it made me feel special and important.

Eventually, I got around to telling him about my past.

I said I had something important to tell him, and if he still wants to continue with our relationship, then great, but if he doesn't, I'll totally understand, I won't be offended, and we'll each go our separate ways.

John looked puzzled, all confused. You could see in his facial expressions, he was wondering what the hell you going on about.

Then I told him about my past, all about the porn films, and all about being a call-girl. I told him just about everything. I said I no longer did these things, and haven't done since February.

He listened intensely.

I told him I was trying to enter the music industry, and had been recording demos for Tony, a music mogul. I didn't tell him to begin with, that I'd had a brief fling with Tony. Because obviously, I had just dropped a bombshell as it was, and I didn't think telling him about my affair with Tony would make it any easier.

Also I didn't tell him about Ray, again, I didn't feel John needed to know about him, just yet.

So there it was. The truth as I knew it, and I waited for John's reaction.

I felt really relieved to have told him everything. Honesty is the best policy.

John just sat there. He was genuinely shell-shocked. No doubt about that. Well and truly shell-shocked.

Then, to my surprise it was his turn. It was as if we'd entered the confessional box in a Catholic church, and were confessing our sins to each other.

It was now John's turn, to tell all...

He told me he too had many secrets, and began to tell me some of his deepest darkest secrets.

But, I'm not going to elaborate on those secrets. They were told to me in confidence and I'm honouring that confidentiality. Like me he felt quite relieved to have talked openly about himself with someone, who was open-minded and wasn't going to judge him.

I mean come on the amount of things I've seen and done, in my short space of time, nothing shocks me, nothing does shock me.

So that night he dropped me off, back at my house and he remained a gentleman and didn't stay the night.

He said he had a puppy, and needed to get back, he then asked if he could come round to see me tomorrow, and he'd like to bring the puppy to meet me.

I agreed.

I felt so relieved, I'd got everything off my chest. It had been the right thing to do, and I was so happy I'd been honest with him.

I wasn't sure if he would come and see me the next day. Maybe after processing everything I told him, he might have had second thoughts. My past is far from normal and it's a lot for someone to digest and take on-board.

So would John take me on board? I'm constantly being judged for what I did in my past. I guess that's the price to pay for the work I did.

Would John be different?

But what I did in my past, didn't hurt anybody. The only person that was being hurt was me. Confessing all, in this book, has enabled people to read the truth, and hopefully, finally understand the reasoning behind everything I did.

The next day John messaged me, and said he'd be over later, with the puppy. Now, Dexter, his puppy, had been ill. I was later to discover it had been in veterinary care to recover. I had to seriously consider where his ex-girlfriend fitted into John's life. I assumed she was his ex, and a business partner. But, they still lived in the same house together, but in separate bedrooms.

Was she his ex, or was John lying?

I got the impression from John that they were separated. The only time spent together being for their business. I wasn't quite sure if he was being truthful, because it would soon become apparent his alleged ex-girlfriend would find out about me and become the woman scorned. John would make out she was some kind of psycho-crazy woman. It would all become quite complicated, but that comes later.

As sure as clockwork, John came round with Dexter the puppy. The dog was very cute. He was a character, from the word go. However, he could be vicious, if provoked. The animal had its dangerous side, so you had to be careful with it. That I blamed on the fact that Dexter spent a long time housed in the vets, receiving treatment which might have caused it some distress.

So mine and John's relationship intensified, a crazy whirlwind romance.

I'd never experienced such intensity. We were two people looking for escapism.

Two people trusted each other's darkest secrets. So we officially started dating...

John asked me out. I said yes. Within a week he said he'd found a flat and was moving out from his ex-girlfriend... and so dangerously true to my ADHD form, I impulsively would sacrifice my own house, by putting it up for sale to move in officially with John. An intense whirlwind of a bad romance with the Diet Coke man, called John, would intensely flourish, impulsively would see me moving with him to Wales and the next phase of renewing my life.... To be continued in book two....

STOP THE PRESS! In an interesting twist between finishing the first draft of this book and publication, I've got some exciting news to add....

..... an amazing coincidental opportunity has come knocking. (I've always said I'm a white witch and I believe things all happen for a reason.)

In 1999 when recording demos with Nick H, an opportunity came to me in the form of Paul Deighton. Paul ironically was also originally from Grimsby and, like myself at the time, was living in Manchester. He had connected with Nick H musically and was looking for a female vocalist for a dance track he was producing.

Nick H had kindly recommended myself to Paul, and with our Grimsby connection we clicked so I recorded my vocals on a dance track titled 'Love Thing' which Paul gave me a copy of it on a CD that I kept in my car for years. We lost touch in typical ADHD fashion and like most of the songs that I recorded, nothing more came of the track, which was left gathering dust in my car, never to be heard again.

However, in recent years through social media, Paul and I have become Facebook friends and it was interesting to find out he had, like myself, moved back to Grimsby after spending years living away. Whilst working as a resident DJ at the legendary Ministry of Sound he had produced and recorded some records which were huge hits on the dance scene. Since moving back to Grimsby his life has taken a change of direction and he is now a happily married family man and a teacher.

The crazy coincidence though, is that whilst writing my book I took a trip back down memory lane into my past, found the old demo CDs and was only recently listening to 'Love Thing'. Meanwhile, across town, Paul was setting up his own recording studio again, where he had been making new dance tracks and other music which he'd released on Spotify.

I commented on Paul's Facebook post how I was only just recently listening to 'Love Thing' on CD. He replied and asked if I would be up for recording vocals again, as he had a great House anthem with pianos and saxophone. I was keen to collaborate and we arranged to reconnect on my day off work. I laid down the vocals to an up-to-date version of 'Love Thing', rewritten and retitled 'You are my Thing'.

So, after 24 years we reconnected and recorded a track together, coinciding with the launch of this book, that you have just finished reading!

The song is 'You are my Thing' by Paul Deighton featuring myself, Hannah Huxford, on vocals and it officially is available to download on Spotify from 30th January 2023 if anyone is interested in giving it a listen.

This is the beginning of something amazing as Paul and I plan to record more music together... so watch this space and I'm sure more of our new journey will be written in Book Two.

As I said, it's incredible how, after 24 years it's come full circle and I want to thank you Paul for giving me an opportunity to shine.

Released on Spotify
30th January 2023

 @dreamwalls

My story will continue. Come with me, on my journey to explore and understand more of my complicated life with my undiagnosed ADHD, post-traumatic stress. More heartache and pain to overcome, more lessons to learn. My journey through life would see me become a first-time mum. Fighting for my freedom...Which would eventually take me full circle back home to Grimsby, back to my family and to my beloved Ed... And finally finding my truth by being officially diagnosed with ADHD...
Want to read more...to be continued in Book Two:
'The Secret Diary of an ADHD Martyr:
A GIRL GONE GOOD'

Printed in Great Britain
by Amazon

17795652R00173